FOREIGN INVESTMENT IN CHINA

Also by Feng Li

THE GEOGRAPHY OF BUSINESS INFORMATION

Foreign Investment in China

Feng Li
Strathclyde University
Glasgow

and

Jing Li
Freelance consultant

First published in Great Britain 1999 by
MACMILLAN PRESS LTD
Houndmills, Basingstoke, Hampshire RG21 6XS and London
Companies and representatives throughout the world

A catalogue record for this book is available from the British Library.

ISBN 0–333–66241–5

First published in the United States of America 1999 by
ST. MARTIN'S PRESS, INC.,
Scholarly and Reference Division,
175 Fifth Avenue, New York, N.Y. 10010

ISBN 0–312–21913–X

Library of Congress Cataloging-in-Publication Data
Li, Feng, 1965–
Foreign investment in China / Feng Li, Jing Li.
p.   cm.
Includes bibliographical references and index.
ISBN 0–312–21913–X (cloth)
1. Investments, Foreign—China.   I. Li, Jing, 1964–   .
II. Title.
HG5782.L477   1999
332.67'3'0951—dc21   98–45602
                                                              CIP

This book is printed on paper suitable for recycling and made from fully managed and sustained forest sources.

10   9   8   7   6   5   4   3   2   1
08   07   06   05   04   03   02   01   00   99

Printed and bound in Great Britain by
Antony Rowe Ltd, Chippenham, Wiltshire

To Jeffrey

Contents

List of Figures	xi
List of Tables	xii
Preface	xiii
Acknowledgements	xvi

1 INTRODUCTION: FOREIGN INVESTMENT IN CHINA UNDER THE OPEN DOOR POLICY — 1

The Background of the Reform and Open Door Policy in China	3
The Evolution of the Open Door Policy in China	8
The Role of FDI in China	9
Previous Studies and This Book: A Brief Review of Related Literature and the Main Sources of Information for the Study	11
The Structure of the Book	18

2 CHINA'S MAIN ATTRACTIONS TO FOREIGN INVESTORS — 26

The World Economy and the Rapid Growth of FDI since the Early 1970s	26
The structural crises in the global economy	26
FDI – the new engine of world economic growth	31
Multinational corporations – the key players in the world economy	33
The Key Motivations for Investing in Foreign Markets	35
China's Main Attractions to Foreign Investors	39
A classification of FDI in China: who are the main investors?	39
What have attracted foreign investors to China?	40
Summary	45

3 OPENING THE DOOR TO FDI: THE EVOLUTION
   OF RELEVANT POLICIES IN CHINA   51

The Main Forms of FDI in China   51
The Evolution of FDI-Related Policies in China   54
   The first phase: late 1978 to early 1983   54
   The second phase: mid-1983 to early 1986   58
   The third phase: mid-1986 to early 1989   62
   The fourth phase: mid-1989 to late 1990   65
   The fifth phase: from late 1990 to early 1994   67
   The sixth phase: from mid-1994 onwards   69
   Summary: A gradualist approach to reform and
   opening up   72
From Reactive to Proactive Policy Making: The Main
Causes for Policy Changes in the Aspect of FDI in China   74
   Internal forces   74
   External forces   77
Summary   78

4 THE FOREIGN INVESTMENT ENVIRONMENT
   IN CHINA: THE HARD ENVIRONMENT   82

The Hard and the Soft Investment Environments   83
China's Hard Investment Environment for FDI   86
   Energy shortage   87
   The inadequate transportation infrastructure   94
      The railway   95
      Other transportation infrastructure   99
   The poor quality and insecure supply of raw materials   103
   Telecommunications   106
Summary   108

5 THE FOREIGN INVESTMENT ENVIRONMENT IN
   CHINA: THE SOFT ENVIRONMENT (I)   116

'Waking up from the Past' – The Historical Background of
China's Opening up   118
The Political Environment in China – The Fluctuation,
Stagnation and Continuation of the Reform and
   Opening up   123
The Social Environment – The Cultural and Structural
Transformation in Contemporary Chinese Society   130

Guanxi in Chinese Society 139
  The cultural root 140
  The institutional root 143
Summary 147

6 THE FOREIGN INVESTMENT ENVIRONMENT IN
  CHINA: THE SOFT ENVIRONMENT (II) 151

Insufficient Foreign Exchange Facilities 151
Problems with FDI Related Legislation and the Quality of
China's Legal Environment 155
  The Chinese legal tradition 156
  The Chinese Communist Party and the main sources
  of Chinese law 157
  The 'flexibility' and ambiguities of Chinese laws 159
  Two legal frameworks for foreign investors in China 162
  The legal environment in China 164
Human Resource Related Problems 165
Other Issues 171
  Social security and welfare 171
  Bureaucratism and corruption 172
Conclusions: The Main Features of the Investment
Environment for FDI in China 174

7 DISTRIBUTION, MARKETING AND CONSUMER
  BEHAVIOUR IN CHINA 179

Distribution and Sales in China 180
Consumer Behaviour and Marketing in China 185
  How big is the Chinese consumer market? 187
  Market segmentation and consumer behaviour in China 191
  Competition and marketing in China 194
  Consumer buying habits 197
Summary 198

8 THE ECONOMIC AND SOCIAL INFLUENCES OF
  FDI IN CHINA 202

The Major Economic Influences of FDI in China 204
  Relieving capital supply bottlenecks 205
  Technological progress 208
  Enterprise management 211

Foreign trade 214
Employment opportunities 215
Uneven regional development 216
Income distribution 217
The influences of FDI in the Chinese economy 218
FDI and the Social Transformation in Contemporary China 218
   FDI and changes in the mainstream ideologies and
   values in Chinese society 219
   FDI and the re-fabrication of Chinese society in the
   context of reform and opening up 223
   The rapid completion of FDI-related legal systems and
   the improvement in relevant government services 225
Summary of the Chapter 226

9 CONCLUSIONS: FOREIGN INVESTMENT
   ENVIRONMENT IN CHINA UNDER THE OPEN
   DOOR POLICY 231

The Foreign Investment Environment in China 232
FDI and the Chinese Economy: Problems and Future
Prospects 237
   FDI in China: emerging problems and new trends 237
   The Chinese economy and society: problems and future
   prospects 240

Bibliography 247

Index 263

List of Figures

2.1 Foreign Direct Investment in China by Origin
(per cent of Total)   41
4.1 The 'Great Coal Base' in China   88
7.1 The Relationship between Growth in Income and
Product Demand   192
7.2 The Average Income in Eight Cities
(August, 1996, yuan)   193
8.1 Foreign Direct Investment in China
(Utilized, 1983–1996; US$bn)   207

List of Tables

3.1 Pledged Foreign Investment in Equity Joint Ventures   61

4.1 The Key Elements of the Foreign Investment
Environment   85

6.1 Discretionary Concessions Allowed by Chinese Foreign
Investment Law   160

8.1 A Comparison between Chinese and Western
Approaches to Management   213

Preface

Since opening its door to foreign investment in the late 1970s, China has undergone tremendous changes. In addition to the profound political and social transformations, the economic regime in China is gradually being converted from a centrally planned economy to a market system. A legal system for foreign investment and trade has been built up from a virtual void to one of the most complete legal systems in a developing transitional economy today. The lucrative opportunities unleashed by the reform and the continuous rapid growth of the Chinese economy have attracted numerous foreign investors from all over the world, making China the second largest recipient of foreign direct investment (FDI) in the world since the early 1990s.

Although the Chinese government has adopted what is known as the gradualist approach to its reform and opening up, the changes in China over the past two decades – in its political system, economic regime, social structure and international relations, amongst many other aspects – have been very profound. The age of revolution is certainly not over! After nearly two decades of rapid growth and even faster-rising expectations, China has since the mid-1990s embarked on a new round of radical reform. *The Economist* magazine regarded the current change in China as the third revolution, which is 'more complex than Mao's self-preserving turmoil and more far-reaching than Deng's economic modernisation'. This will open up new markets for foreign capital, technology and products.

Until the mid-1990s, China has been very cautious in maintaining social and political stability while undertaking reform. Since then, some radical reforms have been implemented, including reforming the loss-making state-owned sector and the banking system. At the fifteenth Party Congress in 1997, President Jiang Zemin further removed ideological obstacles to the reform by emphasising that China would remain in the 'primary stage of socialism' for a long time, and that China would continue to use 'Deng Xiaoping theory' to guide its development. Nevertheless, the practical difficulties and uncertainties involved in the current reform are enormous, and if not handled properly may jeopardise the two-decades-long reform programme.

With the new reform, the need for central control and stability will increase, as everyone in China will be affected and there will be clear winners and losers. However, the new reform will also by definition require the Chinese government and the Chinese Communist Party to further decentralise power to enterprise owners and to an independent judiciary and other arbiters of conflict rights and claims. Ordinary Chinese people will also demand greater control over their own lives – for example, where they live and how they work, and indeed, a greater say in how they should be governed. How to resolve such conflicting demands and strike an appropriate balance between central control and economic, political and social freedom remain the most difficult challenge facing the Chinese government.

The foreign investment environment in China has been improving steadily and, in some aspects, rapidly. However, many foreign investors, particularly those from the developed economies, have found that doing business in China is far more difficult than they anticipated. The difficulties have been derived from many sources, including the on-going transition from planning to market; the extremely rapid pace of development; the frequently changing policies and priorities of the Chinese government; the enormous cultural differences between China and the West; the growing competition between foreign investors themselves and between foreign investors and Chinese local companies; and the rapidly changing and profoundly different consumer market in China. Other factors, such as international market fluctuations, China's entry to the World Trade Organisation (WTO), Hong Kong's stability, Taiwan issues, and China's relationship with the USA, as well as environmental and human rights issues, may further complicate the situation. Understanding the rapidly evolving and extremely complex foreign investment environment in China is becoming increasingly essential to the operation and development, and indeed the survival, of any foreign invested enterprises in China.

Until the mid-1990s, FDI in China was dominated by overseas Chinese investors, and FDI from Hong Kong and Taiwan accounted for over 70 per cent of all FDI in China. Hong Kong's return to China in 1997 has further boosted such investment. However, in recent years, FDI from the USA, Europe and Japan has been on the increase, as the strategic importance of China as a huge market for foreign capital, technology and products has been increasingly recognized. Although many foreign investors continue to enter

China by forming joint ventures with local partners, the number of wholly owned foreign ventures in China has been growing very rapidly. More and more foreign invested enterprises are now run by local Chinese managers, and it has been found that ventures run by local managers tend to perform better than those run by foreign expatriates, and local managers also cost less. The shortage of qualified local managerial staff remains a serious problem facing foreign invested enterprises.

The continuous development of China will require massive new foreign capital, particularly large-scale investments in various infrastructures and in the middle and western provinces. Reforming the state owned sector also requires major capital injection and technology transfer, and so does the development of the high-tech and service industries. Therefore, the demand for FDI in China will continue to increase. The experience of the past two decades has clearly indicated that China is a huge and rapidly growing market, and there are numerous lucrative commercial opportunities. The hard and soft investment environment for FDI has been improved considerably today. However, the difficulties involved in doing business in China are greater than ever. This book is our attempt to help foreign investors, as well as researchers, business consultants, politicians, business school students and other people who are interested in the Chinese market, to understand the nature and characteristics of China's investment environment.

Acknowledgements

Numerous people have helped us with this book and it is a real challenge to acknowledge everyone properly. First of all, we would like to thank Dr Shaun Breslin (Now at Warwick University Business School in England), Dr Tim Gray and Dr Martin Harrop (Both at the University of Newcastle upon Tyne, England) for their critical comments and constructive suggestions on earlier versions of the book. The encouragement from Dr Chris Gentle (The Henley Centre in London), as well as many other friends and colleagues, has also been extremely valuable.

Although we only started writing this book in 1995, some of the original ideas went back much further and many people have shaped our ideas. Among the most influential people was the late Professor Yang Shuzhen, of the Renmin University of China in Beijing, who was a respected scholar and a father figure for us. In particular, he taught one of us how to conduct valid research in the Chinese context. Other people that have significantly influenced our thoughts include Professor Jin Ling, Professor Zhao Ji, Professor Wu Yuguang, Professor Feng Jiaping, Professor Cheng Liansheng, Professor Yang Ruyi, as well as Li Chunping, Yi Daichang, and Jiang Xianhua. Numerous friends and colleagues also helped us collect relevant data for this book.

We are indebted to Jane Powell, Commissioning Editor at Macmillan for recognizing the importance of this topic and for her enthusiastic encouragement to turn our ideas into this book. She also helped us to get in touch with Giovanna Davitti who commissioned the book. After Giovanna left Macmillan, Sunder Katwala took over and we would like to thank him for his understanding when we had to delay the delivery of the manuscript due to reasons beyond our control. We would also like to thank Linda Auld, Editorial Consultant for Macmillan for her excellent editorial work.

We would like to acknowledge the following publishers and individuals for granting us the right to use some extracts of which they hold copyrights:

Professor Robert Kleinberg for allowing us to reproduce Table 6.1 Discretionary Concessions Allowed by Chinese Foreign Investment

Law, from his book on *China's Opening to the Outside World*, published by Westview Press, Boulder in 1990.

Euromonitor and Gordon Cousland for allowing us to reproduce Figure 7.1 The Relationship between Growth in Income and Product Demand, from *China: A Directory and Source Book*, published by Euromonitor, London in 1994.

Routledge for allowing us to reproduce Table 8.1 A Comparison between Chinese and Western Approaches to Management, from Child, John and Yuan Lu (1996) 'Introduction: China and international enterprise', in Child, John and Yuan Lu (Eds) *Management Issues in China: Volume II, International Enterprises,* Routledge, London.

Finally, we would like to thank our families for their continuous support. Our parents, as always, have encouraged us in their different ways. Most of all, Jeffrey has been extremely supportive and tolerant throughout the last two years – he must have been puzzled from time to time by the heated debate between us. We would like to dedicate this book to him.

Feng and Jing Li, Glasgow

1 Introduction: Foreign Investment in China under the Open Door Policy

Since the implementation of the economic reform in late 1978, China has achieved impressive results, including rapid economic growth, major structural changes and unprecedented improvement in living standards for the majority of its 1.2 billion people.[1] In spite of challenging political, social and economic problems,[2] annual economic growth (GDP) during 1978–92 averaged 9 per cent, further increasing to 12 per cent during the eighth five year plan (1991–95), with industrial growth in the coastal region far exceeding these 'modest' figures.[3] In 1993, the UBS International Finance predicted that the Chinese economy would have quadrupled that of 1980 by 1994 (which actually happened in 1995[4]), and it could double again by 2002.[5] The calculations made by the World Bank and the International Monetary Fund (IMF) concluded that on a comparable basis, China had become the world's second largest economy after the USA, with an estimated GDP of US$2850 billion in 1990 by 'purchasing power parity' (PPP), and over US$2000 billion by 'new country weight' in 1992.[6]

The growth of the Chinese economy has been particularly impressive during the eighth five year plan (1991–95). Total GDP reached 5760 billion yuan in 1995, which quadrupled that of 1980, five years ahead of the planned schedule. In spite of serious problems, such as economic over-heating and high inflation in 1994 and early 1995, annual GDP growth averaged 12 per cent in the five years (9.3 per cent and 14.2 per cent for the lowest and highest years), and economic fluctuation during this period was the lowest in China's eight five year plans since 1950.[7] In particular, using indirect measures such as monetary policy, financial policy and interest rate (rather than administrative measures as it did in the past), China successfully managed a soft landing from the economic over-heating of 1993/94 in 1995/96, and the runaway inflation and rapid growth was brought under control without causing major

1

damage to the economy. A series of radical reforms in areas ranging from taxation and finance, banking, foreign currency and foreign trade, investment, price control, distribution system and
organization management, to social welfare and housing, are being
implemented. Reforming the loss-making state owned sector has
also been underway, and some early results have been fairly positive.[8]
It is widely considered that China, along with some Asian economies, has made up the world's most dynamic and rapidly growing
regional economy of the 1980s and 1990s, and the tendency is
projected to continue over the next two decades.

China's transition from a planned economy to a market system
has created numerous opportunities for foreign investors. For many
world-leading companies, China is simply too big a strategic opportunity to miss in spite of the perceived political risks, potential
cultural clashes and other difficulties in doing business in China.
In combination with China's renewed effort to open up further to
the outside world since 1992, foreign investment has poured in at
an accelerating speed. By the end of 1995, the total number of *San
Zi* or foreign invested enterprises[9] in China reached 258 903, with
a total utilized foreign direct investment (FDI) of US$133.37 bil-
lion, making China the second largest destination for FDI in the
entire world after the USA. By the end of 1996, the figure increased
to over 280 000 foreign invested enterprises, with a total utilized
FDI of US$176.59 billion (US$469.39 billion contracted).[10]

China's main attractions to foreign investors include its abundant,
cheap, but reasonably educated labour resources, its potentially
enormous and rapidly growing market, the preferential taxation and
policies for foreign invested enterprises, and its rich reserves of
natural resources (such as coal and oil). Also, the absolute number
of educated, skilled people in China is very large – a big-country
advantage which many people tend to neglect. However, China's
remarkable progress may tempt unwary foreigners to believe that
they can simply invest in the country, sit back and wait for the
profits to roll in.

In reality, this is obviously not the case, and investing in China
requires careful preparation and constant attention.[11] Many investors have learnt this lesson in the hard way. The Chinese economy
has moved some way towards the market, and the quality of China's
investment environment has been improving steadily and rapidly.
However, the nature of Chinese society and economy, including its
political system, economic regime, social structure, prevailing culture,

consumer behaviour, and the level of socio-economic development, is profoundly different from western countries. Many well tested management and marketing techniques in the USA, western Europe and Japan may simply not work in China. For example, the so-called 'just-in-time' (JIT) strategy currently used in the developed world is unlikely to work in China, because the transportation infrastructure and the supply of raw materials are often unreliable; and the price fluctuation for certain materials can sometimes be very volatile due to general short supply and incomplete market mechanisms. The potential benefits of cost-saving from JIT may not even be able to offset the potential risks of production disruption. As such, it is essential for potential investors to develop a comprehensive understanding of the quality and main characteristics of China's investment environment if they intend to achieve the projected returns on their investment.

This book intends to systematically examine the characteristics and conditions of China's investment environment within the wider context of its economic and political reform and opening up to the outside world. The unique characteristics of Chinese consumer behaviours are also analysed in detail, and the contributions made by FDI and the main problems it has brought to China are also examined as they inevitably affect the perception and attitude of Chinese leaders and ordinary Chinese people towards FDI, which in turn will be reflected in China's future policies and regulations for FDI in China.

THE BACKGROUND OF THE REFORM AND OPEN DOOR POLICY IN CHINA

The Chinese Communist Party came to power in 1949, and until the late 1950s China maintained close economic relations with the former Soviet Union and some East European countries. After Sino-Soviet political and economic ties gave way to conflict, the Chinese economy became highly isolated internationally – primarily 'a self-reliant, centrally planned, Socialist state-owned economy'. To withstand potential sudden military attacks from the then Soviet Union or the hostile Western countries, efficiency in production was subordinated to requirements of national security and ideology. Agriculture was collectively managed; industry was relocated to the least accessible provinces in the interior. A high degree of provincial self-sufficiency was encouraged. High level investment rate was maintained during the period to ensure a reasonable rate of output growth.

The problems of central planning and self-reliance were particularly serious during the Cultural Revolution (1966–76), and by the early-1970s these problems were increasingly recognized by some senior Chinese leaders. The normalization of Sino-US and Sino-Japanese relations in 1972 and 1973 symbolized China's intent to break out of the situation of international isolation from the West. In 1975, Zhou Enlai (the Premier of the Chinese State Council at the time) suggested the 'four modernization'[12] as the guiding principle of China's economic reform. However, the actual reform process did not begin until the Third Plenum of the Eleventh Central Committee of the Communist Party (*San-Zhong-Quan-Hui*, or 'The Third Plenum' for short) in December 1978. The Third Plenum challenged Mao's legacy with the radical ideological shift from 'class struggle' to modernization as the Chinese Communist Party's legitimate purpose. It also called for a major shift of investment from heavy industry to agriculture and consumer goods and the legitimization and expansion of markets.

Domestic economic reforms were first introduced on an experimental basis with the dissolution of collective agriculture in some parts of Anhui, Sichuan and Guangdong Provinces. By the mid-1980s, the communes had been re-constituted as townships and villages throughout China. These new units only have indirect responsibility for economic activities, and virtually all agricultural production was conducted by household farming on leased land. Agricultural output grew by 8 per cent per annum between 1978 and 1986, and rural markets re-emerged. Farmers used their increased purchasing power to buy consumer goods, and to diversify into light manufacturing – hence the rapid growth of the privately or collectively owned town and village enterprises or *Xiang Zhen Qi Yie*, which are playing an increasingly important role in the rapid growth of the Chinese economy.

In urban areas, similar experiments with enterprise autonomy during the early 1980s led to the introduction of the enterprise responsibility system in 1984 and the contract management system in 1986. By the end of the 1980s, contracting had become a major feature of the urban economy. However, the retaining of central planning in certain industries created a complex multi-tiered pricing and resources allocation system, which formed the basis for many forms of corruption and in particular *Guan Dao* (that is, people with power – including their relatives and friends – can obtain materials in short supply at state controlled price and re-sell the materials at market prices to make hyper profits over night). This was one of the main factors that evoked the massive student movement in 1989. The urban reform also created several other difficult problems, such as in the area of bankruptcy law and penalties for poor decision-making and enterprise management. Nevertheless, the vitality injected into the national economy led to unprecedented economic growth in China.

Increased enterprise autonomy was accompanied by a decentralization of decision-making from the central to local governments, which enabled provinces and lower level administrative units to pursue their own industrial policies within the overall framework set out by the central government. However, increased local autonomy resulted in a poorly co-ordinated national economy, and problems such as investment boom and bust, inflation and unemployment forced the central government to re-adjust its reform policies several times during the 1980s. In the early 1990s, the central focus of the Chinese economic reform was on the creation of the market economy in China, particularly in the area of macro-economic policies in fiscal, banking, taxation, foreign exchange and investment sectors. Since the mid-1990s, the focus has been moving towards micro-economic issues such as reforming the loss making state owned enterprises and the commercialization of Chinese banks.

China's domestic economic reform has been paralleled by its increasing opening up to the outside world. The open door policy refers to a set of foreign economic policies adopted by China after 1978 that invite and control outside participation in national and regional development, which has been a key area of China's overall economic and political reform. The open door policy includes not only the policies that concern foreign investment, international trade, technological transfer and special economic zones, but also reforms such as accepting foreign aid and concessionary loans; sending thousands of graduate students abroad to study; letting foreigners travel quite freely in China; and allowing the Chinese people to see and learn more about the outside world particularly through the state controlled mass media.

China's opening up to the outside world represents a radical ideological change in the Chinese leadership's economic and political thinking. Instead of dividing the world into Socialism and

Capitalism, China now engages in trade and investment relations with all kinds of countries to increase its national productive capacity. In other words, China has adopted a more pragmatic approach to economic development, and it is prepared to use any measures possible to improve its national economic power and the living standard of its people – both are essential to China's social and political stability and international position.

China's opening up primarily means the adoption by the state of new methods to promote national economic strength, methods that replace class struggle and global class conflict. The state encourages the involvement of foreign partners in China's economy, subject to government laws and policies. China offers special concessions to those who bring capital and technology. Such measures have facilitated rapid growth and led to many local economic success stories. However, these stories also had destabilizing effects that challenged the government to devise new methods of control. The experience of the 1980s and the first half of the 1990s has proven that managing the balance between local initiative and central intervention is an extremely difficult task.

The reform in China has been characterized by shifts from planning to market mechanisms, from ideological to material incentives, from centralized to a comparatively decentralized decision-making and, most importantly, from an isolated self-reliant economy to an open economy. The first move of the Chinese reform involved readjusting investment priority to give more resources to agriculture and light industry. The hallmark of Mao's cellular, self-reliant economy – the commune – was gradually abandoned. The second move, prompted by the urgent and immediate need for new financial resources, was to create special economic zones to attract foreign investment. These policies represented attempts to use the local market and the international market as supplements to the state owned planned economy.

The initial success of agricultural reform urged the Chinese leadership to spread its new economic policies to industries, which led to the beginning of the urban reform in 1984, followed by a series of measures to transform the Chinese economy from a centrally planned economy to a market system throughout the 1980s and early 1990s. In spite of reoccurring economic booms and busts, as well as emerging social and political problems, the reform in China led to an extremely rapidly growing economy. Since 1993, a series of policies have been implemented to unshackle the financial sector in China. To a large extent, the steps being taken to liberalize the financial sector were driven by the underlying wishes of the Chinese central authority to unlock the estimated equivalent of US$250 billion of untapped local currency savings in the banking systems and re-direct it towards financing industrial development.[13] This figure had grown to nearly US$450 billion (3708.52 billion yuan) by September 1996 and is still growing.[14] A series of radical steps have since been implemented, and China's own financial system has gone through several overhauls. Equally important is the opening up of the financial sector to foreign financial institutions, and by the end of 1995 well over one hundred foreign banks and other financial institutions had set up branches in China,[15] with total assets in China exceeding of US$19.1 billion.[16] Since the mid-1990s, the focus of the national economic reform has shifted to the loss making state owned enterprises, and foreign investors are increasingly encouraged to participate directly in the process through joint ventures and technology transfer.

It is emphasized that the open door policy is only one part (however important) of China's political and economic reform, and its nature is determined by the overall framework setting out China's new political and economic regime. The relationship between China's foreign economic opening up and other elements of the reform (such as China's internal economic reform and cultural and legal liberalization) are very complex, and they are not always logically linked, nor are they always mutually supportive or beneficial. Sometimes, they even move towards opposite directions.[17]

In spite of frequent fluctuations and re-adjustments of these policies, market mechanisms have increasingly been introduced in China, and FDI has been regarded as a major source of capital supply and a key channel for technology transfer in China. Although so far the political and economic reform has suggested that the open door policy is not intended to move China towards Western-style liberalism, the open areas (that is, areas that are open to foreign investors) have been extended to the whole of China, and the foreign investment environment has been improving rapidly. It is increasingly recognized by the Chinese leadership that the opening up in general and the rapid growth of FDI in particular have been essential to China's phenomenal economic success since 1978, and FDI can play an even greater role in the next stage of China's economic development.

THE EVOLUTION OF THE OPEN DOOR POLICY IN CHINA

The open door policy is an integral part of China's new development strategy and a key element of China's political and economic reform. Generally speaking, the open door policy consists of the following three key elements:[18]

- attracting foreign investment
- promoting foreign trade
- introducing advanced technologies, skills and management techniques.

The central focus of this book is on the first aspect, and it will systematically examine the quality and the key characteristics of China's foreign investment environment. In order to do so, it is necessary to examine how the growth of FDI has evolved in China; the policies and key measures designated to attract (specific forms of) FDI; and the main influences of FDI in Chinese society and economy.

So far, China's open door policy has undergone five major steps of progress. The designation of special policies for Guangdong and Fujian provinces, and the setting up of the four special economic zones in 1979 as windows of China's opening up, marked the first major step. Then, in 1984, the geographical coverage of the 'open area' was extended to fourteen coastal cities as the front-line of China's open door, and Hainan Island was also designated as a special administrative region at this time. The third step started in 1985, with the creation of Changjiang and Zhujiang Deltas, and the Minnan Triangle in Fujian province as 'coastal economic open areas' to act as bridges for the opening up of inland areas in the future.[19]

With these three steps, China's open area covered the entire coastal belt stretching from the far North to the South. This belt is of strategic importance to China, as it produces over half of China's industrial and agricultural outputs, and has a population of over 200 million.[20] The success of this region is important in boosting the development of the national economy and in removing the obstacles for further opening up in the future.

The opening of Pudong New Development Zone in Shanghai in September 1990 as a special economic zone marked the fourth major step in China's opening up.[21] This step is not simply an extension of the geographical coverage of open areas, as in the first three steps. Rather, it marked the beginning of a new round of China's opening up, characterized by further opening up within an 'open area'. This step is significant in that the focus of China's opening up has progressed from extending the size of the open area to one which also emphasizes quality. More importantly, designating a special economic zone at the very heart of the most important economic centre in China also demonstrated China's determination to open up the national economy. This objective was further boosted and materialized by the visit of Deng Xiaoping to southern China in 1992. In the meantime, the geographical coverage of open areas was continuously extended.[22]

The latest step in China's opening up started from 1994, which shifted the central focus of the opening up to 'quality' and 'long term development'. A wide range of measures has been planned and implemented, including further relaxing foreign currency control and making Chinese currency fully convertible as soon as practical and feasible; phasing out preferential policies for foreign investment in special economic zones and Pudong new development zone by the end of the century; slashing tariff and non-tariff barriers for the import and export of a wide range of products; further opening up the domestic market particularly in sectors such as the financial sector and retailing; adopting special measures to attract foreign investments in infrastructure development, agriculture and other primary industries; and encouraging foreign investors to invest in the middle and western parts of China. In particular, special economic zones – the show piece of China's opening up and economic miracles – will be converted from 'preferential economic zones' to 'functional economic zones' with the gradual disappearance of preferential policies.[23] This stage of opening up will provide part of the basis for China to join the World Trade Organization (WTO). It is also a key step in China's wider economic reform in establishing socialist market economy and in transforming China's economic development strategy from an 'extensive' to an 'intensive' one.[24]

THE ROLE OF FDI IN CHINA

China's economic achievement since 1978 owes much to the adoption of radical initiatives in most areas of international economic relations.[25] Unlike other aspects of China's opening up (such as foreign trade, which has to be financed by extra export earnings), FDI brings foreign capital and foreign experts, together with the necessary technical and managerial know-how, directly into China, thereby providing an important physical learning ground for its Chinese employees, suppliers and customers. Although the major beneficiaries of FDI in China are the coastal provinces (which aggravates the regional imbalance between the coast and the interior), FDI is now a sustainable endeavour and its contribution to China's capital formation, its impact on income in priority areas and its ability to earn foreign exchange has been phenomenal. In particular, since China's recovery from the 1989 Tiananmen Square tragedy, the role of FDI has been undergoing a radical change: it no longer simply plays a symbolic role in China's opening up to the outside world, it has become one of the key driving forces in the development of the local and national economy.

In early 1992, a new round of reform and opening up was initiated by the visit of Deng Xiaoping to southern China.[26] He urged swifter growth of the Chinese economy through further opening up by employing a simple slogan: 'Do it faster', and the message was widely publicized in all major Chinese official media.[27] Officials at all levels of the Chinese government rushed to do his bidding, culminating in a frenzy of activities in the last quarter of 1992. In attracting new FDI, China was particularly successful. Over 47 000 new joint ventures, co-operative enterprises and wholly-owned foreign ventures were established in 1992, which exceeded the total number of foreign invested enterprises attracted to China during the entire preceding 14 years. More than US$30 billions of FDI contracts were signed, which accounted for about one quarter of the total fund invested in developing countries world-wide.[28]

The year 1993 was even more successful, and 83 265 new foreign investment projects were approved, with a total pledged and deployed (utilized) foreign capital of US$110.852 billion and US$25.759 billion – increases of 70.6 per cent, 90.7 per cent and 134 per cent respectively from 1992. The size of foreign investment in these new projects averaged US$1.33 million, an increase of 12.9 per cent from 1992. Total FDI attracted to China in 1993 equalled that for the entire period of 1978–92, and there is no sign of slowing down. By the end of 1993, the total number of foreign invested enterprises in China reached 167 500, with a total pledged FDI of US$216.91 billion, and actual utilized FDI of US$56.48 billion.[29]

By the end of 1995, the figures had further increased to 258 903, with a total utilized foreign investment of US$133.37 billion (which more than doubled that by the end of 1993), making China the second largest destination for foreign investment in the entire world after the USA.[30] The average size of foreign investment in new projects increased to US$1.77 million in 1994, and US$2.45 million in 1995 – with many world-leading companies flocking into China. In spite of repeated warnings from the Chinese central government over the danger of economic over-heating,[31] many local leaders stated openly that their local economies were simply not hot enough and they wanted them hotter.[32]

Since 1993, China has taken a series of important steps towards liberalizing its economy by loosening restrictions on exchange rate. Other measures, such as the relaxation of restrictions on investment in real estate and some infrastructure projects, are also fuelling foreign investment surge in China. The soft-landing of the Chinese economy from the 1993/94 boom in 1995/96 without using the familiar administrative measures of re-centralization indicated that the Chinese authority has learnt important new economic measures of the market system in managing the Chinese economy, which further boosted international business confidence in China. However, for potential foreign investors, a comprehensive understanding of the investment environment in China – including its unique history, culture, political system, socio-economic regime, legal system, infrastructure, and consumer behaviour, to mention but a few aspects – is essential for the establishment of successful ventures in China. This issue is the central focus of the book.

PREVIOUS STUDIES AND THIS BOOK: A BRIEF REVIEW OF RELATED LITERATURE AND THE MAIN SOURCES OF INFORMATION FOR THE STUDY

This book intends to examine the quality and key characteristics of China's foreign investment environment, and highlight their implications for FDI. However, these issues can only be fully understood in the wider context of the contemporary world economy and the general economic and political reforms in China. As a result, the study will highlight the main attraction of China to foreign investors in the contemporary world economy, outline the evolution of China's open door policy particularly in respect of FDI, identify the unique characteristics of consumer behaviour in China, and evaluate the major economic and social influences of FDI in China. The nature of these key issues has determined that this is primarily a qualitative research, although a large number of quantitative figures will be used to support the findings of the book. The fact that both authors have lived and worked in China and Britain for many years provided us with the essential background knowledge in understanding the nature and characteristics of the problems and issues that will be examined in the book.

FDI is still a relatively new phenomenon, which has only appeared in China since 1979. Despite the growing interest in FDI-related issues by the Chinese authorities and by the international business and academic communities, very few systematic studies have been published about the foreign investment environment in China. Adding to the already enormous difficulty of understanding this environment is the extremely rapid pace of change in almost every aspect and every area in China. Over the last few years, many 'how to' or 'guide' types of books and reports have been published both in China and in the West, mainly targeting business people intending to invest in China or people interested in the Chinese market.[33] Some surveys and reports about the Chinese market and foreign invested enterprises in China have also been published.[34] Some of these books and reports can be very useful for people who know very little about China. However, many such publications are overly simplistic, fragmented, and superficial, and some can even be misleading, if not potentially harmful, to potential investors.

For example, a report published by the prestigious Andersen Consulting and the Economist Intelligence Unit in 1995 found that about two thirds of all multinational companies they studied were profitable, and it took most of them only two years to make money after setting up. Many findings of the report were original and interesting, which can be very valuable to potential foreign investors and to academic researchers. However, the report also concluded that 'there is no black magic, special *Guanxi* (connections) or business practices unique to China', and the best performers of foreign invested enterprises in China focused on 'the things that make them successful in other parts of the world'.[35] There might be some truth in these findings, but anyone familiar with China would suspect the validity of such conclusions. We believe such conclusions may be related to the methods they adopted for the research – the type of methods people normally use in the West, such as questionnaire surveys and interviews – which may not always be valid in China. Would you realistically expect a businessman to tell you how he bribed some powerful government officials, or that he was hiding profit for tax reasons, or his success was related to special connections or *guanxi* with certain powerful people in China? Without paying special attention to the highly personalized style of business dealings in China and the critical importance of networks and *guanxi*, a foreign investor may soon find himself paying extremely dear prices for the mistake.

As will be discussed later in the book, a key characteristic of business dealings in China is the extensive use of personal networks or *guanxi*.[36] This network ensures the free flow of information within the network, and to gain access to such information one first has to enter the network. Network entry has to be earned and people in the network need to be useful to each other. It is thus understandable that a researcher who is essentially an outsider would find it hard to tap into such network information. As a Chinese businessman once said to a researcher while being interviewed: 'You asked me very sensitive questions both at a personal and a company level. I can't tell you that we are not doing well here. On the other hand, there is no point telling you how well we are doing'. Thus, we need to be extremely cautious in treating research findings about business practice and related issues in China. In particular, a realistic evaluation of the quality of China's foreign investment environment depends critically on a comprehensive understanding of the nature of the contemporary Chinese society and economy – especially Chinese politics and culture.

This is, however, not to say nothing can be learnt from previous studies. On the contrary, some factual surveys and policy studies can be very useful to foreign investors. Several scholarly studies about the early years of the open door policy provided an initial guide to the way foreign investment operated in China (for example, Ho and Huenemann;[37] Moser;[38] Wang;[39] and Chai[40]), with important descriptive value. Since the late 1980s, some more insightful studies have increasingly appeared, many of them based on primary data gathered from pioneer foreign invested enterprises in China, whilst others were about the reform and opening up and the management of enterprises in China in general. Of particular relevance to this study are the works of Pomfret,[41] Pearson,[42] Shen,[43] Thoburn *et al.*,[44] Lee *et al.*,[45] Aiello,[46] Harwit,[47] Kamath,[48] Chan *et al.*,[49] Lockett,[50] Child,[51] and Warner, to name but a few.

Pomfret described the chronological evolution of China's open door policy (mainly between 1978 and 1988), and the geographical spread and other characteristics of foreign direct investment in China, focusing particularly on joint ventures in the manufacturing sector. His work provided an extensive (albeit sometimes superficial) guide for private sector investors from the West with limited knowledge and experience about China. The background and contextual knowledge on investing in China outlined in the book were particularly useful.

A more in-depth study by Pearson examined the evolution and underlying political thinking of the open door policy and foreign investment in China between 1979 and 1988. She highlighted that at the core of China's foreign investment policy is the attempt to use foreign capital to spur economic development while maintaining control over that capital (at national, regional and enterprise levels); and examined the Chinese government's effort to control the terms of foreign investment, particularly in equity joint ventures. Her study examined the Chinese government's goals of both absorbing and controlling foreign investment, and how China attempted to realize these goals, by describing China's foreign investment programme and changes in the programme over time, and the patterns of foreign direct investment in China. It also investigated the various forces that shaped foreign investment policy throughout the 1980s, and examined how effective China actually was at meeting its goals. This study is particularly valuable for potential foreign investors in understanding the general context of the open door policy and to appreciate the importance of politics in Chinese society and the economy.

Shen Xiaofang looked at the first decade of China's experience with FDI, examined the erratic course FDI took and the factors that caused such a pattern. She emphasized that in spite of the difficulties and setbacks, initial FDI performance made a significant contribution to the Chinese economy during this period. She also pointed out that before the Tiananmen Square tragedy in 1989, FDI had already reached a critical stage in which fundamental socioeconomic problems were destined to hinder its further development. What happened on the fourth of June 1989 simply added to the difficulties the Chinese authority has to fare and put the future of FDI in China in question. To maintain the growth rate of FDI in China during the first decade of the opening up, the Chinese government needed to recommit itself strongly to carrying through the reform and open door policy. Her analysis of the impact of FDI on Chinese society and economy, and the problems encountered by foreign invested enterprises (often based on empirical evidence) was particularly insightful.

The studies by Aiello, Harwit, Lee *et al.*, Thoburn, Lockett, and many other studies, were based on evidence gathered from either individual cases (for example, Beijing Jeep-Chrysler) or specific geographical areas (such as some Special Economic Zones or the Pearl River Delta). They described the problems foreign investors encountered in China, speculated on how they had gone about resolving those problems, and elaborated on their implications for other foreign investors. Some studies also examined specific aspects of FDI in China such as culture and the problems of Chinese management (Lockett), and labour relations in foreign invested enterprises (Chan *et al.*). These studies provided valuable insights on specific aspects of the foreign investment environment in China.

Child's book reviewed a large number of previous studies, and by drawing upon information (albeit limited) he obtained directly from case studies in China, his book provided a good account of management in China during the age of reform. The book not only covered joint ventures and their contribution to Chinese management development, but also management of Chinese state owned enterprises in general in the context of reform and socio-economic transition in China. The background information provided in the book may be particularly useful for someone intending to develop a good understanding of Chinese political, social and economic systems. He recognized that the Chinese model is one of reform by incremental and experimental innovation, with the state retaining a major role in the overall regulation of the economy and probably a significant stake in the ownership of industrial property as well.

Child also recognized that although much had been written about the intentions of the reform at the enterprise level and the management of joint ventures both by Chinese and foreign authors, he suspected the validity of many studies. Many papers were written by non-Chinese authors on the basis of quick, one-off and generally superficial studies, which concentrated on one aspect of Chinese management attitude or experience. These studies often employed a questionnaire-based methodology, which might not be valid or reliable in China. Such studies may be stimulating in terms of their propositions and in the range of issues they address, but they were rarely informative in terms of their results. Many studies by Chinese authors failed to reveal the sources of their information, therefore the readers cannot assess the quality of the information. Even studies that are not so limited by their methodology, depth or comparative coverage are often not sufficiently up-to-date in their materials. By emphasizing that China is an industrializing and modernizing economy, the unique system of industrial governance and most of all, Chinese culture, Child's book provided valuable insight into management issues in China. His work on joint ventures is particularly relevant to this book.

This research also referred to a number of business guides to doing business in China. For example, Euromonitor published *China: A Directory and Source Book 1994*,[53] which discussed key issues in China ranging from the Chinese economy and consumer market in the 1990s, the main issues of doing business in China by foreigners, to various sources of useful information. Another useful business guide by Brahm and Li published in 1996 provided a broad outline of the legislation and various issues involved in establishing an investment and conducting business activities in China.[54] We also obtained a large number of business guides for investing in various parts of China published by Chinese local authorities. The information contained in such guides can be extremely useful to foreign investors in developing an initial understanding of various aspects of doing business in China.

In spite of the valuable contribution made by previous studies, and the insights they advanced, many authors have so far failed to appreciate the unique nature of Chinese culture, history and politics, and many other aspects of Chinese society and economy, and their implications for the negotiation, implementation, maintenance, operation and development of foreign invested enterprises in China. The unique characteristics of consumer behaviour in China, its differences from the western world and its implications for doing business in China were also largely absent from previous studies. Most of all, few researchers have systematically examined the nature, quality and characteristics of China's investment environment for FDI, its current situation and future prospect. This research systematically examines the characteristics and quality of China's hard and soft investment environments, identify their most important elements and factors, and evaluate their quality from the perspective of foreign investors. It will particularly highlight the unique nature of the Chinese culture, politics and history, examine the differences between China and the West, and speculate on their implications for the management of foreign invested enterprises in China.

The materials for the study have mainly been gathered from documentary sources, including Chinese and foreign newspapers and magazines, published statistics and reports by Chinese central and local governments and international organizations (such as the Almanac of Foreign Economic Relations and Trade; the World Bank Country Report), press releases by Chinese central and local governments and foreign investors/groups, scholarly studies such as books, journal and conference articles, and research notes published both in Chinese and English inside and outside China. Some evidence from published case studies on particular foreign invested enterprises (such as Beijing-Jeep, Shanghai-Volkswagen and many others) is also used. Materials as up-to-date as 1998 have been gathered and incorporated in the analysis.

These various sources of information provided the basis for this research. Chinese press and journal articles (for example, the Chinese official newspaper, the *People's Daily*, and the weekly *Beijing Review* and *Liaowang*) provided information about official policies and regulations and the justifications for them. The latest figures about the Chinese economy, foreign investment in China, new economic targets and so on are also first released to the public via such media by various official sources (for example, the State Council, the State Statistics Bureau, various Ministries, and local governments). Information from such sources often reflected less opposition to and problems with the negative effects of FDI than in fact may have existed, though on the other hand, the concerns they did express were probably not especially controversial, or at a minimum, were issues to which leaders had to respond. Some foreign newspapers and journals (for example, *The Financial Times*, *The Economist*, and the *Far East Economic Review*) offered up-to-date coverage of particular FDI cases in China and of statistics and trends in the general policy from an extra-China account. The combination of these two sources provides a proper balance on the real situation in China. More importantly, these sources of information enable us to keep up with the latest developments in China, which is a major challenge to any researcher as the pace of change has been so rapid. The relevance of scholarly publications such as journal articles and books has been discussed earlier in this section.

Before turning to the next section, it is emphasized, once again, that in spite of numerous previous studies on Chinese reform and

open door policy in general and on foreign investment in particular, the number of high quality, up-to-date, systematic studies of
China's investment environment is rather limited. So the number
of scholarly studies that this book can refer to is not as wide ranging as we originally anticipated. The authors fully understand the
potential problems associated with the popular press (such as *The
Financial Times*, *The Economist*, the *Wall Street Journal,* the *Far
East Economic Review*, and Chinese publications such *The People's
Daily*, *Beijing Review*, *China Daily* and *Liaowang)* when preparing a
piece of academic work. Therefore, although the book relies heavily on such popular press, the use of information from such sources
is mainly restricted to factual information such as figures, specific
laws, regulations and policies and, sometimes, information about
the development of particular cases (for example, the market share
or production capacity of a particular joint venture).

The reliability of Chinese statistics has long been a problem not
only for researchers but also for Chinese government officials and
policy makers. Many people in Chinese central and local governments admit privately that these figures are often unreliable. However, in the absence of better ways of getting more reliable figures
(they simply do not exist in China because of increasing local
autonomy, the rapidly growing grey and black economy and the
private sectors), official figures may be the only option in getting a
reasonable account of the current situation in China. The Chinese
government often releases latest economic figures, new policies and
regulations through its official newspaper – *The People's Daily* – so
to keep this research up-to-date, we have to rely on the popular
press for the latest information release (but we often confirm such
figures via other sources). A wide range of new policy initiatives
are also made known to people in the West via newspapers such
as *The Financial Times* and *The Economist*. The reliance of the
book on popular press thus should not undermine the reliability of
the findings and arguments.

THE STRUCTURE OF THE BOOK

There are nine chapters in this book. After the Introduction (Chapter 1),
the next chapter (Chapter 2) will examine the investment attraction of China under the contemporary world economic climate, and
highlight the key motivations of foreign investors in China: in other

words, why foreign investors want to put their money in China instead of somewhere else. Then, in Chapter 3, the main forms of FDI in China, and the evolution of China's open door policies for foreign investment (in particular the adjustments in related laws and regulations and their underlying causes) are systematically examined within the context of China's political and economic reform.

Chapters 4, 5 and 6 examine issues related to China's investment environment for FDI in detail. The investment environment is divided into two categories, namely, the 'hard environment' and the 'soft environment'. Chapter 4 will focus particularly on issues related to the hard environment, such as the general condition and characteristics of the basic infrastructures (transportation and telecommunications) and the supply of energy and other raw materials, which can have an immediate impact on the operation and development of foreign invested enterprises in China. From the historical, political and social perspectives, Chapter 5 will analyse the characteristics and quality of China's soft investment environment, and speculate on their implications for the operation and management of foreign invested enterprises. Some operational problems encountered by foreign investors with China's soft investment environment and how foreign investors should go about resolving these problems are examined in Chapter 6 (such as the unique labour relations, incomplete legal system and insufficient foreign exchange facilities in China).

In Chapter 7, key issues (problems in particular) in the area of sales and distribution, marketing, and consumer behaviour in China are examined, and their implications for FDI in China are discussed. In Chapter 8, the major influences of FDI in the Chinese economy and the problems and changes that FDI has brought to Chinese society are examined. The social and economic influences of FDI may significantly affect the perception and attitude of Chinese leaders and ordinary Chinese people towards FDI in China, and therefore, many such influences will be reflected in China's future FDI related policies and regulations. Finally, in the Conclusion (Chapter 9), the main findings of the book are summarized, and the future prospect of the Chinese economy and foreign investment environment in China are discussed.

China is still in the process of a radical socio-economic transformation, and the pace of change has been extremely fast. It is, therefore, important for the readers to understand the arguments and findings of the book within a dynamic and rapidly changing context. The reform and opening up in China is an on-going process, so constantly updating the materials used in the book poses an extremely difficult challenge. The real situation in China may have changed by the time this book goes to print! Combining with the fact that China is a large country with growing regional differences, many problems identified in the book may not apply in certain regions. However, the principles highlighted in the book will be relevant and valid for a long time to come, and a proper focus in time and geography is necessary for foreign investors in making specific decisions.

Notes

1. *The Economist*, 28 November – 5 December 1992, 'China: The titan stirs'.
2. Such as the reoccurring cycles of economic boom and bust, a still bloated state sector, high inflation, the growing disparity in income divide both within and between regions, and the enormous challenge in maintaining social and political stability during the transition.
3. *The People's Daily* (Overseas edition), 20 March 1996, 'The People's Republic of China National Economic and Social Development: Outline of the "ninth five year plan" and long term targets for the year 2010' (*Zhong Hua Ren Min Gong He Guo Guo Min Jing Ji He She Hui Fa Zhan 'Jiu Wu' Ji Hua He 2010 Nian Yuan Jing Mu Biao Gang Yao*), p. 1. This report was presented at and approved by the fourth plenary session of the Eighth People's Congress on 17 March 1996. Also see figures published in 'The People's Republic of China National Statistical Bureau Report on China's Economic and Social Development' for 1993, 1994 and 1995 [*Zhong Hua Ren Min Gong He Guo Guo Jia Tong Ji Ju Guan Yu 1993 (1994, 1995) Nian Guo Min Jing Ji He She Hui Fa Zhan De Tong Ji Gong Bao*], in *The People's Daily* (Overseas edition), 4 March 1994; 2 March 1995; 5 March 1996. Figures published in 1996 revised earlier figures on national economic growth rate to 12 per cent for 1993, 11.8 per cent for 1994 and 10.2 per cent for 1995.
4. *The People's Daily* (Overseas edition), 20 March 1996, *op. cit.*
5. *UBS International Finance*, Issue 15, Spring 1993, 'China's great leap forward', pp. 1–8.
6. These figures were reported in *The Economist*, 15 May 1993, 'Chinese puzzles', p. 95. In 1996, however, the World Bank revised its figure about the size of the Chinese economy. The World Bank's 1996 *World Development Reports* put Chinese GDP (per capita), measured on PPP basis, at US$2500 in 1994. A later report (also in 1996), *Poverty in China: What do the numbers say?* put the figure at US$1800, reducing the estimated size of the Chinese economy by over a quarter. Never-

theless, the size of the Chinese economy is still over US$2000 billion. Also see *The Economist*, 12–18 October 1996, 'How poor is China?', pp. 79–85.

7. Wang, Qingxian and Rong Huang (1996) 'We Start from Here'(*Wo Men Cong Zhe Li Qi Bu*), *The People's Daily* (Overseas edition), 7 March 1996, pp. 1 and 3.

8. An important step in reforming the state owned enterprises in China was the 'optimisation of capital structure'. This programme was first tried out in 18 cities as pilots, which at the beginning of the 'ninth five year plan' (1996–2000) was extended to over 50 cities in China, see *The People's Daily* (Overseas edition), 10 August 1996, 'An important step in vitalising the state owned economy' (*Gao Huo Guo You Jing Ji De Zhong Yao Yi Bu*), p. 1. Some initial results of the experiment began to appear in newspapers in 1996, for example: *The People's Daily* (Overseas edition), 27 March 1996, 'Modern enterprise system experiment in Sichuan achieving positive results' (*Sichuan Xian Dai Qi Yie Zhi Du Shi Dian Gong Zuo Jian Xiao*), p. 1. It reported on its front page that experiments in Sichuan Province with 80 large and medium sized state owned companies have achieved impressive results. The experiment started with 22 large companies in 1993 (among the earliest in China), and extended to 80 in 1994. In 1995, total sale and profit of these 80 companies on average increased by 20 per cent and 15 per cent respectively. Some of their experiences would be extended to other places in China. Similar experiments were conducted in Hebei Province with 130 state-owned companies since May 1994, and a wide range of initial benefits began to emerge recently: *The People's Daily* (Overseas edition), 1 November 1996, 'Hebei deepens its pilot reform in modern enterprise system' (*He Bei Shen Hua Xian Dai Qi Ye Zhi Du Shi Dian Gai Ge*), p. 1.

9. *San Zi* enterprises, 'the three types of foreign funded enterprises', refer to equity and contractual joint ventures and foreign wholly-owned firms. Such enterprises are generally referred to as 'foreign invested enterprises' in this book.

10. *The People's Daily* (Overseas edition), 5 March 1996 and 7 April 1997, 'The People's Republic of China National Statistical Bureau Report on China's Economic and Social Development' for 1995 (1996). [*Zhong Hua Ren Min Gong He Guo Guo Jia Tong Ji Ju Guan Yu 1995 (1996) Nian Guo Min Jing Ji He She Hui Fa Zhan De Tong Ji Gong Bao*]. p. 2.

11. The Economist Intelligence Unit (EIU) and Andersen Consulting (1995) *Moving China Ventures out of the Red into the Black: Insights from best and worst performers*, The Economist Intelligence Unit, London.

12. The 'four modernisation'(*Si Ge Xian Dai Hua*) refers to the modernization of industry, agriculture, national defence (military), and science and technology.

13. *Banker*, 18 March 1993, 'Follow the leader', p. 18.

14. This new figure was released by the People's Bank of China. See *The People's Daily* (Overseas edition), 4 November 1996, 'Savings by Chinese urban and rural citizens increasing steadily, total saving reached 3708.5 billion yuan by the end of September 1996' (*Quan Guo Ge Di*

Cheng Xiang Ju Min Chu Xu Cun Kuan Zeng Zhang Wen Ding, Dao Jiu Yue Di Chu Xu Yu E Da 37085 Yi Yuan), p. 1.

15. *The People's Daily* (Overseas edition), 1 April 1996, 'Over 100 foreign financial institutions set up in China's coastal region' (*Bai Jia Wai Zi Jin Rong Ji Gou Zai Wo Yan Hai Xing Cheng Qi Hou*), p. 1.

16. *The People's Daily* (Overseas edition), 12 June 1996, 'Total assets owned by foreign banks in China exceed US$19.1 billion' (*Zai Hua Wei Zi Yin Hang Zong Zi Chan Da Yi Bai Jiu Shi Yi Yi Mei Yuan*), p. 1. According to a senior official from the People's Bank of China (Mr Jin Qi), by the end of 1995, 519 banks and other financial institutions had set up offices in China, with 142 of them with operational branches.

17. Frankenstein, John (1995) 'The Beijing Rules: Contradictions, ambiguities and controls', *Long Range Planning* 28(1): 70–80.

18. Li, Peng (1991) 'Report of the outline of the ten year National Economic and Social Development Plan and the eighth five year plan' (*Guan Yu Guo Min Jing Ji He She Hui Fa Zhan De Shi Nian Yuan Jing Gui Hua He Ba Wu Ji Hua De Bao Gao*), *The People's Daily* (Overseas edition), 11 April 1991, pp. 1 and 4.

19. Gao, Shangquan (1987) *Nine Years of Chinese Economic Reform (Jiu Nian Lai De Zhong Guo Jing Ji Ti Zhi Gai Ge)*, The People's Publishing House (*Ren Min Chu Ban She*), Beijing.

20. Zhang, Youwen, Duan Xiping, and Jin Bu (1986), *The Opening up of Our National Economy (Wuo Guo Jing Ji De Dui Wai Kai Fang)*, Shanghai Publishing House (*Shanghai Chu Ban She*), Shanghai.

21. *Beijing Review*, 33(14), 22–28 October 1990, pp. 12–15.

22. For example, *Yian Hai Kai Fang* was being extended to *Yan Jiang Kai Fang* and *Yan Bian Kai Fang*, that is, designating open areas along the coast is being extended to areas along rivers and national borders.

23. *The People's Daily* reported responses from Puodong and Shenzhen local authorities after the Chinese government announced phasing out of preferential policies for foreign investors in special economic zones. *The People's Daily* (Overseas edition), 23 March 1996, 'China adjusts preferential policies for special development zones and special economic zones, what could Pudong do?' (*Zhong Guo Tiao Zheng Kai Fa Qu He Te Qu Yiu Hui Zheng Ce, Pu Dong Ze Mo Ban?*), p. 1; 26 March 1996, 'Shenzhen progresses towards functional special economic zone' (*Shen Zhen Kua Xiang Gong Neng Xing Te Qu*), p. 1.

24. *The People's Daily* (Overseas edition), 6 March 1996, p. 5. Speaking at the Fourth Plenum of the Eighth People's Congress, the Director of National Planning Committee, Chen Jinhua highlighted the dual transformation in China: from planning to market economy, and from extensive to intensive growth strategy. On 11 December 1995, Chinese Vice Premier Wu Bangguo had already announced these changes in economic regime and growth strategy when answering questions about the central focus of the national economic development and trade for 1996.

25. Ash, Robert and Y. Kueh (1992) 'Introduction', *China Quarterly*, September 1992, No. 31, Special Issue: The Chinese Economy in the 1990s.

26. *The Economist*, 21–28 March 1992, 'Running to keep up with Deng', p. 71.
27. *The People's Daily* on 12 March 1992 proclaimed the Chinese Politburo's decision to speed up reform and opening up before the opening of the National People's Congress on 29 March 1992. In particular, it emphasized the decision to adopt a more pragmatic approach by claiming that a measure is 'Socialist' and good, rather than 'Capitalist' and bad, if it 'benefits the development of the productive force' and 'improves the living standard of the people'. These were later formally approved by the National People's Congress.
28. *The Financial Times*, 14 June 1993.
29. Wu Yi, the Minister for the Ministry of Foreign Trade and Co-operation, announced some of the figures at the State Council news conference, which were reported in *The People's Daily* (Overseas edition), 29 January 1994. Some of the figures were announced at the Working Conference for the Registration Management of Foreign Invested Enterprises: *The People's Daily* (Overseas edition), 26 April 1994. Also see *The Financial Times*, 14 June 1993, 'Lure of the billion-buyer market'; *The Financial Times*, 20 May 1994, also reported relevant information obtained from the Ministry of Foreign Trade and Economic Co-operation.
30. According to figures released by the Chinese authority and the United Nations. *The People's Daily* (Overseas edition), 25 September 1996, 'United Nations trade and development report indicated China as No. 2 in attracting foreign investment' (*Lian He Guo Mao Fa Hui Bao Gao Xian Shi Zhong Guo Xi Yin Wai Zi Liang Ju Shi Jie Di Er*). Also see *The People's Daily* (Overseas edition), 1 February 1996 and 16 November 1995.
31. For example, *The Financial Times*, 14 May 1993, 'China puts the brake on rapid economic growth'.
32. For example, the Vice-Mayor of Tianjin (the third largest city in China) in charge of attracting foreign investment, told *The Financial Times*, 14 June 1993, that 'It's not nearly hot enough in Tianjin. We want more heat'.
33. For example, The Economist Intelligence Unit and Andersen Consulting (1995) *op. cit.* Bucknall, Kevin (1994) *Kevin B. Bucknall's Cultural Guide to Doing Business in China*, Butterworth Heinmann, Oxford.
34. For example, *Gallup Survey of Consumer Attitudes and Lifestyle Trends in the People's Republic of China* in 1995; *Yue Gang (Guang Dong and Hong Kong) Information Times (Yue Gang Xin Xi Shi Bao)*, 1 March 1995, 'An eye-catching research about China's investment environment' (*Yan Tao Zhong Guo Tou Zi Huan Jing, Yi Xiang Cheng Guo Bei Shou Zhu Mu*), which reported a systematic study of 188 large and medium cities in China, using a framework consisting 8 aspects, 32 categories, and 61 criteria, including urban infrastructure development, market conditions, labour supply, social development, economic development, foreign investment absorbed and so on. This study will be discussed in Chapter 4 in detail.
35. The Economist Intelligence Unit and Andersen Consulting (1995)

op. cit. Some key findings of the report were also briefly reported in *The Financial Times*, 22 September 1995, 'Myths of business in China debunked'.

36. Schuster, Camille P. and Michael J. Copeland (1996) *Global Business: Planning for Sales and Negotiations*, The Dryden Press, Harcourt Brace College Publishers, Fort Worth, USA.

37. Ho, Samuel and Ralph Huenemann (1984) *China's Open-Door Policy: The Quest for Foreign Technology and Capital*, University of British Columbia Press, Vancouver.

38. Moser, Michael J. (1984, ed.) *Foreign Trade, Investment and the Law in the People's Republic Of China*, Oxford University Press, Hong Kong.

39. Wang, N.T. (1984) *China's Modernization and Transnational Cooperations*, Lexington Books, Lexington, Mass.

40. Chai, Joseph (1983) 'Industrial co-operation between China and Hong Kong' in Youngson, A.J. (ed.) *China and Hong Kong: The Economic Nexus*, Oxford University Press, Oxford, pp. 104–55.

41. Pomfret, Richard (1991) *Investing in China: Ten years of the open door policy*, Harvester Wheatsheaf, New York.

42. Pearson, Margaret M (1991) *Joint Ventures in the People's Republic of China: The control of foreign direct investment under Socialism*, Princeton University Press, Princeton.

43. Shen, Xiaofang (1990) 'A decade of direct foreign investment in China' in *Problems of Communism*, March–April, 1990.

44. Thoburn, John T., H.M. Leng, Esther Chau and S.H. Tang (1990) *Foreign Investment in China under the Open Policy: The Experience of Hong Kong Companies*; Avevury, Aldershot; Thoburn, John T. (1991) 'Investment in China by Hong Kong companies', *IDS Bulletin*, Vol. 22, No. 2.

45. Lee, Keun, Chung H. Lee, and Won Bae Kim (1990) 'Problems and profitability of direct foreign investment in China: An analysis of the survey data', *Journal of Northeast Asian Studies*, Vol. IX, No. 4, Winter 1990.

46. Aiello, Paul (1991) 'Building a joint venture in China: The case of Chrysler and the Beijing Jeep Corporation', *Journal of General Management*, 17(2), Winter.

47. Harwit, Eric (1992) 'Foreign passenger car ventures and Chinese decision-making', *Australian Journal of Chinese Affairs*, Issue 28, July 1992.

48. Kamath, Shyam J. (1990) 'Foreign direct investment in centrally planned developing economy: The Chinese case', *Economic Development and Culture Change*, Vol. 39, No. 1, October, 1990.

49. Chan, J.C.M., N.Y. Li and D. Sculli (1989) 'Labour relations and foreign investors in the Shenzhen special economic zone of China', *Journal of General Management*, 14(4), Summer 1989.

50. Lockett, Martin (1987) 'China's special economic zones: The cultural and managerial challenges', *The Journal of General Management*, Vol. 12, No. 3, Spring 1987; Lockett, Martin (1988) 'Culture and the problems of Chinese management', *Organization Studies*, 9(4).

51. Child, J. (1994) *Management in China during the Age of Reform*, Cambridge University Press, Cambridge.
52. Warner, Malcolm (1996) 'Managing China's enterprise reforms: A new agenda for the 1990s', *Journal of General Management*, 21(3), Spring 1996: 1–18.
53. Euromonitor (1994) *China: A Directory and Source Book 1994*, Euromonitor Plc, London.
54. Brahm, Lawrence and Li Daoran (1996) *The Business Guide to China*, Butterworth-Heinemann Asia, Singapore.

2 China's Main Attractions to Foreign Investors

This chapter examines the main attractions of China to foreign investors in the context of the contemporary world economy. Three key issues are addressed here. First, the process of globalization in the evolving world economy since the early 1970s is analysed, and major tendencies in the growth of FDI are identified. Then, the necessity and key motivations for investing in foreign markets (in third world countries in particular) are discussed. Finally, in the third section, the different types of FDI in China are identified, and the main attractions of China to each type are highlighted.

THE WORLD ECONOMY AND THE RAPID GROWTH OF FDI SINCE THE EARLY 1970s

This section discusses three main issues. First, the structural crises in the global economy since the early 1970s and the underlying reasons for these crises are analysed. Then, the proposition of FDI as a new engine for the growth of the world economy is established. Finally, the growing dominance of multinational corporations in the world economy is highlighted. The rapid growth of FDI in China has happened within such a context.

The structural crises in the global economy

Since the early 1970s, the world economy has experienced a series of crises. These crises are far deeper than conventional cyclical economic recessions. They not only broke out simultaneously in several sectors in many countries, but also each new crisis was deeper than the old ones. The time gap between crises has become increasingly shorter, and the difficulties and uncertainties involved in economic recovery have increased substantially.[1]

The first recession in the early 1970s was triggered by the oil crisis, which reflected the growing political and economic conflicts between developed countries and oil producing third world countries. The recession started first in developed countries, then quickly spread to developing countries, resulting in one of the most serious global economic crises since the second world war. Although by the mid-1970s most countries had recovered reasonably well from the initial shock, successive oil price increases, coupled with a series of other problems, made the recovery rather short-lived. By the late 1970s and early 1980s, many countries found themselves plunged into an even deeper recession.

Different from traditional cyclical economic recessions, which mostly occurred as a result of temporary mismatch between supply and demand in certain markets, new crises since the early 1970s have reflected the growing structural imbalance in national and international economies, and a series of profound, deeply rooted, political and economic conflicts between developed and developing countries, and between developed countries themselves. Although the total global economic output did not decline in any single year of the recession (mainly as a result of increased production in socialist countries and some Far East economies), a drop in production was experienced in most developed countries, which was accompanied by a major slow down in the third world economies. In particular, a decline in GNP was experienced in north America and western Europe, where the drop in industrial production assumed even greater proportions.[2] The number of companies which went bankrupt increased considerably, and was the highest since the 1929–33 economic crisis. Several famous companies were rescued only by substantial public subsidies. The level of unemployment soared to levels never reached before. Similar crises repeated several times during the 1980s and early 1990s.[3]

A wide range of possible explanations for these crises were put forward by various experts, one of them being that the global economy was caught in a major shift in economic strength. The developed countries (particularly those in north America and western Europe) have dominated the world economy for over 150 years, but since the 1950s and 1960s many economies elsewhere have pushed aggressively into western markets and have thus been rapidly catching up – firstly Japan, then the four 'Asian Dragons' (that is, Taiwan, Hong Kong, Singapore and South Korea) and, more recently, scores of third world countries in Asia and Latin America and in the former eastern bloc. However, Japan and the 'Four Dragons' only have a combined population of 200 million (the 'Four Dragons' have only

73 million). In contrast, this latest round of catching up has a combined population of two to three billion! History has suggested that global shifts in economic power are rarely smooth, therefore the worst crises in the global economy may be yet to come![4]

A shrinking gap in income between the rich and poor countries is quite natural, as catching up is often easier than being the economic leader. Producers in less developed countries can copy others' methods at comparatively low costs, whereas rich countries have to develop new technologies or new production methods to maintain their growth. Just as Britain became richer than Holland in the late 18th century, the United States of America swept ahead of Britain in the late 19th century, and some of today's developing countries will one day overtake the rich countries. However, what is astonishing about the current global shift of economic power is its pace, which seems to have quickened considerably. Therefore, any new shocks associated with the global economic shift will be concentrated in a much shorter space of time.

A World Bank report[5] pointed out that after the Industrial Revolution took hold in about 1780, Britain needed only 58 years to double its real income per head. From 1839, America took 47 years to do the same. Starting in 1885, Japan took 34 years; from 1966, South Korea took 11 years; and more recently, China took less than ten years (in fact, the size of the Chinese economy quadrupled in 15 years between 1980 and 1995).[6] For most of the recorded human history, China was the world's largest economy. It had the highest income per head until around 1500. As late as 1830, China still accounted for 30 per cent of world manufacturing output, and was the world's largest economy until 1850 when it was overtaken by Britain.[7] For centuries, the speed of growth in China had been very slow, and it was only after the late 1970s that China began to develop very rapidly. The continuation of its rapid growth over the next few decades will enable China to catch up with the developed countries, although opinions vary about when China will become the world's largest economy again.[8]

Rapid growth in developing countries does not mean growth in developed countries will decline – quite the opposite. Fast growing economies in developing countries create rapidly growing markets for export and higher return on investments for developed countries. However, it does cause painful structural changes in developed economies, and some sectors are often badly hit. Developing countries are now no longer solely exporters of raw materials from which they earned revenue to pay for imports of manufactured goods from developed countries. Manufactured goods now account for almost 60 per cent of developing countries' exports (up from 5 per cent in 1955). The third world's share of world exports of manufactured goods jumped from 5 per cent in 1970 to 22 per cent in 1993.[9] As a result, developed economies have to go through a major shift of labour to sectors in which they have a comparative advantage within a fairly short space of time. Unfortunately, those who lose their jobs in developed countries often do not possess the skills to move to new industries and services, hence high unemployment in developed economies is inevitable, and the level may continue to rise over the next few decades – unless radical measures are taken to remedy the situation.

The political and economic conflicts between developed countries themselves are probably even more significant to the global economy in the short to medium terms. One major lesson learnt from the recessions in the early 1970s was the importance of large trade imbalances among major developed countries. Worries about the US deficit and the Japanese and German surpluses dominated the international economic policy debate since the 1980s. Until the mid-1990s, economists and policy-makers from Europe, the USA and Japan showed a remarkable degree of agreement that the 'twin deficits' of the United States were a grave threat to world economic growth and a major source of difficulties and uncertainties for the global economy.

Since the late 1970s and early 1980s, national governments and various international organizations made a series of policy adjustments in order to achieve economic recovery and development, which in the mid-1980s did produce a period of economic expansion. Confidence returned in the private sector and the growth of both world trade and cross-border investment accelerated.[10] However, many deeply rooted problems which had caused the repeated crises since the early 1970s remained unresolved, and their accumulation only led to the outbreak of a new round of deep recession in the late 1980s and early 1990s.[11]

The recovery from the latest recession was rather weak and unstable, and only became more firmly established in 1994, when continental western Europe and Japan began to emerge from some of the deepest recessions in half a century, and when upswings began to gain momentum in the UK, Canada and Australia and, most of all, when a high level of capacity utilization was restored in the USA.[12] In 1995, due to slower than expected growth in western Europe, and the slowdown of the world economy, some doubts were expressed about the strength of the recovery.[13] Even with strong signs of recovery in 1996 and 1997, doubts still existed about whether and for how long this recovery was going to last. Many difficult tasks continue to confront policy makers endeavouring to ensure a strong and durable expansion with low inflation, low unemployment, and low fiscal imbalance (lower public debt in particular). Since early 1998, the recovery has been over-shadowed by the Asian financial crisis and concerns about the over-valued stock market in the USA.

In spite of repeated economic crises, views about the long term future of the global economy have been rather optimistic. It has been predicted that the third world will continue to prosper, and the rich countries will gain (rather than lose) from the growing prosperity of the third world. In particular, the world economic recessions are not evenly distributed across the globe, so certain parts of the world have maintained rapid economic growth even during world economic recessions. For example, some Far East economies, particularly the 'Four Dragons' and, more recently, China, have been developing rapidly and continuously for a long time. The rapid growth of the 'Four Dragons' since the 1960s has been well documented. Stating in the late 1970s, the Chinese economy achieved an average annual real growth of 9 per cent (between 1978 and 1992); and between 1991 and 1995 the annual growth averaged 12 per cent (3–4 per cent higher than the planned economic growth rate for the 'eighth five year plan').[14] The Chinese government experienced considerable difficulties in slowing the economy down to under 10 per cent in order to control the run-away inflation.[15] Even with the Asian financial crisis, the Chinese economy is still projected to grow at 8 per cent in 1998 by stimulating domestic demand.

Since the mid-1990s, some transitional countries in eastern and central Europe also bottomed out of the recession as market mechanisms became established, although the future of Russia is still fragile and Africa's future remains gloomy.[16] The rapid growths of third world economies have not only provided much needed export markets for developed countries, they are also attracting large sums of capital investment from countries that are experiencing economic decline or slow growth.[17] The current growth of FDI in China has happened under such a world economic climate, and further elaboration on this issue will be given later in the chapter.

FDI – the new engine of world economic growth

There is no doubt that international trade has contributed enormously to the growth of the world economy since the second world war. With the rapid decrease of trade barriers, world trade volume increased over the period from 1950 to 1975 by more than 500 per cent, compared with an increase in world output by only 200 per cent. Between 1970 and 1995, the average annual growth for world trade was about 5.5 per cent, while that for world real GDP was just over 3.5 per cent. As such, international trade has for a long time been regarded as a main engine for the growth of the world economy.[18]

The dismantling of trade barriers among developed countries in the 1950s and 1960s contributed to a period of unprecedented world economic growth. In the 1970s and the 1980s, an increasing number of developing countries adopted outward-looking trade policies as part of their strategy of structural reform. Countries which succeeded in implementing these reforms experienced a significant and durable improvement in economic performance. Since the early 1990s, countries in transition in central and eastern Europe also liberalized their previously distorted trading regimes as an essential part of their transformation to market-based economic systems.[19] The completion of the Uruguay Round in April 1994 extended trade rules to areas previously exempted as too difficult to liberalize (agriculture and textiles) and to important new areas not previously included in GATT (General Agreement on Tariffs and Trade), such as trade in services, intellectual property, investment policy, and trade distortion. The formation of the World Trade Organization (WTO) in January 1995 gave permanence to GATT. These measures served to reduce trade barriers dramatically, and it was estimated that their implementation would raise world real income permanently by several hundred billion dollars.[20]

While international trade continues to grow and its contribution to the growth of the world economy is increasingly recognized, a significant new trend began to appear in the late 1980s, with international capital flows emerging as a prime motor for further global economic growth.[21] In particular, the growth in FDI since the late 1980s has far outstripped that of international trade and of real GDP! Although the major flows of FDI were between developed countries, in recent years an increasing volume of investment has flowed from developed countries to developing countries and between developing countries themselves.[22]

During most of the 1980s, developing countries annually received about US$15 billion in the form of FDI (about one-third of total global FDI), of which the east Asian economies (excluding China) received about $5 billion.[23] The growth has been particularly fast in the 1990s, and the total inflow of FDI into developing countries has surged from US$31 billion in 1990 to US$80 billion in 1993, with almost 60 per cent going to Asia.[25] Annual utilized FDI in China increased steadily from US$0.92 billion in 1983 to US$3.77 billion in 1990, and jumped to US$11.29 billion in 1992, US$37.7 billion in 1995, and US$42.35 billion in 1996![24] This surge helped developing countries to sustain relatively rapid growth during a period of protracted weakness in the developed countries. The sluggish economy and low interest rate in developed countries, coupled with the efforts by governments in developing countries to stabilize their national economies, have also contributed to the trend.

Although the total FDI flow into developed countries is still bigger (around US$110 billion in 1993) than that into developing countries, FDI in developing countries has been increasing steadily over the past two decades, and now constitutes one of the largest components of aggregate capital inflow to developing countries. Countries in Asia have been among the main recipients of the recent surge in FDI; of the top ten recipients of FDI between 1988 and 1992, seven of them were in Asia.[26] Between 1979 and 1996, China alone attracted FDI (utilized) worth US$177 billion, of which US$159 billion was since 1990, and US$150 billion since 1992 (see Chapter 8 for a more detailed discussion)!

Throughout the 1980s and early 1990s, the 'Four Dragons', the ASEAN (Association of South East Asian Nations) countries (including Thailand, Malaysia, Indonesia, Brunei, and the Philippines) and China have maintained their remarkably high rates of economic growth, which offered investors higher returns than the mature, slow growing industrial economies. During this period, Korea, Taiwan, China and several other Asian economies increasingly liberalized their historically restrictive policies towards inward investment, while Hong Kong and Singapore renewed their historical effort in attracting foreign investment. Coupled with the proximity of these economies to the fastest growing international investor – Japan – there was a major expansion of FDI flows in this region in recent years.[27] The 'Four Dragons' themselves have also become important sources of FDI as their economic structures shift to higher levels. Moreover, it is no longer just the large companies that have gone global; a growing proportion of FDI has originated from medium-sized and even small companies.[28]

Different from international trade where import has to be balanced by export, and foreign loans have to be repaid, FDI gives the host countries greater access to capital, new technology, increased scope for rapid growth of exports and increased competition in domestic markets. For example, by the end of 1994, China had a total of 90 784 foreign invested enterprises in operation. These enterprises employed a total of 12.6 million people, with an annual industrial output of over 500 billion yuan (about US$60 billion), which accounted for 12.2 per cent of China's total industrial output.[29] By the end of 1995, China actually utilized FDI worth US$135 billion, with over 120 000 foreign invested enterprises in operation, employing a total of 17 million people. These enterprises paid a total tax of over 70 billion yuan, about 10 per cent of the national total. These enterprises also exported over 60 per cent of their output, which accounted for 31.5 per cent (US$46.88 billion) of China's total exports, and this proportion has been increasing steadily and rapidly.[30] Total FDI attracted to China in 1996 reached US$42.35 billion! These enterprises played an increasingly important role in China's rapid economic development over the past two decades.

Multinational corporations – the key players in the world economy

The rapid development of multinational corporations, whose operations are characterized by direct investment across national borders, has been a key feature of the world economy. Since the second world war, these corporations have gained enormous economic and political power and they have been the key players in global economic affairs.[31] Today, the largest 100 multinational corporations possess total assets of over US$4000 billion, and they are responsible for 85 per cent of world trade, and almost all monumental new product developments.[32] Although, since the early 1980s, some small and medium sized companies have been able to find a competitive edge in certain niche markets using computer-based flexible technologies and flexible production systems, the power and position of large companies in the international, national, regional and local economies are continuously being enhanced.[33] Today, large multinational corporations remain the key shapers of the world economy. It is the activities of these companies that form the key dynamics of the world economy at the present time.[34]

The rise and rise of multinational corporations has been very dramatic over the last few decades, and since the mid-1980s the turnover increase in the world's largest companies has consistently outstripped economic growth in Europe, Japan and the US.[35] Indeed, many multinational companies are now economically more powerful than sovereign states. For instance, in 1994, Toyota – a Japanese car manufacturer – had net sales of over US$94 billion, and Du Pont – a US chemicals and plastics producer – had sales totalling nearly US$37 billion. By contrast, Ireland had a GDP of US$23 billion in 1993. Large multinational companies are also pioneers in organizational innovations, particularly through innovative use of information and communications technologies (ICTs).[36] Their restructuring in recent years has had a profound impact on the geographical patterns of the world economy.[37] The expansion and integration of capital markets on an international basis allowed large companies to finance and manage the risk on their investment more easily, because the new capital markets were more suitable for providing liquidity and spreading the risk for multinational companies.

Changes are not only happening in the manufacturing sectors. There is a growing cohort of companies in a range of service industries that are now exploiting the differentials that exist around the world with increasingly sophisticated telecommunications networks.[38] For instance, since the late 1980s, Swiss Air has had a reservation and administration centre on the Indian sub-continent. In addition, Bangalore (the 'electronic city', as it has become known) has become a popular centre for software writing with multinational companies such as IBM, Hewlett Packard and Sanyo. The labour intensive process of machine code writing (the basis for software operating systems) now takes place in vast offices staffed by well-educated, but low paid (by western standards) Indians. Such activities have undoubtedly had a major impact on the patterns of economic development in different parts of the world.

Since the mid-1980s, the pace of globalization has accelerated, because advanced ICTs have increasingly been used to remove some of the constraints of time and distance, which enables multinational companies to perform effective control and co-ordination of their global activities.[39] Also, by frequently transacting large sums of money and information across national borders, such companies can make the best use of geographical differentials in production factors at the global scale and by-pass unfavourable national regulations. The enormous economic and political power of some multinationals can significantly influence the policy making in many countries.

A major tendency of FDI in China in recent years is the rapid growth of direct investment by large, multinational corporations and, by the mid-1990s, over 200 well known multinational corporations had invested in China.[40] The main characteristics of FDI in China, and their profound social and economic influences, will be discussed later in the book.

THE KEY MOTIVATIONS FOR INVESTING IN FOREIGN MARKETS

People invest in foreign markets for a wide variety of reasons. The most common ones include:[41]

- Penetrating new markets.
- By-passing heavy duties at the national border.
- Rationalizing production by making use of the best locational advantages (for example, low wages).
- Exploiting economies of scale within the company group at the global level.
- Taking advantage of tax incentives, preferential policies and government grants for FDI in foreign countries.
- Developing new sources of raw materials and energy supply.
- Securing sources of supply to other parts of the company group.
- Internalizing profit through vertical integration along the value chain.
- Exploiting the benefits of monopoly power in new geographical areas.
- Achieving higher returns on investment by investing in fast growing economies.
- Getting closer to main customers in foreign countries in order to respond to their changing demands more quickly.
- Establishing better access to newly developed technology.

The above list is not exhaustive, and needs to be understood in the context of the evolving global economy and the rapidly changing business environment in different parts of the world. In fact, many FDI projects have been developed as responses to changes in the world business environment. For example, after the oil shocks in the 1970s and early 1980s, all G-7 (firstly G-5) countries invested heavily in oil and other raw materials supplies overseas. In the 1980s, Japan invested in several large projects in Indonesia in the mineral and oil extraction industries.[42] Similarly, in early 1991, a Sino-Japanese coal pulp joint venture was set up in Shangdong, with an annual production capacity of over 250 000 tons, which was to expand to one million tons in 1992 – all for export to Japan. In the meantime, eight large global oil companies have been involved in the joint exploration and development of China's Tarim Basin oilfield, and some of these companies have also invested heavily in the joint exploration and development of China's offshore oilfields.[43] In addition to securing supplies, such investments also showed the enhanced profitability in energy and other raw material extraction industries over the last few decades.

Securing supplies is not restricted to energy and minerals, and it has also happened in many other industries. For example, a British clothing company invested in Egypt in order to secure the supply of cotton fabric for its UK production. Originally, this company was responsible for no FDI and it simply imported cotton fabric from Egypt, manufactured clothes in Britain and sold its products in the domestic market and the USA. However, in recent years, as its production volume increased, the company began to have trouble with the reliability of the delivery of cotton fabric from Egypt. In order to secure the main sources of supply, the company decided to buy out the Egyptian supplier and run the factory in Egypt as a subsidiary. By replacing the market relationship with internal administration, the supply is now guaranteed. In the meantime, the demand in the USA for its products has been growing steadily, so the company decided to set up its own chain of retail outlets, intending to internalize potential profits within the group. The latest movement of the company is to set up manufacturing facilities in Egypt, where labour and other operating costs are low, and in the USA in order to avoid the US duty for imports from the UK and Egypt. The US production facility has also been intended to respond quickly to changing customer demands in the US market.

Another main reason for FDI is to bypass heavy duties at the national borders and penetrate new markets. Since the early 1980s, Europe has attracted a large sum of foreign investment particularly from the Far East and the USA. These companies invested in

Europe in the build-up of the single European market, mainly because – among a number of other reasons – they were worried that heavy duties would be imposed on imports from outside Europe. The potential new market opportunities unleashed by European integration are also a major attraction. Three major Japanese car manufacturers, Nissan, Toyota and Honda, have all set up new production facilities in the UK to supply the European market. Nissan also set up research and development facilities in the UK in order to make Nissan cars more suitable for European customers. The strong yen and Japan's huge trade surplus in the 1980s also contributed to these projects. Moreover, since these three car manufacturers have all implemented the so called just-in-time production strategy, many Japanese and European component suppliers have also set up new production facilities in the UK.

Japanese investment in Europe is not restricted to the car industry: since the early 1990s, companies from other Far East economies (for example, Samsung from South Korea and Chunghwa from Taiwan) have also invested hundreds of millions of pounds in greenfield production facilities in the UK in order to supply their European customers. Investment from American companies has happened at similar scales since the early 1980s. Apart from entering the European common market, these companies have been attracted by factors such as the comparatively cheap but skilled labour force in the UK's declining regions, good infrastructure, favourable regulations and tax systems, as well as generous government regional grants and subsidies. The ratification of the Maastricht Treaty and the formation of the Single European Market also facilitated a large number of cross-border investments between European countries, including mergers, acquisitions, and radical rationalization of production and logistics in the 1980s and early 1990s.[44]

Another main reason for FDI is the global economic shift and structural changes in national economies. For example, some FDI from developed countries to developing countries involved the shift of existing production capacity of certain industries, particularly those 'sunset', 'dirty' or labour intensive industries, and such investment was often intended to avoid the high labour costs and higher safety and environment protection standards imposed by developed countries.[45] Also contributing to the globalization of production since the mid-1980s was the rapid development of information and communications technologies (ICTs) which enabled large companies to manage geographically distributed activities more effectively.[46] More recently, some newly industrializing economies are doing the same by shifting labour intensive production to developing countries with even lower costs.

Profit is obvious one of the most important considerations for all FDI, and investing overseas can often bring investors higher profit than investing in the domestic market. Some large companies have been enjoying high profits from their overseas investments for decades.[47] These companies can take advantage of preferential policies of the host countries, and they often have technological and/or managerial advantages compared with local companies in those markets. The profit they earn can either be shifted back to the home countries or be re-invested overseas to make even more profit. In some cases, investing in foreign countries can also be an effective way to break down trade barriers by importing components for the final products and the necessary equipment for overseas production.

For East Asia as a whole, the largest investor is Japan,[48] although both the US and EU are still the most important partners for certain economies (for example, the US is the largest investor in Taiwan, Hong Kong and the Philippines). The research by Grosser and Bridges concluded that post-war Japanese investment in East Asia falls into the following four main categories:

- resource development, particularly minerals and oil
- import substitution industries, such as home electronics and automobile components
- export production using cheaper labour, investment incentives and other benefits
- service sectors, such as banks, security and insurance.

The rapid appreciation of the Japanese yen, combined with other conditions (such as the rapidly increasing production costs in Japan, and the upgrading of Japanese economic structure), facilitated significant restructuring of Japanese industries, which frequently involved the relocation of production facilities in some industries to cheaper off-shore sites. Since 1985, this has led to an increased level of investment from Japan to other Asian economies. Since the early 1990s, the newly industrializing economies (NIEs) are faced with similar problems, such as rising labour costs and the upgrading of national economic structure, and many labour intensive activities are being shifted to other countries in the region. In the case of China, the divergent levels of development in its provinces and cities have provided some of the most attractive places for both the relocation of Japanese companies and companies from the NIEs. This point will be discussed in detail in the next section.

For most large investors, a massive, politically stable market probably offers the greatest attraction. However, in exchange for access to such markets, the host country may impose certain conditions in order to secure some benefits for the host country (such as restrictions on ownership and the proportion of local content in the final products, or demanding that the foreign investor export a certain proportion of the output). There is obviously a point, different from company to company, beyond which such conditions would become unacceptable.[49] The motivations behind FDI are extremely complex, and a comprehensive understanding of these issues is extremely important, both to potential investors in selecting the best overseas locations for their investment, and to national and local governments intending to attract FDI when devising relevant policies.

CHINA'S MAIN ATTRACTIONS TO FOREIGN INVESTORS

The analysis of the world economic climate in the first section of the chapter concluded that in spite of repeated world economic fluctuations, international capital flows (particularly in the form of FDI) have been growing steadily and rapidly; and FDI has increasingly been regarded, together with international trade, as the main engine of world economic growth. In recent years, an increasing proportion of FDI is destined for developing countries, and some Asian economies have been doing particularly well in attracting FDI. In the last section, the key motivations for investing in foreign markets are discussed: these can range from penetrating new markets to securing sources of raw material supply. This section examines the key attractions of China to various groups of foreign investors. Two issues will be addressed here. First, the main types of FDI in China and their key characteristics are examined; and then the main attractions of China to each group are analysed.

A classification of FDI in China: who are the main investors?

Today, China has attracted FDI from over 150 countries (and other economic entities) around the world, and these investors have been attracted to China by a wide variety of factors. According to the place of origin and some other key characteristics, FDI in China can be classified into two broad categories. The first category compromises investors from developed countries such as the USA, Japan, and some western and northern European countries (for example, UK, Germany, France, Italy and Sweden). From 1979–95, foreign investment from these countries accounted for approximately a quarter of the total FDI (value) in China.[50] The second category mainly consists of investors from Asian economies (excluding Japan), such as Hong Kong and Macao and, towards the end of the 1980s, Taiwan, South Korea and Singapore. The second category accounts for the greatest number of projects concluded in China and for approximately three quarters of the value of FDI in China (Figure 2.1).[51]

There are a number of main differences, although not clear cut, between these two categories of FDI in China. The ventures in the first category were often located in the largest cities in China, such as Shanghai, Guangzhou, Tianjing, Dalian and Beijing. They often brought new technology and new management and marketing techniques to China, and the scale of each investment tended to be large. An increasing proportion of investment from this category has come from well known multinational companies.[52] In contrast, the second category investments were mostly labour intensive production geared towards export, the average size of each investment was often smaller, and few of them brought new technologies to China.

What have attracted foreign investors to China?

The biggest attractions of China to foreign investors include its huge, rapidly growing market, and the abundant supply of raw materials and cheap labour. However, there are major differences between the two categories of investors discussed earlier in this section. For investors of the first category, the main attractions of China are its enormous and rapidly growing market and the huge potential for future development; while for the second category, cheap labour and raw materials are probably the main attractions. Tax incentives and preferential policies in China also form an attraction for both categories. More recently, the richness of China's human resources (for example, engineers) is increasingly recognized – although the shortage of qualified managerial talents has become a compelling problem for many foreign investors.[53]

Figure 2.1 Foreign Direct Investment in China by Origin
(per cent of total)

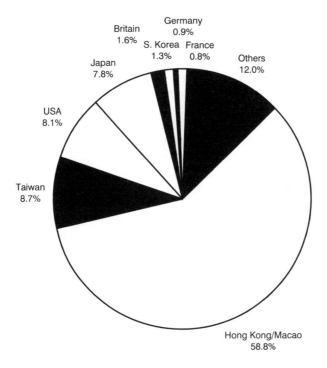

**Total FDI in China
(1979–95)
US$133.2 billion**

Britain
1.6%

Germany
0.9%

S. Korea
1.3%

France
0.8%

Japan
7.8%

Others
12.0%

USA
8.1%

Taiwan
8.7%

Hong Kong/Macao
58.8%

Sources: China Statistical Year Book, 1996

In the context of the contemporary world economy, the new economic and political systems in China and its new global position (both in world politics and economy) since the late 1970s and early 1980s formed the main background for the rapid growth of FDI in China.[54] The gradual implementation of the open door policy represented a sharp break from the past in China's development strategy (which will be discussed in detail in the next chapter). The decision to seek foreign investment and loans in China was initially not aimed at filling a domestic savings gap, but a serious foreign exchange gap created by China's economic development. The rapid growth of FDI in China has been accompanied by a rapid growth of China's international trade, and by the early 1990s China had become the eleventh largest trader in the world (tenth in the late 1990s). Today, China has acquired membership in various international organizations. It is a member of the United Nations Security Council, the World Bank, the International Monetary Fund (IMF), and the Asia Development Bank. It has participated in the activities of these organizations in a constructive and responsible manner.[55] Currently, China is also negotiating to join the WTO (although China failed to meet the conditions to become a founding member on 1st January 1995), and it is only a matter of time before China becomes a formal member. All these suggest that China has become increasingly integrated into the world economy.

For the first category foreign investors in China, the primary attraction of China is its potentially huge domestic market. As such, the investment in this category has mostly been geared towards long-term strategic considerations, together with a variety of secondary, short-term considerations. For example, Shanghai Volkswagen Automotive Co. Ltd was the largest joint venture in the machine building industry in China when the project was launched. The German multinational came to China with two major considerations. The first was economic. China is a huge potential market, therefore it is natural for a large multinational group like Volkswagen to find this market attractive. The second was political. Volkswagen has traditionally been very experienced at exploiting the locational advantages of the third world countries, and China is simply too big a strategic opportunity for Volkswagen to miss by failing to get a foot in the door at a time when the domestic market is being opened up.[56]

Despite various problems, Shanghai Volkswagen has been a major success, and it has gained as much as 65 per cent of the Chinese car market.[57] More importantly, to reward early investors with long term commitments, China in 1994 decided not to allow anyone to set up new car assembly lines until 1997 and, after this, any car maker intending to produce finished cars in China has to start with 60 per cent local contents. This measure has certainly gave Volkswagen a clear, distinctive advantage over other foreign competitors. Since China might shut its door permanently in this sector, several world-leading car manufacturers began to invest heavily in car components in China and negotiate with relevant authorities to set up car manufacturing facilities after the two year ban. A similar practice was soon extended to many other sectors, and in 1995, China published a new regulation and a comprehensive list of industries in which FDI is encouraged, restricted, allowed or prohibited.[58] This selective policy has sent a clear message to potential investors: for a slice of the Chinese market, foreign investors need to show their long term commitment to China.

To break into a market already occupied by the first comer is extremely difficult. General Motors hesitated about entering China in the first round of China's opening up, so now not only has to invest heavily in joint ventures making various car components (ten already in operation, and another twenty five in negotiation), it also has to set up a joint venture to design and develop new cars alongside a deal to jointly manufacture 100 000 cars per year in Shanghai.[59] Chinese partners claimed the biggest mistake in China's first round joint ventures in the car industry – including Volkswagen – is that local development and design capability was not part of those deals.[60] Similarly, AT&T found that they could not break the strong hold of Alcatel on the Chinese market for telephone switching equipment unless it competes with more advanced products.[61] In other words, to share a slice of the Chinese market, many foreign investors have to share their latest technologies.

Another example was the first solely foreign-owned company opened in China since the promulgation of the Provisions for Encouraging Foreign Investment on October 11th 1986 – the China subsidiary of Grace Co. of the US in Shanghai's Minhang Development Zone. According to the Chairman and President of Grace Co., the primary attraction of China was the huge domestic market.[62] This company's products were all sold in China, and in the early days China even paid for its products in foreign currency by exporting tinned food.

Similar evidence has been found in many other sectors ranging from refrigerators to colour television and air-conditioning. Many world leading companies have been fighting an increasingly bloody battle for at least a foothold in China.[63] For most investors in this category, the major attraction of China is its huge domestic market (although short-term profits are also important, and most foreign investors begin to make profits from the second year in operation[64]). Many investors in this category are often willing to forego immediate profits in China in exchange for the strategic opportunities that their Chinese ventures offer when the domestic market is fully opened up. Such investments are of strategic importance, and many investors believe that they cannot afford to lose the chance for even a small slice of the Chinese market. Getting a foot in the door will put them in a favourable competitive position – as has recently been demonstrated in the car industry.

Some investors in the first category are also in the process of looking for low cost manufacturing bases for their Asia production. The opening up of China offered them an additional option for their global production restructuring.[65] In addition, a new trend in China in recent years has been the rapid growth of joint exploitation and development of natural resources (such as coal and oil) with leading western companies such as British Petroleum (BP) and Shell. These are all long term collaborations with huge foreign investment involved.

For the second category (mainly from Asia excluding Japan) investors, considerations for investing in China are significantly different. In recent years, wages in newly industrializing economies (NIEs, such as the 'Four Dragons') have been rising steadily and rapidly, which has begun to erode the competitiveness of their light, labour intensive manufacturing industries that initially led to their rapid growth. As a result, many companies in these economies have to find cheaper locations for their production if they intend to remain competitive in the global market. Their investment in China and other low cost areas represents a major shift of labour intensive production from Asian NIEs to cheaper developing economies.

For example, the single largest investor in China's mainland is Hong Kong, and this investment has mainly been in the same labour intensive industries as those comprising most of Hong Kong's exports, such as textiles and clothing, electronic products and plastics. As labour and other operating costs soared in Hong Kong, the attraction became clear of moving production to China, so close in distance, sharing the same culture and language, but where labour costs are less than 20 per cent of the Hong Kong level.[66] Equally, Taiwan companies, particularly those in low-tech, labour intensive industries, faced similar difficulties to those from Hong Kong. The rapid appreciation of Taiwan dollars in recent years also served to force some companies to look for a cheaper production base in order to compete in the global market. China is particularly attractive, as labour costs are extremely low, labour supply unlimited, geographically close, and most of all, people share the same culture and language. FDI in China from Hongkong, Macao and Taiwan, between 1979 and 1995, accounted for 67.5 per cent of total FDI in China (Figure 2.1).

To sum up: whilst the main attractions of China to the first category investors are the potentially huge domestic market and the strategic opportunities it offers; the main attractions of China to the second category investors are the richness of China's unlimited supply of cheap labour, low operating costs and various preferential policies. For investors from Taiwan, Hong Kong, Macao and Singapore in particular, the common Chinese culture and language also formed a unique attraction. The huge potential market is also very attractive to many of them. In addition, investors from Taiwan are often offered even more preferential policies than others, because Taiwan is regarded as part of China, therefore investments from Taiwan are regarded as a special category of domestic investment rather than 'foreign'.[67] In the early 1990s, Taiwan overtook the USA and Japan as the second largest investor in China after Hong Kong.

SUMMARY

This chapter has examined three main issues. In the first section, the evolving world economy since the early 1970s and some major tendencies of FDI are discussed. A key feature of the world economy during this period has been the reoccurring structural crises, far deeper than the traditional cyclical economic recessions, and the situation has been clearly reflected in the main patterns of FDI. In particular, since the late 1980s, several significant new trends have emerged. One is that FDI, alongside international trade, has become a prime motor for global economic growth. Another is that medium- and small-sized companies are playing an increasingly important role in the growth of FDI, although the dominance of multinationals in the globalization of the world economy is not affected. Last but not least, although the major flows of FDI are between developed countries, considerable volume of investment has flowed from developed countries to developing countries and between developing countries themselves.

The chapter also discussed the key motivations for investing in foreign markets, which vary significantly between individual investors. However, there are a number of common features among them. Exploiting new market and locational advantages (cheap labour) are very common features. Securing the supply of raw materials and energy is another important consideration. In some cases, FDI is the result of industrial restructuring in the evolution of national economies. For many large multinational companies, FDI also involves the strategic consideration of 'getting a foot in the door' in order to place themselves in a competitive position while waiting for the market to grow and to be opened in the near future.

In the third part, foreign investors in China were classified into two broad categories according to their origin and other key characteristics: namely, those coming from the developed economies such as Japan, the USA, Germany and other Western European countries (which accounts for about one quarter of all FDI in China in value); and those from Asia (except Japan), such as Hong Kong, Singapore, Macao and, towards the end of the 1980s, Taiwan and South Korea (which accounts for about three quarters of all FDI in China in value). The political and economic background and the main attractions of China to each category were discussed in detail. In the next chapter, the evolution of China's open door policy in respect of foreign direct investment, and the related laws and regulations, are systematically examined.

Notes

1. IMF (1980–96) *World Economic Outlook*, published twice each year in May and October by the International Monetary Fund (IMF), Washington D.C.; Barclays Bank (1990–96) *Barclays Economic Review*, published quarterly by Barclays Bank, London; OECD (1990–96) *OECD Economic Outlook*, published twice each year in June and December by OECD, Paris.
2. United Nations (1983) *Economic Survey of Europe*, United Nations (UN), New York.
3. IMF (1980–96) *op. cit.*
4. *The Economist*, 1–7 October 1994, 'Survey of the Global Economy'.
5. Boltho, Andrea (1994) *China's Emergence: Prospects, Opportunities and Challenges*, The World Bank, Washington D.C.; *The Economist*, 1–7 October 1994, *op. cit.* p. 10.
6. *The People's Daily* (Overseas edition), 6 March 1996. Chinese Premier Li Peng announced at the Fourth Plenum of the Eighth People's Congress that China's GNP quadrupled between 1980 and 1995, five years ahead of the planned schedule: 'Our National GNP quadrupled five years ahead of plan' *(Wuo Guo Guo Min Sheng Chan Zong Zhi Ti Qian Wu Nian Fan Liang Fan)*, pp. 1 and 3.
7. Boltho (1994) *op. cit.*

8. *The Economist*, 12–18 October 1996, 'How poor is China?' pp. 79–85; The World Bank (1996) *World Development Report*, The World Bank, Washington D.C.; The World Bank (1996) *Poverty in China: What Do the Numbers Say?* The World Bank, Washington D.C.

9. *The Economist*, 1–7 October 1994, *op. cit.*

10. Julius, DeAnne (1990) *Global Companies and Public Policy: The growing challenge of foreign direct investment*, Pinter Publishers Ltd, London; Julius, DeAnne (1991) 'Direct investment among developed countries: Lessons for developing world', *IDS Bulletin*, 1991, Vol. 22 No. 2.

11. *The Financial Times*, 24 September 1990, 'Financial Times Survey: The world economy'; Britain, Samuel (1992) 'Tour of world economy after Berlin wall', *The Financial Times*, 19 November 1992.

12. IMF (1994) October, *op. cit.*

13. IMF (1996) October, *op. cit.*

14. The *Chinese Science Newspaper (Zhong Guo Ke Xue Bao)* (Overseas edition), 25th August 1995, 'China quickly marching towards modernisation: The national economic and social development in China underwent major changes during eighth five year plan' (*Zhong Guo Kuai Bu Zou Xiang Xian Dai Hua*), p. 3; *The People's Daily* (Overseas edition), 20 March 1996, 'The People's Republic of China National Economic and Social Development: Outline of the "ninth five year plan"' and long term targets for the year 2010' (*Zhong Hua Ren Min Gong He Guo Guo Min Jing Ji He She Hui Fa Zhan 'Jiu Wu' Ji Hua He 2010 Nian Yuan Jing Mu Biao Gang Yao*), p. 1.; *The People's Daily* (Overseas edition), 6 March 1996, *op. cit.*

15. *UBS International Finance*, Issue 15, Spring 1993, 'China's great leap forward', pp. 1–8; Wang, Qingxian and Huang, Rong (1996) 'We start from here' (*Wo Men Cong Zhe Li Qi Bu*), *The People's Daily* (Overseas edition), 6 March 1996, *op. cit.*

16. IMF (1994) October, *op. cit.*

17. IMF (1996) October, *op. cit.*

18. *Ibid.*

19. *Ibid.*

20. IMF (1995) May, *op. cit.*; Cline, William (1995) 'Evaluating the Uruguay Round', *The World Economy*, 18 (1) January 1995, 1–24; Nguyen, Trien, Carlo Perroni and Rardall Wigle (1995) 'A Uruguay Round Success?' *The World Economy*, 18 (1) January 1995, 25–30.

21. Soete, L (1991) *Technology in a Changing World*, A report of policy synthesis of the OECD Technology Economy Programme by MERIT, University of Limburg, Maastricht, Netherlands; *The Economist*, 1–7 October 1994, *op. cit.*; IMF (1994) October, *op. cit.*

22. Howells, J. and M. Wood (1991) *The Globalization of Production and Technology*, a report under the Programme of Forecasting and Assessment in the Field of Science and Technology (FAST), Directorate-General For Science, Research and Development, Commission of the European Communities. Available from CURDS, Newcastle University, Newcastle upon Tyne NE1 7RU, England; *The Economist*, 1–7 October 1994, *op. cit.*

23. Grosser, Kate and Brian Bridge (1990) 'Economic interdependence

in East Asia in the global context', *The Pacific Review*, Vol. 3 No. 1.

24. Figures released in 'The People's Republic of China National Statistical Bureau Report on China's Economic and Social Development' for 1993, 1994, 1995, 1996 *[Zhong Hua Ren Min Gong He Guo Guo Jia Tong Ji Ju Guan Yu 1993 (1994, 1995, 1996) Nian Guo Min Jing Ji He She Hui Fa Zhan De Tong Ji Gong Bao]*, in *The People's Daily* (Overseas edition), 4 March 1994; 2 March 1995; 5 March 1996; 7 April 1997, p. 2.

25. *The Economist*, 1–7 October 1994, *op. cit.*, p. 29.

26. According to figures released by the Chinese authority and the United Nations. *The People's Daily* (Overseas edition), 25 September 1996, 'United Nations trade and development report indicated China as No. 2 in attracting foreign investment' (*Lian He Guo Mao Fa Hui Bao Gao Xian Shi Zhong Guo Xi Yin Wai Zi Liang Ju Shi Jie Di Er*).

27. Julius *op. cit.* Grosser and Bridge (1990), *op. cit.*

28. Julius (1990) *op. cit.*

29. The *Chinese Science Newspaper (Zhong Guo Ke Xue Bao)* (Overseas edition), 25 August 1995, 'New characteristics in China's utilisation of foreign investment' (*Zhong Guo Li Yong Wai Zi Cheng Xin Te Dian*), p. 3.

30. *The People's Daily* (Overseas edition), 13 August 1996, 'Commentary: We are determined to utilise foreign investment effectively' (*Jian Ding Bu Yi Yong Hao Wai Zi*), p. 1.

31. Amin, A., D. Charles, T. Frazer, J. Goddard and J. Howells (1992) 'Large firms and regional cohesion in the European Community', paper presented to DGXVI, Commission of the European Community, Brussels. This paper is available from CURDS, University of Newcastle upon Tyne, Newcastle upon Tyne, NE1 7RU, England.

32. *The People's Daily* (Overseas edition), 4 September 1996, 'What have multinational corporations brought to China?' *(Kua Guo Gong Si Gei Zhong Guo Dai Lai Le She Mo?)*, p. 2.

33. Martinelli, F. and E. Schoenberger (1989) 'Oligopoly alive and well: Notes for a broader discussion on flexible accumulation', paper presented at the international conference on *Les nouveaux espaces industriels: un survol international*, Paris, 21–22 March 1989; Amin, A. and M. Dietrich (1991) 'From hierarchy to hierarchy: the dynamics of contemporary corporate restructuring in Europe', in Amin, A. and M. Dietrich (eds), *Towards a New Europe*, Elgar, London; Howells and Wood (1991) *op. cit.*

34. Robins, K. and A. Gillespie (1992) 'Communications, organization and territory', Robins, K. (ed.), *Understanding Information: Business, Technology and Geography*, Belhaven, London; Li, F. (1995a) *The Geography of Business Information*, John Wiley and Son, Chichester.

35. Li, F. and C. Gentle (1995) *Corporate Location in the New Europe*, Henley Centre for Forecasting, London.

36. Li, F. (1995b) 'Structural innovations through information systems: Some emerging tendencies in Europe', *Journal of Management Systems* 7(3): 53–65.

37. Li (1995a) *op. cit.*

38. Hepworth, M. (1989) *Geography of the Information Economy*, Belhaven Press, London; Li (1995a) *op. cit.*
39. Hepworth (1989) *op. cit.*; Goddard, J. (1992) 'New technology and the geography of the UK information economy', Robins, K. (ed.) *Understanding Information: Business, Technology and Geography*, Belhaven, London; Li (1995a), *op. cit.*
40. *The People's Daily* (Overseas edition), 29 October 1996, 'The systemisation of investment by multinational corporations in China' (*Kua Guo Gong Si Zai Hua Tou Zi Xi Tong Hua*), p. 2; *The People's Daily* (Overseas edition), 26 July 1995, 'New characteristics of foreign investment in China' (*Zhong Guo Li Yong Wai Zi Cheng Xin Te Dian*), p. 1.
41. For example, Sekiguchi, Sueo (1991) 'Direct foreign investment and the Yellow Sea Rim', *Journal of Northeast Asian Studies*, Spring; Julius (1991), *op. cit.*; Ishigami, Etsuro (1991), 'Japanese business in ASEAN countries: New industrialization or Japanese?' *IDS Bulletin*, Vol. 22 No. 2.
42. Grosser and Bridge (1990) *op. cit.*
43. Reported in *The People's Daily* (Overseas edition), 23 November 1995; *The Financial Times*, 31 March 1993, 'Everything to play for in China's Tarim basin'.
44. Howells and Wood (1991) *op. cit.*; Li & Gentle (1995) *op. cit.*
45. Frank, Andre Gunder (1980) *Crisis in the World Economy*, Heinemann Educational Books Ltd, London.
46. Hepworth (1989) *op. cit.*; Li (1995a, 1995b) *op. cit.*
47. Cai Hangan (1991), 'On the financial position and function of the transnational management of enterprise groups', *Economic Research* (*Jing Ji Yan Jiu*), May 1991.
48. Grosser and Bridges (1991) *op. cit.*
49. Lall, Sanjaya (1977), *Foreign Investment, Transnationals and Developing Countries*, Macmillan Press Ltd, London.
50. Pearson, Margaret M. (1991) *Joint Ventures in the People's Republic of China*, Princeton University Press, Princeton; *The People's Daily* (Overseas edition), 18 October 1995, 'Multinational corporations rush to invest in China' (*Kua Guo Gong Si Yong Yue Tou Zi Zhong Guo*), p. 2.
51. Pearson (1991) *op. cit.*; *The People's Daily* (Overseas edition), 22 June 1995, 'China's great achievement in attracting foreign investment: Investment from Hong Kong and Macao top the league table with a total utilised investment of over US$60 billion' (*Zhong Guo Xi Shou Wei Zi Cheng Jiu Xian Zhu: Gang Ao Tou Zi Shu Liang Zui Duo Yu Liu Bai Yi Mei Yuan*). *The Chinese Science Newspaper* (Overseas edition), 25 April 1995, 'The league table of foreign investors in China' (*Dui Da Lu Tou Zi Zhe Pai Chu Zuo Ci*); *The Economist*, 15 April 1994, 'Multinationals in China: Slow car to China'.
52. The Economist Intelligence Unit (EIU) and Andersen Consulting (1995) *Moving China Ventures out of the Red into the Black: Insights from best and worst performers*, The Economist Intelligence Unit, London.

53. *Ibid.*
54. Dernberger, Robert F. (1988) 'Economic Cooperation in the Asia-Pacific Region and the Role of the P.R.C.', *Journal of Northeast Asian Studies.* Spring 1988, Vol. VII, No. 1.
55. *Ibid.*
56. *Beijing Review*, Vol. 29, No. 29, 21 July 1986, p. 24.
57. *The Economist*, 2–8 March 1996, 'Has Europe failed Asia?', pp. 63–65.
58. *The People's Daily* (Overseas edition) 1 July 1995, 'Regulation on guiding the direction of foreign investment' (*Zhi Dao Wai Shang Tou Zi Fang Xiang Zan Xing Gui Ding*) and 'Index of foreign investment industrial guide' (*Wai Shang Tou Zi Chan Ye Zhi Dao Mu Lu*), p. 2.
59. *The People's Daily* (Overseas edition), 27 March 1997, 'The largest Sino-US joint venture signed, two automobile companies established in Shanghai' (*Zhong Mei Zui Da He Zi Xiang Mu Qian Yue, Liang Jia Qi Che You Xian Gong Si Zai Hu Cheng Li*), p. 1; *The Chinese Science Newspaper* (Overseas edition), 25 April 1997, 'The largest Sino-US joint venture will be set up in Pudong' (*Zhong Mei Zui Da He Zi Xiang Mu Jiang Luo Hu Pu Dong*), p. 3.
60. *The People's Daily* (Overseas edition), 30 March 1996, 'General Motors has come to China: An interview with General Motors' China Chief Executive' (*'Tong Yong' Lai Dao Zhong Guo Lai*), by Lin Gang (journalist) p. 2.
61. *The Economist*, 2–8 December 1995, 'How and why to survive Chinese tax torture' pp. 89–90; The Economist Intelligence Unit & Andersen Consulting (1995) *op. cit.*
62. *Beijing Review*, Vol. 29, No. 45, 1986, p. 31.
63. *The Economist*, 3–9 December 1994, 'How not to sell 1.2 billion tubes of toothpaste', pp. 95–96.
64. The Economist Intelligence Unit and Andersen Consulting (1995) *op. cit.*
65. Haggard, Stephan and Tunjen Cheng (1987) 'State and foreign capital in the East Asian economies' in Frederic C. Deyo (ed.) *The Political Economy of the New Asian Industrialism*, Cornell University Press, Ithaca, N.Y., pp. 84–135.
66. Thoburn, John T., H.M. Leng, Esther Chau and S.H. Tang (1990) *Foreign Investment in China under the Open Policy: The experience of Hong Kong companies*, Avebury, Aldershot; Thoburn, John T. (1991) 'Investment in China by Hong Kong companies', *IDS Bulletin*, Vol. 22 No. 2.
67. *Almanac of China's Foreign Economic Relations and Trade* (1990) 'Regulation of the State Council of the P.R.C. for encouraging Taiwan compatriots to invest in the mainland'. Ministry of Foreign Economic Relations and Trade, Beijing.

3 Opening the Door to FDI: The Evolution of Relevant Policies in China

In the last chapter, the main attractions of China to foreign investors in the context of the contemporary world economy were examined. This chapter identifies the key steps of China's opening up to foreign investment since 1978. The central focus of this chapter is on the evolution of FDI related policies (regulations and laws) and their underlying causes in the context of China's political and economic reform. Understanding how FDI related policies have evolved to their current state is essential to assess the quality of China's foreign investment environment.

This chapter consists of three sections. In the first section, the various forms of FDI in China are outlined briefly. Then, the evolution of the open door policy in the aspect of FDI and the main reasons behind these policy adjustments are analysed in detail. Finally, in the third part, the implications of these policy adjustments for foreign investment in China are highlighted.

THE MAIN FORMS OF FDI IN CHINA

Since 1979, FDI in China has taken several different forms. Until July 1994, the most important ones included:[1]

- equity joint ventures
- wholly foreign-owned ventures
- co-operative business operations or contractual joint venture
- joint development
- compensation trade
- processing trade.

Under an equity joint venture, as defined by the 1979 law on joint ventures, Chinese and foreign investors operate the venture and

51

share the risks, profits and losses jointly. All parties involved agree on the equity share of each party. Equity investments may be in the form of equipment, cash, factory buildings or industrial property rights, and profits are distributed to the parties in proportion to their equity share.

A wholly foreign-owned venture, as its name suggests, is wholly owned by foreign investors. This form of foreign investment was not allowed in China by the 1979 law, but it was subsequently found acceptable. This form of FDI has been growing very rapidly in recent years – especially in the 1990s.

In a co-operative business operation or contractual joint venture, the Chinese partner provides land, natural resources, labour and equipment/facilities, while the foreign partner provides capital/technology, key equipment and materials. Both parties decide on the proportions in which products, revenue and profits are distributed.

Joint development applies mainly to activities such as offshore oil exploitation, and returns are normally specified shares of the physical output.

Compensation trade refers to cases where the Chinese partner provides the factory building and labour, while the foreign investor supplies production equipment, technology and, sometimes, technical and supervisory personnel. The foreign partner is paid by means of the goods produced or by a combination of some other products and cash as agreed by both parties.

Finally, processing trade refers to the arrangement whereby the foreign partner supplies materials while the Chinese partner processes them into finished products according to the foreign partner's specifications. All products are passed on to the foreign partner, and the Chinese partner receives a processing fee.

Most other countries do not consider compensation trade and processing trade as FDI, and since the late 1980s, Chinese statistical sources have begun to report these two categories as separate groups. This study excludes these two categories and focuses particularly on joint ventures and wholly foreign-owned ventures.

At the end of 1993, the investment code in China went through a thorough overhaul. The new Company Law came into effect on 1st July 1994. For the first time it provided a firm legal foundation for the establishment of both large and small companies within the framework of the socialist market economy.[2] This new law did not do away altogether with the forms of foreign investment discussed above. Instead it attempted to reclassify them under one of two new and distinct classes of companies: the limited liability company (*You Xian Ze Ren Gong Si*) and the joint stock company (*Gu Fen You Xian Gong Si*).

The limited liability companies are little different from joint ventures already operating in China, and are more obviously targeted at foreign investors. They are cheaper to set up and more flexible than their joint stock equivalents, because although they require more shareholders, the Board of Directors can be smaller and the influence of workers' representatives to the Board is limited to just one per company. The joint stock companies, however, are quite different from the joint ventures in China before 1994. They are more tightly regulated, and place more emphasis on the role of Chinese investors, who must numerically outweigh their foreign counterparts in the early stages of a flotation even though the actual weight of money probably favour the foreigners. This gives a higher degree of protection to shareholders.

The legal systems in operation before the 1994 Company Law were put together in a piece meal fashion – first the joint venture law, then the law for wholly foreign-owned enterprises, and then that for special projects in the investment regions. These laws were so full of contradictions and loose definitions that the scope for misunderstanding was huge. The 1994 law gives China not just a single unified platform for foreign enterprises, but also a means of integrating them seamlessly with a domestic business environment which is itself changing rapidly from central planning to market principles.

With the 1994 Company Law, foreign companies were also allowed to run wholly-owned and fully empowered branch offices in China for the first time (before 1994 the Chinese branches of foreign companies were barred from trading directly with the Chinese public). Some multinational corporations in China have also been given approval by MOFTEC (Ministry of Foreign Trade and Economic Co-operation) to establish foreign invested holding companies (also know as umbrella companies, or *San Xing Qi Ye*) – either as joint ventures or wholly foreign-owned ventures – but in order to do so the foreign company must have a sound reputation in China and must meet some strict conditions (for example, the total assets of the company must be over US$400 million, and the registered capital of the holding company must be over US$30 million).[3] An umbrella company could do everything from procuring raw materials to manufacturing, distribution and eventually retailing its products, although the actual functioning of a holding company is limited by various restrictions. However, this has provided many multinational companies with a structure through which to operate nationally and to co-ordinate and manage investment companies already established in China.

THE EVOLUTION OF FDI-RELATED POLICIES IN CHINA

In December 1978, the Third Plenary Session of the Eleventh Central Committee of the Chinese Communist Party (The Third Plenum or *San Zhong Quan Hui*) took place, which marked the historical turning point and the symbolic beginning of China's reform and opening up. Since then, China's open door policy in the aspect of FDI has undergone six main stages of evolution: late 1978 to early 1983; mid-1983 to early 1986; mid-1986 to early 1989; mid-1989 to late 1990; late 1990 to early 1994; and from mid-1994 onwards. In this section, these policy changes and the underlying causes are analysed in detail. In particular, this evolution trajectory of China's open door policy will be used to illustrate how, and why, China's foreign investment environment has gradually evolved to its current state.

The first phase: late 1978 to early 1983

The open door policy in China began with the symbolic announcement in The Third Plenum in December 1978 that China would be 'actively expanding economic co-operation on terms of equality and mutual benefits with other countries', and would be 'striving to adopt the world's advanced technologies and equipment'.[4] Within a few days of The Third Plenum, Li Xiannian, the president of China at that time, told a group of foreign visitors that, provided China's sovereignty was not impaired, the country was prepared to accept not just technology but also investment from the capitalist world.[5]

On 8 July 1979, with the promulgation of the new law – Law of the People's Republic of China on Joint Ventures Using Chinese and Foreign Investment, the open door policy in China was formally implemented. This new law established the basic legal framework for equity joint ventures.[6] The promulgation of this new law was a significant event in China's opening up. It not only offered a variety of incentives and specified the terms designed to ameliorate concerns of foreign investors, but also marked the beginning of the process of codifying the terms under which China would maintain control over joint ventures (in the aspects of foreign exchange and management, for example). These terms were complemented by a series of new laws and regulations promulgated over the next few years, as well as by rules negotiated into particular contracts.

This new law had an immediate effect on potential foreign investors, and soon after its promulgation, China managed to attract some foreign investment and successfully concluded some deals. Between 1979 and 1982, a total of 83 equity joint ventures, with US$141 millions worth of FDI, were agreed between China and foreign investors. These figures may seem rather modest according to today's standard. In fact, even in the early 1980s, the amount of FDI attracted to China was regarded by the Chinese government as inadequate.[7] However, the symbolic implications of these deals far exceeded their economic value. The real significance of the open door policy during this period did not lie wholly, indeed not even primarily, in how much FDI China attracted, how many new technologies were transferred or obtained, or how much foreign trade increased. Rather, the real significance lay in the symbolic implications of the open door policy in showing the world that China intended to break out of international isolation and become actively involved in the world economy; in shaking up Chinese people's values and ideology after over thirty years of international isolation and central planning; and, indeed, in convincing Chinese leaders at various levels of government of the great potential of opening up to the outside world. In spite of the modest direct benefits China obtained from FDI during this period, the enormous future potential unleashed by this policy formed the basis for China's further opening up in the following years.

It was understandable that China experienced many problems during this period, and reactions to such problems were clearly reflected in subsequent policy-making. The first problem was that the total amount of FDI attracted to China during this period – particularly the amount of foreign capital attracted in equity joint ventures (the form of foreign investment most favoured by the Chinese government) – was very low. This gave rise to the need for subsequent open door policies to address concerns of potential foreign investors by offering more attractive incentives, relaxing government control and providing practical assistance and political and legal assurance.

Secondly, of growing concern to both the Chinese government and foreign investors were the so-called 'ideological obstacles' in Chinese society. These obstacles were derived from a wide variety of sources, with one of the most important being the historical legacies of both the pre-1949 period and the period between 1949 and 1978 in China. On the one hand, the bitter, humiliating experience of the unequal treaties imposed on China in the mid-nineteenth century at the conclusion of the Opium War was still clearly remembered. Under these treaties, western powers demanded the opening of key Chinese ports and established their own enclaves, which were not subjected to Chinese law. On the other hand, the trade embargo imposed on China by the United States in the 1950s as part of Washington's backing of the Nationalist government in Taiwan, combined with the predominant Maoist style of economic management in China, virtually isolated China from world trade and investment for the best part of twenty years. During this period, self-reliance was the goal and foreign trade was merely a temporary way to plug gaps in the domestic economy in China.

For many Chinese people, since China is a big country with very rich natural resources, economic exchanges with other countries were not essential and the country could survive easily and happily on its own. The achievement of such a national desire only became possible after 1949 when the Chinese Communist Party came to power and made China an independent country. Between the late 1950s and the late 1970s, the one-sided emphasis on self-sufficiency reached its peak and became increasingly linked to patriotism and national pride in China, and it was widely accepted that China should be an independent, self-sufficient economy at all costs. The reform and opening up in China initiated in 1978 was, therefore, to change not only national economic policies, but also this deeply rooted and widely accepted ideology in Chinese society. Although economic policies can be changed relatively quickly, ideological changes always take much longer. Such a time lag made it very difficult for the open door policy to be implemented smoothly, particularly during the early days of the reform, and resistance to the opening up was very strong at almost all levels.

Adding to the difficulty was the fact that many people in China failed to understand the strategic significance of opening up the Chinese economy to the outside world. Post-war world economic history demonstrated that market mechanisms and free international trade and investment were more effective than self-sufficient, centrally planned economic regimes in bringing about prosperity and rapid and sustained economic development. The over emphasis on self-sufficiency and central planning in China for over two decades significantly enlarged the already enormous gap between China and the industrialized western countries in economic development. If China intended to improve its economic position in such a world, it had to become actively involved in world economic activities and play by the rules of the free market. Although this theory was increasingly understood (even if only partially) by a small number of Chinese leaders and intellectuals, to communicate this idea to the more 'conservative' leaders and to the general public was no easy matter. Indeed, after decades of international isolation and central planning in China, this idea was probably more difficult to accept than to understand. If not handled properly, it could cause major social and political turmoil in China.

To complicate the situation further, many people believed that foreign investors would only come to China to make money by exploiting Chinese workers, and in the long run they probably would do more harm than good to China. China's own market was so big and its natural resources so abundant that there was no need to develop exports for foreign markets or attract foreign investment. In many people's eyes, the open door policy was merely an expedient measure, and once modernization was achieved, there would be no need for China to expand foreign economic exchanges at all. This view was particularly strong during the early days of the reform, because many people were still strongly affected by the legacy of the ultra-leftist ideology, and their tendency was to equate FDI with the past experiences of imperial colonialism and exploitation of China by western capitalists. There were also many other extremely difficult ideological obstacles to the reform and opening up; and the cumulative effect of these obstacles was to slow down the implementation of the open door policy in China, particularly in attracting FDI.

The third problem that emerged during this period was the inherent conflict between China and foreign investors in their prime objectives. While China sought to attract FDI for capital, new technology, new management and marketing techniques, and hard currency, many foreign investors were more interested in the potentially huge domestic market. The 1979 joint venture law stated that 'a joint venture is encouraged to market its products outside China . . . its products may also be distributed in the Chinese market',[8] but the reality was very different. Domestic sale was strictly regulated, which was partly related to the long-standing policy of protectionism in China.

The expansion of joint ventures in the domestic market meant direct competition with China's fledgling capital goods and consumer industries. Anxieties occurred over the question of whether domestic sales by joint ventures would harm or hamper domestic industries. On the one hand, the relatively high efficiency in foreign invested enterprises associated with foreign technology and management techniques posed a serious threat to domestic industries. On the other hand, experiences from newly industrialized economies after the second world war gave support to the value of joint ventures in helping domestic industries to break away from backwardness through increased competition and the transfer of new technology and management techniques. There were major debates among key decision-makers on this issue.

The dominant view was that 'excessive protectionism' was harmful to the Chinese economy, and some domestic sales by joint ventures should be allowed. In the long run, excessive protectionism would be detrimental to China's economic development, and China would lose its competitiveness and the ability to withstand the strong forces in the world market. Although the protection of domestic industries was often necessary, it had to be handled carefully and in ways that would help the domestic industries to develop. By allowing joint ventures to sell some goods in the domestic market, domestic industries would be forced to improve efficiency and competitiveness, but in a controlled environment, and the process would be less harsh than in a free market. Joint venture sales should be distinguished from foreign imports, as the former would not affect trade balance directly (and might even reduce the need for imports, and contribute to exports and trade balance). The acceptance of these views eventually led to the relaxation of FDI-related policies, which not only included the right to joint ventures for domestic sales, but also the right to make greater profits (together with many other rights). These new rights were formalized in a new law in 1983, which marked the beginning of a new phase in China's opening up.[9]

The second phase: mid-1983 to early 1986

The implementation of the new law in 1983 as a modified version of the original Tax Law in 1980, marked the beginning of a new phase in the evolution of China's open door policy in the aspect of FDI.[10] This law included concessions such as tax breaks, pricing, domestic sales and more latitude for independent operation by foreign investors. The new law was only the beginning of a series of reactions by the Chinese authority to problems which emerged during the first phase and to changes in China's internal conditions and external environment. Internally, there had been an increasing number of complaints from foreign investors about the poor co-ordination among Chinese bureaucracies responsible for the approval and operation of foreign invested enterprises, the inadequate legal infrastructure, and a series of other problems. The total amount of FDI attracted to China was very modest. Externally, other developing countries had adopted similar measures to attract FDI.[11] Therefore, this policy adjustment reflected China's own internal need and its perception of the changing international environment. It is also important to note that this relaxation in foreign investment related policies only occurred in 1983 – about one year after China's shift to an activist phase in its pursuit for more FDI.

During this period, the Chinese government gradually realized that in order to attract more high quality foreign investment, China had to improve the regulatory environment for joint ventures. Therefore, on 20 September 1983, major preferential policies for foreign investment in China were codified in a new set of regulations issued by the State Council: Regulations for the Implementation of the Law of the People's Republic of China on Joint Ventures Using Chinese and Foreign Investment.[12] The '*Regulations*' generally meant that joint ventures' profitability would be enhanced through liberalization in the valuation of their capital contributions and the costs of domestically supplied inputs, increased domestic sales, extended scope for setting sales prices, and tax and duty exemptions. The large body of formal rules contained in the Regulations was widely regarded as a major concession made by the Chinese government in its effort to attract more high quality foreign investment.

For example, on the issue of domestic sales by joint ventures, a major compromise was made by the Chinese government to foreign investors who bring in advanced technologies, although those producing other goods were not included. However, for joint ventures selling mainly in the domestic market, the regulations remained vague on how these foreign investors would be able to convert their profits in Chinese yuan (*renminbi* or *RMB*) into foreign currencies. Also included in the regulations was the right for joint ventures to do business independently within the scope of Chinese laws, decrees, and the agreement. Joint ventures were given preferential treatment over domestic enterprises in the area of supplies in order to guarantee the implementation of their capital construction plans.

During much of the second phase, the general economic environment in China was very favourable for foreign investment.[13] Following the announcement of extensive urban and enterprise reforms in 1984, the central government decentralized major economic control over domestic enterprises to the provincial and local levels. In particular, for the first time, state owned enterprises were allowed to sell a portion of their products outside the plan, and to retain more profit and to decide how to use the profit. Greater access to resources such as foreign exchange and credits were granted to local governments and domestic enterprises. These resources could be used on imports, and credits could be used for establishing new joint ventures and for the expansion of existing ones. These measures also played a vital role in convincing foreign investors that the Chinese government was seriously pursuing the economic reform programme.

The result of these new measures was very impressive. Following the relaxation of restrictions on foreign investment in 1983, the formation of joint ventures from January 1983 to June 1984 jumped over three times in number to a total of 279, from merely 83 for 1979–82.[14] Table 3.1 shows that the formation of joint ventures in China grew steadily from a mere 29 in 1982 to 107 in 1983, 741 in 1984 and 1412 in 1985. Although the figure for 1986 was only 892, it quickly recovered to 1395 in 1987 and 3909 in 1988. The amount of FDI attracted to China grew at a similar pace, which will be discussed later in this chapter.

The period between 1983 and 1985 was widely regarded as one of the most successful periods in China's opening up until the new economic boom started in early 1992. The success was the result of the effective combination of the Chinese government's strong desire to attract more foreign investment and its realistic assessment of the international environment. However, problems began to emerge towards the end of this period for various reasons.

The most serious problem was that the decentralization of economic control from the central to the provincial governments broke the old control mechanisms of the central planning system without creating new ones, which led to an over expansion of credit and a rampant spending on imports. Combined with the drop in oil export revenues and the rising value of the Japanese yen, China's foreign

Table 3.1   Pledged Foreign Investment in Equity Joint Ventures

Year	1980	1981	1982	1983	1984	1985
No. of projects	26	28	29	107	741	1412
Value of projects (US$ bn)	0.040	0.043	0.044	0.19	1.07	2.03

Year	1986	1987	1988	1989	1990	1991
No. of projects	892	1375	3909	3659	4093	8395
Value of projects (US$ bn)	1.38	1.95	3.13	2.65	2.68	6.08

Source: Almanac of China's Foreign Economic Relations and Trade

exchange reserves dropped sharply (Chinese exports were yen-dominated).[15] In July 1984, the figure stood at US$17 billion (up from US$1 billion in the late 1970s), but it fell sharply to US$12.3 billion by February 1985 and further to US$10.8 billion by mid-1985. The central government reacted to these problems in late 1985 by re-centralizing control over activities such as foreign exchange expenditures and imports.

During this time, some leaders in the Chinese central government used the chance to launch a political campaign to regain some of their diminishing power and to reverse the economic reform programme. That was the large scale mass movement, the anti spiritual pollution campaign (*Fan Jing Shen Wu Ran*), in the area of ideology in China, although it was quite unpopular and soon failed. Nevertheless, this movement, directly and indirectly, dampened the enthusiasm and ability of potential foreign investors to negotiate contracts, and made the operation of existing joint ventures very difficult. Complaints from foreign investors consequently soared. Many foreign investors complained about the shortages of foreign exchange, unreliable energy and other supplies, and the widespread corruption and bureaucratism in local governments. Foreign investments fell sharply in both the number of new joint ventures formed and the value of new foreign investment attracted in 1986 (Table 3.1), and most foreign invested enterprises failed to bring advanced technologies to China. To address these problems and to stop the situation deteriorating further, the Chinese government reacted quickly. This reaction, combined with several other changes, marked the beginning of a new phase in the evolution of China's open door policy in the aspect of FDI.

The third phase: mid-1986 to early 1989

The Chinese government increasingly realized that in order to improve the quality and quantity of future FDI, the foreign investment environment in China must be improved, and the problems faced by foreign investors must be dealt with quickly. To resolve some of the problems which emerged during the first two phases, the State Council issued a series of new regulations, including the Notices for Further Improvements in the Conditions for the Operation of Foreign Invested Enterprises[16] in July 1986, and the Provisions for Encouraging Foreign Investment in October 1986.[17] These were accompanied by additional regulations to guide their implementation at both the national and local levels. Various municipal and provincial regulations were also produced according to different local conditions, many of which offered even more 'preferential' treatments than those issued by the central government.[18]

The new regulations by the central government went much further than the 1983 regulations by offering major incentives for foreign investment in the two types of joint venture that the Chinese government most favoured: joint ventures using advanced technologies and/or producing exports. Both types of joint venture were eligible for special treatment from local governments. Their expenses, such as land use fees and certain subsidies to be paid to labour, were reduced. They also received preferential tax treatments, and were given priority in obtaining water, electricity and other services in short supply. Several municipalities and open cities, including Beijing, Tianjin, Shanghai, Guangzhou and Dalian, quickly developed a number of joint ventures in these two categories.[19] The regulations also made changes in foreign exchange rules and in the management of joint ventures, which will be discussed in more detail in Chapter 6.

The promulgation of these regulations led to a sudden rise of 41 per cent in pledged investment in joint ventures in 1987 over 1986, and a further increase of 59 per cent in 1988 over 1987 (Table 3.1).[20] Despite the fact that the Chinese government embarked on a severe retrenchment programme in late 1988, the growth of FDI in China remained strong in the first half of 1989 [between January and June of 1989, utilized FDI rose 21.5 per cent over the same period in 1988; pledged investment rose even more (44.2 per cent)].[21] Although a decline in foreign investment did not happen until after June 1989, investors were aware of the effects of the broader economic retrenchment, especially after the Third Plenum of the Thirteenth Central Committee.[22] Efforts to slow down the economy, particularly by tightening *renminbi* credit, took a toll on existing joint ventures. The credit squeeze also made it difficult for some joint ventures to collect bills, which in turn stymied operations.

Many other serious problems – both domestic and international – also began to emerge during this period. Most of these problems were deeply rooted in the ideological, social, political and economic foundations of the Chinese society. Firstly, in the area of ideology, with the rapid growth of FDI, the Chinese door was also opened to foreign ideas, values, philosophy and culture, which were combined with the revitalization of some traditional Chinese values and culture. Many of these ideas had been banned in China since 1949, and the Chinese Communist Party had worked hard for decades to get rid of them across the whole society through a series of political movements and intensive and extensive propaganda and campaigns.

This problem was noticed much earlier, and back in the early 1980s some Chinese leaders tried to launch the anti spiritual pollution campaign in order to regain control over Chinese politics and ideology but failed. This failure allowed the rapid proliferation and penetration of western ideas in China. Central to the process was the increasing demand for western style democracy and freedom in parallel to the rapid improvement in people's living standard. This demand first developed among well educated people (such as intellectuals), but it soon spread to a wide fraction of the urban population who were at the front line of China's opening up. The rapid proliferation of western ideas provided part of the ideological root for the sweeping student movement in 1989.

Secondly, in the area of reform, the Chinese Communist Party had for a long time been criticized for the slow pace of political reform, which was increasingly unable to accommodate the new demands from the economic reform. This mismatch appeared in Chinese society as a series of crises in the transition from traditional socialism to a new 'socialism with Chinese characteristics' (that is, socialist market economy). For instance, during the transition, market price and government controlled price for certain products (particularly for those in short supply) co-existed, which allowed people with access to such products (including their relatives and friends) to exploit the price difference and become overnight millionaires. This was known as *guan dao* in China, and it caused a lot of dissatisfaction and resentment among ordinary Chinese people (particularly people without access to such networks). There were many other serious problems, such as bribery, using public resources for private purposes (for example, eating out, travel), and wasting state-owned resources. However, such problems were difficult to deal with due to the nature of the existing political system in China – one ruling political Party, incomplete legal system, state ownership and so on. Therefore, there was a growing call for more democracy and political liberalization in China.

Many social problems also emerged during this period, and some of them were closely related to the nature of China's political and economic systems. For instance, the income distribution system in China was not compatible with a market system, because, as a famous joke (which was true!) stated, an expert making atomic bombs (*Yuan Zi Dan*) might earn less than someone who sells tea flavoured eggs (*Cha Yie Dan*); a highly trained brain surgeon might earn less than a barber; and a professor might earn less than someone selling tea and soft drinks (*Mai Da Wan Cha*). Growing inflation was also a major concern. These elements were among the direct causes for the mass student movement in 1989.

The enormous difficulties which emerged during the transition in China apparently called for quick solutions, particularly political solutions from the very top. However, there were major differences of opinion – indeed, open conflicts – among top leaders over what those solutions should be, and in particular, over how to integrate the new system with the old. Decentralization in the political system and in state-owned enterprises, combined with the incomplete legal system in China, had worsened the problems of corruption, bribery and bureaucratism among those in power at all levels of the political and economic hierarchy. These problems caused growing dissatisfaction among Chinese people. The political uncertainty was further exacerbated by growing polarization in people's incomes both within and between regions. These problems formed the political and economic background of the 4 June event in 1989.

The dramatic event in 1989 marked a new phase of China's open door policy, in that the top leaders in China realized that a wide range of political, social, and ideological issues associated with the open door policy needed to be re-assessed. This new phase did not begin with a new gesture of concessions from the Chinese government, such as a reactive new law or a new set of regulations. However, this period was very special, because of the changing internal forces caused by factors such as confusion among Chinese people, political struggles among Chinese leaders, and the passive resistance from those affected by the event, and external forces such as political and economic sanctions from Western countries. The 1989 event also caused an enormous destruction of the great achievements of the 1980s – not only economically, but also ideologically and in many other aspects.

The fourth phase: mid-1989 to late 1990

During this period, the central task confronting the Chinese leadership was to control the domestic and international damage and to recover from the enormous destruction caused by the 4 June event in 1989. In the journal *Asian Survey*, the year 1990 in China was summarized as 'The year of damage control'.[23] The Chinese government faced huge difficulties during this period, including:

> ... restoring the appearance of unity in the leadership, ensuring loyalty of the military, re-establishing social order, reasserting central control over the provinces, re-centralising and retrenching the economy, and re-defining China's role in a post-cold war international environment.[24]

Despite the difficulties and many remaining problems, by the end of 1990 China had recovered quite successfully from the crisis. Social and political stability was restored; economic growth was underway (albeit modestly); foreign relations with most countries were re-established. In fact, several foreign governments deliberately down-played what happened on 4 June 1989 for their own economic and political interests in China. The sweeping and dramatic events in Eastern Europe and the former Soviet Union and the Gulf crisis also served to divert international attention away from China.

During the second half of 1989, China's open door policy virtually came to a halt, not only because of internal reasons (that is, the whole country was busily restoring order in the political, economic, ideological and military systems), but also because of external factors, particularly the economic and political sanctions from western countries. Many joint ventures had either cut back production or postponed new investment. Some investors were also reported to have shifted away from China to other south east Asian countries.[25] The impact of the 4 June event in 1989 on China's open door policy, and in particular on FDI, was enormous, although it was rather short-lived.

This situation remained unchanged during the first half of 1990. Internally, there was still passive resistance from Chinese people. Externally, the relationship with the West remained frozen by the ban on high-level official contacts and economic sanctions imposed in 1989. It also became clear to the Chinese government that after one decade of opening up, the Chinese economy had become so dependent on its relations with the outside world that China could no longer rely exclusively on itself for development. The combination of these factors forced China to return to reform and opening up in the second half of 1990.

The Chinese government made substantial concessions to foreign investors, and attracting new foreign investment was unofficially regarded as a major criterion for the recovery. Many new measures were proven to be quite successful, because the recovery in China was remarkable. In fact, 1990 could even be regarded as a relatively successful year for China in attracting FDI. Although China was still faced with a low-growth economy, negative market demand, an uncertain political risk climate, and continued economic sanctions resulting from the Tiananmen Square tragedy, foreign investors continued (albeit cautiously) to invest. FDI in 1990 totalled US$5.59 billions, just below the 1985 figure of US$5.93 billions.[26] Many joint ventures actually enjoyed record production and profit in that year, mainly due to special concessions made by China. The strong reactions from foreign investors also encouraged the Chinese leadership to adopt new attitudes towards FDI, which marked the beginning of a new phase of the open door.

Before turning to the next phase, it should be pointed out that during this period, the conflicts between political and economic reform in China remained unresolved. It was widely perceived by some Chinese intellectuals and reformers that political reform in China was too slow to keep up with the emerging demands of the economic reform. The view that political and economic reforms should be taken in parallel to each other or, more radically, political reform should be conducted ahead of economic reform, was further enhanced by the political events sweeping Eastern Europe in the aftermath of the Tiananmen Square tragedy (although this view was soon changed by the economic success in China and the political and economic difficulties in the former Soviet Union and some eastern European countries, which will be discussed later in this chapter).

The fifth phase: from late 1990 to early 1994

The development of the Pudong new development zone was a major event in China's opening up to the outside world. Not only because this zone was in the very heart of China's most important and biggest economic centre, but also, more importantly, this gesture marked the beginning of a major shift in the evolution of China's open door policy – a shift from a policy focusing on extending the geographical coverage of open areas and reacting to criticisms and concerns of foreign investors, to one focusing on deepening the level of opening up and actively designing new policies to attract high quality FDI into desirable areas and industries.

Although the Shanghai people's government published the Ten Preferential Policies and Measures for the Development of the Pudong New Development Zone on 30 April 1990, it was the publication of the Nine New Regulations on the Opening and Development of the Pudong New Development Zone by the Shanghai people's government that marked the beginning of major development for the area.[27] Some of the conditions provided by these regulations to foreign investors were even more 'special' than those for the four Special Economic Zones. They provided much broader areas for possible foreign investment, including the establishment of foreign banks and their branches, joint banks with Chinese and foreign investments, joint finance companies, real estate businesses, retailing and consulting services. They also provided the most preferential treatments in terms of land use and tax relief, including income tax and industrial and commercial consolidated tax. The Shanghai Securities Exchange, the first of its kind in mainland China since 1949, was also formally opened in 1990, which was regarded as one of the top ten events in China.[28]

The opening of a special development zone in China's number one city and its largest and most important economic centre was a major event in China, and its successful development would enable Shanghai to regain some of the functions it had lost to other Asian cities since 1949. Moreover, the opening up of this special development zone also demonstrated to foreign investors the determination of the Chinese government in pursuing its economic reform programme and the open door policy, which significantly boosted international business confidence in China.

Following the opening of the Pudong new development zone in Shanghai, particularly after the tour of Deng Xiaoping to southern China in early 1992, a series of new measures to attract high quality

FDI to China were implemented. Typical examples included the opening of new foreign investment opportunities in sectors where FDI was strictly restricted or prohibited in the 1980s, such as the tertiary (services) sectors including retailing and financial services, some strategic sectors such as road, rail and telecommunications,[29] and primary industries such as the exploitation and development of coal, oil and other minerals both in China seas and inner areas (such as the Tarim Basin[30]). Many other measures were also being developed so as to boost the growth of FDI in China.

Also characterizing this new stage of China's opening up was an ideological shift. In particular, a more moderate view towards political reform was gradually accepted by Chinese people. The disintegration of the former Soviet Union and the resultant economic crisis and social chaos convinced many Chinese people that political reform alone would not automatically lead to rapid economic growth. Rather, if the pace of political reform was taken too quickly in China, the impressive economic achievements in China since 1978 could be ruined overnight. Social and political stability in China and continuous economic development has since become the central focus of government policy and the basis for further reform and opening up.

In the meantime, the success stories of the 'Four Dragons' in south east Asia increasingly became the envy of many Chinese leaders (the Singapore and Hong Kong models in particular), which demonstrated that to achieve continuous rapid economic development, political and economic reforms did not have to be undertaken in parallel to each other. Economic growth can happen very rapidly, but social and political transformation should be undertaken step by step. In particular, many people realized that democracy cannot be achieved overnight – and indeed, it may even be a luxury for materially well-off nations. In a large and poor country like China, many people simply did not have enough to eat, and easing the problems of poverty for a large number of people is an extremely challenging long-term task. Political liberalization – although important – was not a top priority for a large number of Chinese people. Many people accepted that political and social stability was critical to national economic success, and if they wanted to improve living standards quickly, a slower pace of political liberalization might be one of the prices to pay.

This ideological shift has since been reflected in China's reform and opening up. In economic reform, radical but realistic measures were adopted, and the pace of economic reform accelerated again. However, in political reform, China has followed a more moderate route, and in fact the unchallenged political control in China by the Communist Party allowed the Chinese government to adopt a gradualist and experimental approach to reform. In the words of *The Financial Times*, China is seeking a middle way between capitalism and socialism, that is: 'to achieve market-led prosperity without the social disruption of the former Soviet bloc and the political pressures on reformers in the Indian sub-continent.'[31] This has, at least so far, been proven as the right choice for China.

The sixth phase: from mid-1994 onwards

Since mid-1994, China's open door policy in the aspect of FDI entered a new phase, marked by two significant gestures by the Chinese government. One was the promulgation of the new Companies Law on 1 July 1994, which covered a wide range of outstanding legal issues relating to, among others, shareholding and bankruptcy.[32] One of the main aims of the law was to create a platform for reforming the state owned enterprises under socialist market economy (rather than helping foreign investors), but it provided a means to integrate the foreign investment environment with the domestic business environment. In the long run, neither foreign invested enterprise nor Chinese domestic enterprises would have special treatments and they would have to compete on equal ground. Many important issues covered by the law and its relevance to foreign investors have been discussed earlier in this chapter.

The second significant gesture was China's decision to impose restrictions on FDI in the car industry: no foreign investors would be allowed to set up new car assembly lines in China until 1997 (a ban of more than two years on the setting up of new assembly lines in China by foreign investors), and after this, any foreign car makers intending to assemble cars in China had to start with 60 per cent local contents. In particular, one policy stated that foreign car companies expecting to build co-operative or foreign funded car companies in China using its own product, patent and trademark must have developmental capacity and advanced manufacturing technology, an international marketing channel and satisfactory financing ability; and a single car company would not be allowed to set up more than two joint ventures manufacturing the same model of a vehicle in China. This decision was mainly intended to allow the infantile car industry in China to consolidate, but it sent a clear message to potential foreign investors about China's intention to reward early investors with long term commitments, particularly those transferring new technologies and new management techniques.

In mid-1995, this practice was extended to a wide range of industries with the promulgation of a new regulation to guide the direction of future foreign investment.[33] A comprehensive index of industries was published with this regulation which clearly stated in which industries foreign investment would be encouraged, restricted, allowed or prohibited. This regulation further opened up some Chinese industries to FDI (for example, financial services) but at the same time restricted or totally prohibited FDI in selected areas. In the ninth five year plan (1996–2000), China also made it clear that it particularly encourages foreign investors to invest in the western part of China, in infrastructure development, and in the loss-making state owned enterprises.[34]

As the Chinese economy continues to grow at high speed, and as the Chinese market becomes increasingly attractive, and the quality of China's investment environment continues to improve, China is becoming increasingly selective about who should invest where, and under what conditions. In particular, through policy measures, China is actively channelling FDI into key areas essential to the long term development of the national economy (such as agriculture, telecommunications and transportation, coal, electricity and oil industries, high technologies, as well as many other key industries in China). Increasingly FDI in China is being regulated by China's macroeconomic policy, and China will particularly encourage FDI that will contribute to the long term development of the national economy. The central focus of China's open door policy in the aspect of FDI is increasingly put on quality (although quantity remains very important).

In late 1995, China announced that it would introduce a sweeping tax reform for foreign invested enterprises in China – the first step in a general overhaul of preferential tax policies for foreign investors. Under the old regime, foreign funded joint ventures paid 15 per cent corporate tax in special economic zones, 24 per cent in the 400 or so 'open areas', and 30 per cent elsewhere, compared with a 55 per cent tax for state owned enterprises. This tax system would gradually be replaced by a flat 30 per cent national corporate tax plus local taxes on top. Exemptions on equipment import by foreign invested enterprises would also be abolished.

This tax reform would be accompanied by a series of other measures including tariff cuts; limited convertibility of the Chinese currency; the elimination of many import quotas and controls; and easing of restrictions on operations by joint ventures with foreign investment. In particular, China would slash 4000 tariff lines which would lower China's average tariffs by no less than 30 per cent; quotas, licensing and other controls on about 170 tariff lines would be eliminated; foreign exchange transactions by foreign companies would be incorporated in the banking system of foreign exchange procurement and sale; Shanghai and a number of other cities would be designated as pilot bases for joint ventures between Chinese and foreign partners; and a trial scheme for joint retailing ventures with foreign partners would be extended.[35]

Some foreign investors expressed major concerns about the tax reforms and their short term effects on profitability. China reassured them that such measures would be implemented flexibly, sympathetically, and gradually (to be phased in). These measures were part of China's effort to satisfy the conditions for entry to the World Trade Organization (WTO), and it was also part of China's wider reform of the tax system to harmonize national corporate tax and to improve local tax systems. Gradually, foreign investors would have to compete with Chinese companies on an equal basis and they would be treated the same as domestic companies in China.[36] This would eventually contribute to the quality of China's investment environment.

These new policies and regulations would particularly affect special economic zones (including the Pudong new development zone), as a wide range of preferential taxation would gradually be phased out and would not be renewed. However, both central and local governments believed that these special economic zones have acquired a wide range of comparative advantages since the early 1980s, and combined with some of their intrinsic advantages such as good locations, good infrastructure, dominance in certain industries in China, a large pool of foreign investors already there and so on, they would be able to convert from 'preferential' special economic zones to 'functional' special economic zones. By doing so, they would be able to attract high quality foreign investment with long term commitments in China, rather than those investors only temporarily come to China to enjoy the short term preferential policies. They would also be able to exploit their position as centres of economic growth and would continue to be in the vanguard of China's reform, opening up and rapid economic development.[37]

A wide range of difficult reforms have been carried out during this period; and many reforms implemented since 1992 also began to show results. Increasingly, the central focus of reform is shifted from breaking out of the old system to establishing the new system; from reforming individual items/aspects to systematic reform of the economic regime with strategic focuses; and major reforms are legitimized through the establishment of new laws. A market system has been built up, and the planning element in total national industrial output was reduced from 70 per cent in 1979 to 6 per cent in 1994 (and is still dropping!). Progress has been particularly significant in reforming the finance and taxation regime, the banking system, and many other areas such as foreign currency and foreign trade; investment (including foreign investment); state owned enterprises; pension and social welfare; medical insurance; and housing.

One of the main concerns of the Chinese leaders during this period is still to maintain a positive relationship between development and stability. Political and social stability is regarded as critical to China's rapid economic development. So far, China seems to have achieved its twin goals of building a market-based system and achieving integration with the international economy. Reforming the state owned sectors, although extremely difficult, is making progress; and the political transition from the third to the fourth generation leadership has been completed smoothly. Trade balance remains healthy, and national foreign exchange reserves have increased substantially (over US$100 billion by November 1996).[38] China also gave a formal undertaking to the International Monetary Fund (IMF) that from 1 December 1996 the Chinese yuan would become convertible on the current account,[39] which will make foreign investors' life easier. Although economic over-heating and growing inflation have caused, and will probably continue to cause, the central government headaches, macro-economic interventions through indirect measures since 1993/4 seem to be more effective and less destructive than administrative measures of the planned economy.[40] These reforms are clearly reflected in the quality of China's foreign investment environment.

Summary: A gradualist approach to reform and opening up

So far, FDI related policies have undergone six major steps of evolution. These changes have been brought about by a variety of interrelated factors – both domestic and international – which will be discussed in the next section. The evolution of China's open door policy in the aspect of FDI needs to be understood in the wider context of China's political and economic reform, in particular, the difficult transition from a planning to a market economy. As Deng Xiaoping once said, reform in China is like 'crossing the river by feeling the stones on the river bed'. This message has been translated into a series of guiding principles for the reform.

The Twelfth Communist Party Central Committee (*Shi Er Da*) regarded 'planning as the dominant economic regime in China and market as the supporting regime'. This principle progressed in The Third Plenary Session of the Twelfth Communist Party Central Committee (*Shi Er Jie San Zhong Quan Hui*) to a 'planned commodity economy based on socialist state ownership'. The Thirteenth Communist Party Central Committee (*Shi San Da*) stated 'socialist commodity economy should pursue internal harmony between planning and market'; which in the Fourth Plenary Session of the Thirteenth Communist Party Central Committee progressed to 'establishing an economic regime and operation mechanism which combines planning with market intervention'. In 1992, Deng Xiaoping argued that planning was not equal to socialism and market was not equal to capitalism. Capitalism can use planning and socialism can use market. This idea was formally approved by the Fourteenth Communist Party Central Committee in October 1992: that the goal of reform was to 'establish a socialist market economy'. Before the death of Deng Xiaoping in February 1997, the commanding position of the state owned economy was never questioned, and the main guideline for reforming the state sector was to nurture the large state enterprises whilst letting the small ones go their own way (*Zhua Da Fang Xiao*). However, Jiang Zeming's reiteration of Zhao Ziyang's theory about China being in the 'early stages' of socialism and that socialism in China would remain in its early stage for a long time, have cleared further ideological obstacles for more radical reforms.[41]

Many such phrases and statements may sound dull and meaningless to many people, but to reformers and government officials in China, they serve to eliminate – at least to get around – difficult ideological obstacles on the road to radical reform. Without them many measures of reform simply could not be implemented. These evolving guiding principles allowed more and more radical measures to be taken to reform China's economic and political regime. The evolution of China's open door policy in the aspect of FDI has happened within the overall framework outlined by these guiding principles, although a series of internal and external factors have played important roles in shaping the direction of these policies.

FROM REACTIVE TO PROACTIVE POLICY MAKING: THE MAIN CAUSES FOR POLICY CHANGES IN THE ASPECT OF FDI IN CHINA

The evolution of China's open door policy in the aspect of FDI has been reflected in a series of new laws and regulations issued by both the central and local governments, which have been discussed in the last section. The general effect of these laws and regulations is the gradual improvement of China's investment environment and the increasing relaxation of control over foreign invested enterprises. The evolution of the open door policy has been generated by various internal and external pressures in the context of reform and the changing world political and economic climate. It has become increasingly clear to the Chinese leadership that the development of even a big country such as China depends heavily on its interactions with the outside world.

Some of the major domestic and external forces that caused the evolution of China's open door policy were identified in the last section. This section intends to summarize these forces and draw some implications from them. Between 1978 and the early 1990s, the evolution of China's open door policy can be best understood as 'reactive policy-making', that is, major changes had been derived from the reactions of the Chinese government to various internal and external pressures. However, since the early 1990s, a more proactive, as opposed to reactive, approach to policy making has been adopted.

Internal forces

Since 1978, the Chinese government has faced a series of difficult dilemmas in opening up the Chinese market to FDI. On the one hand, to modernize the Chinese economy, China needs foreign capital, advanced technologies, new skills and new management techniques, which are all essential to transform Chinese enterprises into more efficient and internationally more competitive ones. The growth of the Chinese economy also depends critically on the success of Chinese enterprises in the international markets, and joint ventures can help Chinese enterprises to enter the international market through exports. These demands require the Chinese government to relax control over foreign invested enterprises and improve the condition of China's foreign investment environment.

On the other hand, however, FDI is regarded as a potential threat to state control over the national economy. As the amount of FDI increases, the Chinese government is increasingly concerned with extensive foreign influence in the Chinese economy, which may affect China's sovereignty and the direction of China's national economic development. Therefore, the Chinese government wishes to maintain tight control over foreign invested enterprises (for example, in ownership, management control, which sector to invest and where to sell products). In certain 'strategic sectors', FDI is prohibited or strictly restricted. However, in recent years, control over some strategic industries (such as transportation, telecommunications and some primary and service industries – oil, banking, retailing) has increasingly been relaxed, because China needs foreign capital injection and more advanced technologies to speed up the development of these sectors. Nevertheless, a wide range of strict restrictions on foreign involvement in these sectors has been maintained.

The Chinese government has been particularly concerned with the potential damage of FDI to the macro-economy. China wishes to avoid the experience of countries where foreign invested enterprises spend more foreign exchange on imports than they earn through exports, thereby incurring a net drain on these countries' hard currency reserves, which exacerbates their debt problems, and threatens their economic independence. That is probably why the Chinese government has from the very beginning required most foreign investors to balance their own foreign exchange account. More recently, however, control has been relaxed because of the huge and rapidly growing foreign exchange reserves in China (over US$122.8bn by June 1997, according to *The Economist*, 13–18 September 1997).

These dilemmas have been clearly reflected in the different views existing among Chinese leaders at various levels of the government. In the past, Chinese leaders who preferred tight control over foreign invested enterprises (and a slower pace of reform and opening up) were often labelled as 'conservatives' (as opposed to reformers); and the existence of the 'conservative' forces within the Chinese leadership was often regarded by both Chinese and foreign researchers and commentators as something 'bad'. However, the experience of the former Soviet Union and some eastern European countries in the 1990s suggests that this view may need to be re-assessed – not only from China's point of view, but also from that of foreign investors. The gradualist approach adopted by China in the reform and opening up has so far been more successful than the 'big bang' approach adopted by Russia in bringing about rapid and sustained economic development.[42] Without different voices in the Chinese leadership, the moderate pace of reform and opening up might not have been possible.

The point is that both too fast or too slow a pace of reform and opening up can damage rather than benefit the Chinese economy. Only a stable and rapidly developing Chinese economy will provide the commercial opportunities that most foreign investors want. The transformation of a political regime and an economic system cannot happen overnight. Even if the administrative systems and the institutional structures can be set up relatively quickly, these can be easily undermined or overwhelmed by historical legacies. This is especially the case in China where people are used to being controlled by people rather than by law, and a western style democratic culture is something alien to both the feudalistic traditional Chinese culture and to the Communist Party culture. These issues will be discussed again in more details in Chapter 5.

The difficulties and dilemmas discussed above are clearly reflected in the evolution of FDI related policies in China. These new policies (in the form of regulations and laws) not only specified the conditions and terms under which foreign invested enterprises can operate, they were also intended to control and co-ordinate foreign investment in China by limiting the opportunities available to foreign investors. In order to boost the Chinese economy, China needs to attract an increasing amount of high quality FDI, which in turn requires the Chinese government to address concerns and criticisms of foreign investors, relax control and open up more opportunities to foreign investors. Such a reactive policy-making process is understandably uneven, but gradually a more relaxed foreign investment environment is created.

Since the turn of the 1990s, the Chinese government has been actively designating new measures to attract FDI into targeted areas, which is particularly reflected in the shift of emphasis from quantity to quality. In particular, the Chinese government has become increasingly selective about 'which types of FDI to attract into where', which implies that China has progressed beyond passively attracting any FDI, to actively attracting high quality FDI into desirable sectors or areas. The Chinese government recognizes the profound economic and social influences of FDI in China, and how to maintain political, social and economic stability in China while opening up further to foreign investment will remain a major challenge to the Chinese government in the near future.

External forces

The evolution of FDI related policies in China has also been affected by various external forces or pressures. These pressures have come from a number of sources, with the first one being foreign investors already operating in China. In particular, the problems and difficulties encountered by foreign investors in China (such as corruption and venality among local officials, low efficiency of government services, inadequate legal framework and physical infrastructure, and unreliable supplies of energy and raw materials) often lead them to put strong pressure on the Chinese government. To maintain a steady flow of FDI into China, the central and local governments have to react to such problems quickly, because the perception of China's investment environment by foreign investors can significantly affect international business confidence in the Chinese market. China's reactions to such problems and concerns are often reflected in new regulations and policies for FDI.

Another source of external pressure came from outside China, particularly from potential foreign investors. Perceiving the experience of early investors in China, some potential foreign investors realized that certain controls could hinder both their ability to operate effectively and their access to China's domestic market. The result is the withholding of capital by potential investors and reduced total volume of inward investments to China. To attract such investment, the Chinese government has to relax control and open up new opportunities in new sectors or new areas. Such reactions are also reflected in new policies.

In addition, at the macro level, western governments have put strong political and economic pressure on China to speed up reform and to open up new opportunities to foreign investment. Examples include the annual review of China's MFN (most favoured nation) trading status by the USA and the pressure from various national governments and international organizations (for example, the European Parliament) on China to improve the conditions of its internal human rights, or to better protect intellectual property. The policies and measures adopted by other countries in attracting FDI also put pressure on China to adjust its open door policy. Such pressure often leads the Chinese Government to make concessions, responses and adjustments from time to time in FDI related policies. However, in recent years, as the attractiveness of the Chinese market increases rapidly, the bargaining power (and skills) of the Chinese government has improved dramatically. Policy making in the aspect of FDI is increasingly shifted from a reactive to a proactive approach.

In conclusion, the key dynamics in the evolution of China's open door policy have been the interactions between internal and external forces discussed above and the desire of the Chinese leadership to achieve rapid and steady economic development. Until the early 1990s, the process can be described as reactive policy making, but the latest evidence indicates that an increasingly more proactive approach is being adopted.

SUMMARY

In this chapter, the evolution of China's open door policy in the aspect of FDI was systematically examined, with particular reference to the promulgation of FDI related laws and regulations. The terms and conditions made explicit by these laws and regulations lay down the basic legislative and institutional framework for FDI in China. The key forces that led to the major changes in FDI related policies were also identified in this chapter. The key dynamics of China's evolving open door policy in the aspect of FDI have been the interactions between various internal and external pressures and the desire of Chinese leaders to achieve rapid and steady economic development. The resultant 'reactive policy making' process was, understandably, not smooth, but the general tendency is that a more relaxed foreign investment environment is being created. The evidence from the early 1990s indicates that China's open door policy for FDI has shifted from a reactive to a proactive approach, from one emphasizing the geographical coverage of open areas to one emphasizing the quality of opening up within existing open areas, and from one of passively attracting any foreign investors who would come to China, to one actively selecting the most suitable partners with long term commitment in strategic areas. Although the geographical coverage of open areas and new business opportunities in new sectors are continuously being extended, what is increasingly emphasized is the quality of foreign investment. The evolution of the open door policy in the aspect of FDI has been clearly reflected in the quality of the evolving foreign investment environment in China.

Notes

1. For example, Zhang, Youwen, Duan Xiping, Jin Bu (1986), *The Opening Up of Our National Economy (Wuo Guo Jing Ji De Dui Wai Kai Fang)*, Shanghai Publishing House (*Shanghai Chu Ban She*), Shanghai, p. 49; Lo, T.W.X. (1986) 'Foreign investment in the special economic zones: A management perspective' in Jao, Y.C. and C.K. Leung (eds) *China's Special Economic Zones: Policies, Problems and Prospect*, Oxford University Press, Hong Kong; Shao, A.T. and Paul Herbig (1994) 'Marketing inside the dragon, despite China's bureaucracy', *International Marketing Review* 12 (1): 65–76.
2. Euromonitor (1994) *China: A Directory and Source Book 1994*, Euromonitor Plc, London; Brahm, Lawrence and Li Daoran (1996) *The Business Guide to China*, Butterworth-Heinemann Asia, Singapore.
3. Brahm and Li (1996) *op. cit.*
4. *Beijing Review*, 29 December 1978, pp. 6–16.
5. Ho, Samuel and Ralph Huenemann (1984) *China's Open Door Policy: The Quest for Foreign Technology and Capital*, Vancouver: University of British Columbia Press.
6. *Beijing Business Review*, Vol. 10 No. 5, 1983, pp. 30–35.
7. *International Trade*, No. 19 July 1983, p. 55.
8. *Beijing Business Review*, Vol. 10 No. 5, 1983, *op. cit.*
9. *Beijing Review*, Vol. 19 No. 9, May 1983, p. 7.
10. *Ibid.*
11. Wei Yuming (1983) 'Present situation in China's utilisation of foreign investment and suggestions concerning future work', *International Trade (Guo Ji Mao Yi)*, No. 19, July.
12. *Beijing Review*, Vol. 26 No. 41, 10 October 1983, pp. 1–16.
13. Pearson, Margaret M. (1991) 'The erosion of controls over foreign capital in China 1979–1988' in *Modern China*, Vol. 17 No. 1, January 1991.
14. *Beijing Review* No. 47, 19 November 1984, p. 9.
15. *Far East Economic Review*, 27 June 1985, p. 110; National Council for US–China Trade (NCUSCT) (1987) *US Joint Ventures in China: A Progress Report*, Washington D.C.
16. *Almanac of the Chinese Economy*, 1987, Beijing.
17. *Beijing Review*, Vol. 29 No. 43 p. 26.
18. Ji, Chongwei (1987) 'The improvements in China's investment

environment and its future prospects' (*Zhong Guo Tou Zi Huan Jing De Gai Shan Ji Qian Jing*), *Almanac of the Chinese Economy* (*Zhong Guo Jing Ji Nian Jian*), 1987.

19. *Beijing Review*, Vol. 29 No. 4, 1986, p. 4.
20. *Ibid.*
21. Pearson Margaret M. (1991) *Joint Ventures in the People's Republic of China*, Princeton University Press, Princeton.
22. Dittmer, Lowell (1989) 'The Tiananmen massacre', *Problems of Communism*, September – October 1989.
23. Shambaugh, David (1991) 'China in 1990: The year of damage control', *Asian Survey*, Vol. XXXI No. 1 January 1990, pp. 36–49.
24. *Ibid.*, p. 36.
25. Dittmer, Lowell (1990) 'China in 1989: The crisis of incomplete reform', *Asian Survey*, Vol. XXXI No. 1, January 1990.
26. *The China Daily*, 24 December 1990.
27. *Beijing Review*, Vol. 33 No. 44, October 1990, p. 12.
28. *Beijing Review*, Vol. 34 No. 2, pp. 14–20. January 1991.
29. For example, *The People's Daily* (Overseas edition), 25 June 1992, 'Foreign capital extensively entering the tertiary sectors' (*Wai Zi Guang Fan Jin Ru Di San Chan Yie*), p. 1; 30 June 1992, 'The State Council of the central government decided to accelerate the development of the tertiary sectors' (*Zhong Gong Zhong Yang Guo Wu Yuan Zuo Chu Jue Ding, Jia Kuai Fa Zhan Di San Chan Yie*), p. 1; 12 August 1992, '220 foreign financial institutions set up offices in China' (*Wai Zi Jin Rong Ji Gou Zai Da Lu Yi She Dai Biao Chu 220 Jia*), p. 2; 13 August 1992, 'Real estate becomes a new hot spot for investment' (*Fang Di Chan Cheng Wei Tou Zi Xin Re Dian*), p. 1; and 22 August 1992, 'Tertiary sector becomes a new area for foreign investment in the Changjiang Delta area' (*Di San Chan Yie Zai Chang Jiang San Jiao Zhou Cheng Wei Wai Shang Tou Zi De Xin Ling Yu*), p. 2.
30. *The Financial Times*, 31 March 1993, 'Everything to play for in China's Tarim basin'.
31. *The Financial Times*, 24 May 1993, 'China's unique path towards the free market'.
32. Euromonitor (1994) *op. cit.*; Brahm and Li (1996) *op. cit.*
33. *The People's Daily* (Overseas edition), 1 July 1995, 'Regulation on guiding the direction of foreign investment' (*Zhi Dao Wai Shang Tou Zi Fang Xiang Zan Xing Gui Ding*) and 'Index of foreign investment industrial guide' (*Wai Shang Tou Zi Chan Ye Zhi Dao Mu Lu*), p. 2.
34. *The People's Daily* (Overseas edition), 20 March 1996, 'People's Republic of China National Economic and Social Development: Outline of the "ninth five year plan" and long term targets for the year 2010' (*Zhong Hua Ren Min Gong He Guo Guo Min Jing Ji He She Hui Fa Zhan 'Jiu Wu' Ji Hua He 2010 Nian Yuan Jing Mu Biao Gang Yao*), approved by the fourth plenary session of the Eighth People's Congress on 17 March 1996, p. 1.
35. *The Financial Times*, 20 November 1995, 'China plans reforms to break trade stalemate: Beijing to cut tariffs and ease investment rules in attempt to join WTO'.

36. *The People's Daily* (Overseas edition), 29 December 1995, 'China adjusts preferential tax policy for foreign invested enterprises: Creating better investment environment for foreign investors' (*Zhong Guo Tiao Zheng Wai Qi Shui Shou You Hui Zheng Ce Jiang Wei Wai Shang Chuang Zao Geng Hao Tou Zi Huan Jing*), p. 1.

37. *The People's Daily* (Overseas edition) published a series of front page articles to illustrate the situation for special economic zones: 23 March 1996, 'China adjusts preferential policies for special economic zones and special development zones, what shall Pudong do?' (*Yang Du Te You Shi, Zhan Shuang Yi Teng Fei: Guo Jia Tiao Zheng Kai Fa Qu You Hui Zheng Ce, Pu Don Ze Mo Ban?*), p. 1; 26 March 1996, 'Shenzhen is transforming towards a functional special economic zone' (*Shen Zhen Kua Xiang Gong Neng Xing Te Qu*), p. 1; 4 April 1996, 'Li Peng speaks at State Council Special Economic Zone Working Conference: Special economic zones should re-invent themselves, create new advantages and achieve further progress' (*Te Qu Yao Yi Er Ci Chuang Yie Jing Shen Zeng Chuang Xin You Shi Geng Shang Yi Ceng Lou*), p. 1.

38. *The People's Daily* (Overseas edition), 30 November 1996, 'China's foreign exchange reserve exceeded 100 billion US dollars' (*Zhong Guo Wai Hui Chu Bei Tu Puo Qiang Yi Mei Yuan*), p. 1.

39. *The People's Daily* (Overseas edition), 29 November 1996, 'Renminbi will become convertible on the current account from next month' (*Xia Yue Qi Shi Xian Ren Min Bi Jing Chang Xiang Mu Ke Dui Huan*), p. 1; *The Financial Times*, 29 November 1996, 'China moves to yuan convertibility', p. 4.

40. *The People's Daily* (Overseas edition), 18 December 1996, 'Good start for the "ninth five year plan"' (*'Jiu Wu' Kai Ju Hao*), p. 1.

41. *The Economist*, 19–25 July 1997, 'Reform in the air', pp. 59–60.

42. Child, J. (1994) *Management in China during the Age of Reform*, Cambridge University Press, Cambridge.

4 The Foreign Investment Environment in China: The Hard Environment

The last two chapters examined the main attractions of China to foreign investors under the contemporary world economic climate and the evolution of China's open door policy in the aspect of FDI. In the next three chapters, the nature and key characteristics of China's foreign investment environment are systematically examined. This chapter centrally focuses on issues related to the hard investment environment, such as the general condition and future prospects of various infrastructures (for example, transportation and telecommunications, and energy and other raw material supply), which can have immediate impacts on the operation and development of foreign invested enterprises in China. The next two chapters focus on the soft investment environment in China, which comprises factors such as Chinese history, culture, political system, social and economic regimes, legal and regulatory systems, labour relations and business services. The unique characteristics of these factors in China can significantly affect the operation and development of foreign invested enterprises both immediately and in the long run.

This chapter consists of three sections. In the first section, some previous studies of foreign investment environment in China are reviewed briefly, and the concept of the hard and soft investment environment is defined, which formulates the basic framework for this and the next two chapters. Then, in the second section, the condition and key characteristics of China's hard investment environment are illustrated and evaluated, with particular reference to the demands of foreign invested enterprises in China, the general level of China's economic development, and the characteristics of Chinese political and economic systems. Finally, in the third part, the key findings of the chapter are summarized and their implications for foreign invested enterprises are highlighted.

THE HARD AND THE SOFT INVESTMENT ENVIRONMENTS

The investment environment is a very broad concept, which consists of a series of inter-related factors. Some of these factors have been examined singly or systematically by previous studies. Most foreign investors come to China with a series of objectives in mind (see Chapter 2 for a detailed discussion), therefore, they need to consider whether the general condition and the potential partners in China are likely to permit the realization of those objectives. To this end, Geringer examined what he called the 'task related' and the 'partner related' factors.[1] Task related factors concern the quality of the market opportunities, productive skills, resources and other factors, which together determine the economic viability of the proposed venture's operations. Partner related factors refer to the ability of the local partner to work together with the foreign investor, such as the compatibility between the Chinese and the foreign management teams, and the cultural differences between the two organizations. Similarly, De Bruijn and Jia examined what they called the 'environmental factors' (such as the market situation in China, the local supply situation and government policies), the 'key internal factors of the Chinese partner' (for example, their technological and marketing capabilities), and the 'operational criteria' (for example, the requirements for the localization of supply and foreign exchange balance).[2]

In 1995, an independent, comprehensive, quantitative study was conducted by a group of 50 experts from 18 disciplines in China, using government official statistics and first hand data collected from a large number of foreign invested enterprises in China. The study was jointly sponsored by a consortium comprising several newspaper groups, the information centre of the China Federation of Industry and Commerce, and a number of market research companies and large industrial groups. The result was first published in a seminar held in Hong Kong on 'An Introduction and Evaluation of the Investment Environment in Mainland China' (*Zhong Guo Nei Di Tou Zi Huan Jing Jie Shao Ji Yan Tao Hui*) on 27 February 1995.[3] The study systematically examined the quality of foreign investment environment in 188 large and medium cities in China, using a framework consisting of 8 aspects, 32 categories, and 61 criteria, including urban infrastructure development, market conditions, labour supply, social development, economic development, total foreign investment absorbed and so on. The study emphasized that although urban infrastructure development is very important to the quality of foreign investment environment, soft factors such as policy implementation, public security, social stability, inflation and many others cannot be ignored.

The study concluded that the quality of China's overall investment environment was rated 3.53 on a scale of five (between average to satisfactory, 1 = poor, 5 = excellent) by foreign investors in China. Most foreign investors were satisfied with the policies concerning foreign investment and the stability of these policies, but not with the efficiency of local government and the legal protection for foreign investors (their possessions and safety, for example). The quality of the Chinese labour force was not high but cheap and easy to obtain. In terms of the urban infrastructure, there were very few problems with telecommunications but lots of problems with transportation. Some foreign investors were particularly concerned with the lack of market research and consultancy services, which lagged behind many other countries (including many developing countries) and caused serious problems to some investors.

A further finding from the study was that major regional differences existed in China. For example, the quality of the labour force in the coastal region was high but so was the cost, which was increasing very rapidly. In contrast, in inner parts of China, the labour cost was lower and so was the quality of the labour force. However, because 60 per cent of the total purchasing power in China was in the middle and western part of China, the study predicted that more foreign investment would go west and north. A main recommendation to the Chinese government was that preferential policy alone would no longer be enough to attract high quality foreign investment. Instead, the focus should be shifted to improving the quality of policies and the efficiency in their implementation by various local governments and their agencies.

In this book, we will examine a wide range of critical factors, which together make up the foreign investment environment in China. These key factors are classified into two broad categories, namely, the 'hard' environment and the 'soft' environment (Table 4.1). The 'hard' environment refers to the condition and characteristics of the tangible infrastructure, many of which are readily measurable in quantitative terms. In contrast, factors of the soft environment are mostly intangible and are very difficult to measure, but they are often critical to the operation and development of foreign

Table 4.1 The Key Elements of the Foreign Investment Environment

Foreign investment environment	Hard environment	Soft environment
KEY FACTORS	• Transportation • Telecommunications • Energy supply • Public utilities • Other infrastructure • Raw materials and components supplies • Others	• Historical elements • Political background • Culture and social structure • Economic regime • Social securities and welfare • Law and legal system • Human resources • Labour relations • Government services • Business services • Others

invested enterprises. As we shall see in this and the next two chapters, the differences between China and the West in their soft investment environment are probably far more significant than the differences between their hard environment. Failing to understand these differences will seriously misguide potential foreign investors in their risk assessments and in making strategic and operational decisions.

It should be pointed out here that the elements in Table 4.1 are not exhaustive, and many other important factors, such as China's level of economic development and future prospect, market opportunities in different parts and sectors of China (for example, the size of the Chinese market), and foreign investment related policies and regulations, are discussed elsewhere in the book.

Compared with the soft environment, information concerning the hard environment is relatively easy to obtain from government agencies or other information sources. However, such information is often scattered in numerous places (for example, various ministries, government departments, the state statistical bureau and local government agencies) and it is often incomplete, fragmented, not comparable and not up-to-date. The condition of the hard environment can also change very rapidly. The telecommunication link between two cities, for example, can be improved in a short period if it is so intended by the relevant authority and the necessary capital is made available. In contrast, social and political transformations normally take much longer to accomplish, so changes in the soft environment tend to be much slower. Nevertheless, some policy adjustments can have immediate impacts on foreign invested enterprises, which are clearly reflected in the quality of the soft investment environment in China.

China is a very large country in area with enormous regional disparities, both in natural conditions and in socio-economic development, therefore some key factors of the investment environment may vary significantly between places. Equally, the current transformation in China has been happening at an astonishing pace, and the condition of some factors (both hard and soft) can change rapidly in a short space of time. Given the word limit of this book, the geographical variations in the quality of China's investment environment will not be discussed in great detail. However, their significance should not be neglected, and it is essential for foreign investors to adopt a proper geographical and time focus in assessing the quality of the investment environment in China and in making strategic and operational decisions.

CHINA'S HARD INVESTMENT ENVIRONMENT FOR FDI

Because China is a developing country, foreign investors (especially those from developed countries) often find the condition of many taken-for-granted factors in developed countries highly inadequate in China, and many foreign investors are often insufficiently prepared for such inadequacies. This section highlights some major problems encountered by foreign investors in China since the opening up. Both their current situation and future prospects will be discussed.

The most frequently reported problems with China's hard environment have been related to the poor condition of various infrastructures – transportation, energy supply and telecommunications, for example. The Chinese central and local governments fully recognize these problems, and since the early 1980s many measures have been taken to improve the situation – including, more recently, encouraging foreign investors to participate directly in China's infrastructure development. In the coastal region alone, hundreds of billions of yuan have already been invested by the central and local governments, and improvements in energy and raw materials supply, transportation and most of all, in telecommunications have been very impressive.[4] Pomfret even argued that correcting these problems may 'only be a matter of a few years.'[5] There are also numerous attractive opportunities for foreign investors in these industries.

Although the general condition of the hard investment environment has been improving steadily and sometimes rapidly, many problems remain unresolved today due to the even more rapid growth in demand, and the historical legacy of accumulated under-investment in these areas. These factors will remain major obstacles to the operation and development of foreign invested enterprises in China. In this section, the current situation and future prospects in China with energy shortage, inadequate transportation infrastructure, telecommunications, and insecure and poor quality raw material supplies are analysed. Some of these problems are closely interrelated.

Energy shortage

Energy shortage is not only a serious problem encountered by foreign investors, but also a long-standing problem for China's domestic enterprises. This problem has been derived from a number of sources, with the incompatibility between the geographical distribution of energy resources and economic activities as one of the most significant. China's heavy reliance on coal as the primary source of energy significantly exacerbated the problem (coal accounts for over 70 per cent of China's energy consumption,[6] and for many years China has been the world's largest producer of coal[7]). China's inadequate transportation systems also served to worsen the situation considerably (please see the next section).

China has about 30 per cent of the world's total proven coal reserves, but about 84 per cent of them are concentrated in the northern half of China, particularly in Shanxi province and southern Inner Mongolia (Figure 4.1.). In fact, if a line is drawn from Kunlun Mountain, via Qinling Mountain to Changbaishan Mountain, 94 per cent of all China's proven coal reserves are in areas north of the line![8] About 70 per cent of potential hydro-electric power reserves are in the southwest of China, and the biggest hydro power stations are concentrated in the upper Huanghe River (the Yellow River) in remote provinces in the west of China – although the situation will change with the construction of several of the world's largest hydro-electric power stations on Changjiang (the Yangzi river, for example, the Three Gorges Dam) and several other rivers in the south west. The main sources of oil and natural gas supplies are concentrated in the 'Three North Regions' (*San Bei*),

Figure 4.1   The 'Great Coal Base' in China

Figure 4.1. The 'Great Coal Base' in China

that is, the Northeast, Huabei and the Northwest.[9] These three regions have a total proven oil reserve of 60 billion tons (60 per cent of China's total), and 27 000 billion cubic metres of natural gas (70 per cent of China's total).[10] However, the main areas of energy consumption in China have been the coastal provinces in the east of the country.

In the thirteen coastal provinces, energy production only accounts for 13 per cent of the national total output, but they consume 65 per cent.[11] Some energy production in the coastal provinces is often by burning coal obtained from inner provinces; and some of the energy production in the coastal region is for export (for example, some coal produced in Shandong is for export to Japan). Because of the inadequate transportation infrastructure in China and the low capacity of mining and electricity generating facilities, energy shortage has for a very long time been restricting China's economic development. The inefficient generators, burners, and pumps used in China are normally very wasteful, which has made the situation of energy shortage even worse.

FDI in China is highly concentrated in the coastal regions in the east of China (particularly in the southeast). Foreign investors have naturally encountered the problem of energy shortage as soon as they came in, and similar problems have been encountered in inner parts of China. A survey of 42 joint ventures in Tianjin (the third largest city in China) showed that the most serious problem confronting foreign investors was the shortage of energy, particularly in the number of electricity power shut downs.[12] The research by Thoburn *et al.* about Hong Kong companies who invested in the Pearl River (Zhujiang) Delta also suggested that the supply of electricity was a major problem for most investors.[13] As a result of frequent power cuts, many foreign invested enterprises had to maintain their own back-up electricity generators, which increased operating costs. Christofferson reported that even China's first coal mine joint venture – Antaibao coal mine in Shanxi – had to shut down several times because of diesel oil shortage.[14] It is somewhat ironic that even a coal mine has to close because of lack of fuel!

Since the early 1980s, numerous measures have been adopted by both the central and the local governments to relieve this problem. In the case of Hong Kong companies in the Pearl River Delta, some localities such as Panyu built their own electricity generating facilities (instead of relying on the provincial electricity network) to guarantee supply to foreign invested enterprises.[15] Between 1985 and 1990, the sixty-one cities in the coastal provinces completed nearly 100 large and medium sized electricity related projects, which increased electricity generating capacity by over 12.5 million kilowatts. An additional 5700 kilometres of high voltage electricity network was built. The Shatoujiao power station in Guangdong, Zhenhai power station in Ningbo, Macun power station in Hainan, the Qinshan and Dayawan nuclear power stations were only a few examples. By 1990, the total electricity supply in the fourteen coastal open cities and four special economic zones was more than double that in 1983.[16] Some local governments even gave foreign invested enterprises priority in energy supply. All these served to relieve the enormous pressure of energy shortage on foreign invested enterprises in selected areas.

During the eighth five year plan period (1991–95), the energy industries in China achieved even more rapid development.[17] There was even a small over-supply of coal, but a 20 per cent shortfall for electricity remained. Despite rapid growth in production, China also became a net importer of oil (from being a net exporter) during this period – mainly due to the even more rapid growth in demand. Energy consumption was still dominated by coal, which accounted for 72.8 per cent of all energy consumption in China (oil 19.6 per cent, natural gas 2 per cent, and hydroelectric 5.6 per cent). Energy production grew very rapidly during this period. By 1995, annual energy production in China reached 1.3 billion tons of coal (0.22 billion tons more than 1990), 149 million tons of oil (10.78 million tons more than 1990), 17.4 billion cubic metres of natural gas (2.18 billion cubic metres higher than 1990) and 1000 billion kilowatt hours (kWh) of electricity (378 billion kWh higher than 1990). Two nuclear power stations in Guangdong and Qinshan became operational and four new and larger ones are under construction.[18] By the year 2003, China's total nuclear power generation capacity will reach 9 million kW, about 2–3 per cent of national total.[19]

The electricity industry grew by 9.77 per cent between 1991 and 1995, faster than the 8.8 per cent growth rate for this industry achieved during the seventh five-year plan (1986–90). Between 1991 and 1995, electricity generation capacity increased by 75 million kilowatts (that is, newly installed capacity, which accounted for about 35.7 per cent of total electricity generation capacity in China in 1995). Total generating capacity reached 210 million kilowatts, producing 1000 billion kWh of electricity in 1995. Total investments in the electricity industry during the period reached 280 billion yuan, of which US$12.1 billion (utilized) was foreign investment (US$14.5 billion pledged). The high voltage electricity network increased by 31 117 kilometres, and the voltage transforming capacity also increased substantially.[20]

However, due to the continuous rapid growth of the national and regional economies, growth in energy consumption has consistently out-paced the growth in production [the economy grew at 12 per cent per year (17.3 per cent for secondary industries) during the eighth five year plan]. Therefore, energy shortage will remain a serious problem for many years to come. Building more electricity generating capacity in the coastal area will put further pressure on transportation to move large volumes of coal from the north to the south and from the west to the east (also see next section), which re-opens the debate on whether China should build electricity generating capacity in coal producing areas and transport electricity through a national electricity grid, or continue to move coals via transportation. This is an extremely complex issue and a wide range of political, environmental and administrative issues are involved.

For example, environmentally speaking, the west and north are far more fragile than the coast and the south due to climate differences. The lack of water resource in the former areas has understandably constrained the development of electricity generating complexes near the coal pits. Administratively, there are many Ministries and administrative areas (provincial authorities) involved, and collaborations between them are not always straightforward. Politically and economically, there are different interest groups involved, and under the market economy, local interest often overrides national economic well-being as a whole (for example, the not-so-well-off western areas have long felt they have been exploited by the more prosperous areas along the coast, and they are increasingly unwilling to tolerate the situation). Currently, both routes have been taken by China: electricity generating capacity is being built near coal pits in inner provinces; and coal is continuously being shipped to the coastal region – most noticeably by the electrified double tracking railway line between Datong and Qinhuangdao coal dock specially developed for moving coal from Shanxi to the coast. The coal is then moved via sea routes at large quantity to major coastal docks including Shanghai, Ningbo, and Guangzhou. However, resolving the problem of energy shortage in China requires a more systematic approach.

Since the early 1990s, China has been taking a medium- to long-term view towards energy shortage, and major measures have been taken to tackle the problems. For example, apart from opening up several offshore oil and gas fields to foreign investors, twelve additional onshore areas were opened up to foreign exploitation for oil and natural gas, including the opening up of part of the Tarim basin in the remote far western region of China to major global oil companies (for example, Shell, BP, Amoco, Arco, and Unico).[21] The controversial Three Gorges Dam (Sanxia) project was formally approved by the National People's Congress in 1992, and when it is completed at the turn of the century it will significantly increase electricity supply in China.[22] The first phase of Daguangba hydropower and water conservancy project – a key project in the eighth five year plan – was completed in Hainan province in December 1993, and began to supply electricity to the national electricity grid.[23] Numerous other energy projects – including several very large-scale hydroelectric power stations, coal powered stations and four new nuclear power stations – are already underway. Guangxi is constructing a hydropower station in Longtan, which will be the second largest in Asia after the Three Gorges Dam when completed.[24] In 1997, an even larger hydroelectric project, the Xiluodu Dam on Jianshajiang, is under preparation, which will add 11 million kW of new electricity generating capacity (producing 52.6 kWh electricity each year) to China (about two thirds the scale of the Three Gorges Dam). When completed, it will also increase the electricity generating capacity of Sanxia and Gezhouba on Changjiang by 800 000 kWh each year.[25] The four new nuclear power stations will be completed between 2003 and 2005.[26]

These projects will eventually relieve the situation of energy shortage for the booming Chinese economy, and although they were not specifically targeting foreign investors, they will certainly serve to improve the quality of China's foreign investment environment. However, as has been pointed out earlier, the Chinese economy has been developing so rapidly that energy consumption is also increasing at a high speed, and in fact, economic growth is often faster than the growth of energy production.[27] What these projects are doing is to stop the gap from getting bigger. The situation is better in some places, but a great deal remains to be done. The country's economic development is fuelling demand for greater energy consumption, and energy shortage will probably remain a constraint for foreign invested enterprises in China for some time to come.

The energy industry remains a priority area in China's ninth five year plan (1996–2000), and nine key projects have been planned to improve the situation of electricity shortage.[28] The Chinese government is also encouraging foreign investors to get involved in the energy industry. According to the plan, by the end of the century, China will have a total electricity generating capacity of 300 million kW (up from 210 million in 1995); producing 1400 billion kWh electricity per year (up from 1000 billion in 1995). The national electricity grid will be fully integrated. Large-scale electricity generating facilities will be developed in major energy bases to pump electricity into the national electricity grid. The Three Gorges Dam will become operational. A series of new measures will be implemented to improve energy efficiency; and the changing economic structure (rapid growth can come from energy efficient industries) may also serve to reduce the pressure on energy shortage. These projects will together relieve the severe energy shortage in China, but whether the problem can be resolved by the end of the century remains a big question mark.

On 20 January 1997, China's National Electricity Corporation was formally established – a major step in the reform of the electricity industry and in China's transition from planning to market. Its establishment will significantly improve the ability of the industry, in raising new capital from various sources, and in rationalizing the generation and use of electricity in China as a whole.[29] In particular, China will continue to increase its use of foreign investment in the electricity industry.[30] In May 1997, Chinese Premier Li Peng published China's Energy Policy, which, in six sections, systematically outlined the strategies, main targets and other important issues (for example, finance, energy saving, sustained development and environmental issues) for the coal, oil and electricity industries.[31] These measures imply that whilst China continues to explore new ways of speeding up the development of the industry and tackling major bottlenecks, an increasingly systematic approach is being adopted to tackle problems of energy supply in China. These measures will lead to steady and rapid improvements in this area.

Energy shortage in China is closely related to another major problem of the hard investment environment – transportation. Much of the pressure for transportation in China has resulted from the demand for moving large quantities of coal across China; and any new development in transportation capacity can be easily absorbed into the almost bottomless black hole of coal transportation. The inadequate transportation facilities in the country have significantly exacerbated the incompatibility between the geographical distribution of energy resources and the centres of economic activities. Even when more coal has been produced in the northwest, there is no certainty of getting it to the coastal provinces quickly because of the inadequate railway and road systems. Too much transportation capacity allocated to moving coal also leaves little capacity for moving other commodities. The current situation and future prospect of China's transportation infrastructure is the central focus of the next section.

The inadequate transportation infrastructure

The inadequate transportation infrastructure is another serious bottleneck constraining the operation and development of foreign invested enterprises – resulting in high costs of doing business in China and serious delivery problems for domestic inputs.[32] Like energy shortage, this problem has been constraining the development of China's domestic companies for decades. The causes of the problem are diverse. Large disparities in natural conditions, and the uneven geographical distribution of natural resources and economic activities, inevitably demand the transportation of bulk goods. During the cold war, economically rational locational decisions were forced to give way to considerations for national military defence capacity, which often meant locating strategic industries in remote, inaccessible, mountainous areas. For example, the confrontation with the West and with the former Soviet Union forced China to relocate industrial capacity to remote areas, such as the 'third front' and the so-called *Shan* (mountains), *San* (dispersed), *Dong* (underground) location policy, in order to increase the capability of the Chinese economy in withstanding potential foreign military attacks. What made things worse was that economic decisions (such as the location of some large companies) were often made by bureaucratic officials in the absence of scientific support.

   Other factors include the imbalanced structure of different modes of transportation. The outdated equipment and inefficient management of transportation facilities also worsened the situation. Until recently, the underdeveloped road, air, water and pipeline transportation in China meant that the railway had to carry excessive weight for both cargo and passenger transportation. Most of all, China is a developing country, and the transportation infrastructure is generally underdeveloped. Major capital injection, and time, are needed to improve the situation.

The railway

Because of the special importance of railway transportation in China, the main causes for the inadequacy in this infrastructure need to be analysed. Although railway has the advantages of high capacity and low costs for long distance movement of cargo, in China it was also heavily used for small volume cargo over short distance (which is probably more suitable for road). Trains are also heavily used for transporting people across the country. Thus, for a long time, railway transportation has been very inadequate in China, and increase in demand has far surpassed the growth in capacity. The railway system is generally underdeveloped: in 1994, the density of China's railway network was only 56 kilometres per 10 000 square kilometres (lagging behind over seventy countries in the world), whilst the operational mileage was only 0.5 kilometres per 10 000 people – that is, 5 centimetres per person, lagging behind over one hundred countries in the world! Given that railway has been the most important transportation infrastructure in China, these figures clearly indicate the level of inadequacy and the huge potential for future development.

To make the situation worse, most railway facilities available in China were backward and outdated. In 1994, only 16.6 per cent of railway lines were electrified, 26.6 per cent double-tracked, and steam engines still accounted for 35.5 per cent of trains. The top speed of a passenger train was merely 105 km per hour, and the average volume of a freight train was only around 2500 tons.[33] The condition of the railway network in China has been particularly inadequate both for passengers and cargo along some sections, such as Long-Hai (between Lianyungang and Lanzhou), Zhen-Gan (between Zhenjiang and Jiangxi), and Qian-Gui (between Guizhou and Guangxi), Xiang-Qian (Hunan to Guizhou), Bao-Lan (Baotou to Lanzhou). The total capacity of these railway links can only meet between 50 per cent and 70 per cent of the demand. Some companies located in affected areas have to plan production and sales carefully according to the availability of transportation capacity, rather than according to production capacity or market demands.

The sheer geographical scale of China and the uneven distribution of natural resources and economic activities also made the development of an efficient and adequate transportation systems very difficult. China, in area, is as large as the entire continent of Europe. A large part of China's natural resources – including energy resources – is located in the west and middle of the country, but economic activities and population are mainly concentrated in the coastal belt in the east of the country. This has created a huge demand for the transportation of natural resources and commodities across the country.

As has been pointed out in the last section, a large part of China's coal reserves – the main form of energy consumption in China – are concentrated in Shanxi province and southern Inner Mongolia, but the main areas of consumption are the coastal provinces. This has inevitably produced a demand for bulk transportation of coal from north to south and from west to east. The insufficient capacity of China's transportation systems is thus a main cause of energy shortage in the coastal region. The geographical distribution of many other natural resources is equally uneven, and many natural resource reserves are concentrated in remote areas, which creates demand for long distance transportation across the country. Adding to this, the enormous climate variations between the north and the south, and between the east and the west, have created a demand for long distance transportation of agricultural products.[34]

The geographical distribution of economic activities created enormous demand for high volume transportation of industrial products over long distances. Because of the high level concentration of production in the coastal region, there is a demand for moving finished commodities from the east to inner parts of China. Heavy engineering industries are highly concentrated in the northeast of China while the east provinces are particularly good at light industries such as textiles and home electronics. These commodities need to be re-distributed to different regions in the country.[35]

The very rapid development of the Chinese economy since 1979 has significantly exacerbated the historical inadequacy of China's transportation system, and today, it remains one of the weakest links in the Chinese economy.[36] Railway today remains the most important form of transportation in China, which accounts for between 30 per cent and 50 per cent of China's total transportation (both passengers and goods). The railway network operates some of the most intensively used lines in the world and yet facilities for transporting grain, coal and other industrial goods remain inadequate due to the historical underdevelopment of the infrastructure and the rapid increase in demand (cargo and passenger traffic has been growing at 9 per cent annually).[37] Measures such as developing more rail lines to relieve coal bottlenecks, double-tracking and electrifying along the main north-south corridors [for example, from Beijing to Guangzhou (Jing-Guang Line) and Shanghai (Jing-Hu Line)], and east-west lines from Zhejiang province to Changsha in Hunan province, are being implemented, but the inadequate railway services for both cargo and passengers cannot be resolved within the short term.

Both the central and local governments in China have been working hard to relieve the serious situation with China's railway infrastructure. Some major railway developments – along with other transportation infrastructure (water, road, air and pipeline) – were incorporated in the list of national key projects of the eighth five year plan (1991–95) and the same is happening with the ninth five year plan (1996–2000). During the eighth five year plan, the Ministry of Railway Transportation completed 5800 km of new lines (3.4 times that completed during the seventh five year plan between 1986 and 1990), and newly double-tracked 3400 km of line (1.4 times that achieved during the seventh five year plan) and newly electrified 2600 km of existing lines. In terms of the scale of investment and the speed of development, the eighth five year plan period was the most important in China's railway development history.

Since the end of 1992, the Ministry of Railway Transportation has made it their strategic focus to firstly complete Jing-Jiu (Beijing–Kowloon) and Lan-Xin (Langzhou–Xinjiang) lines; then Hou-Yue and Bao-Zhong lines; to continue the work in Huadong (southeast China) and Xinan (southwest China) and to improve Da-Qing (Datong–Qinghuangdao) railway links. A large number of new trains have been developed and produced. Heavy trains carrying 6000 tons of coals are in operation on the Da-Qing line (the heaviest now carries 10 000 tons); and on busy lines such as Jin-Guang and Jing-Hu, 5000 ton cargo trains have become operational along all main trunk routes. New management methods have been adopted which have significantly improved the efficiency of China's railway systems.[38] Train speed has been increased to 140 km per hour between Shanghai and Nanjing,[39] and 160 km per hour between Guangzhou and Shenzhen.[40] In particular, the Jing-Jiu line, a double-tracking line linking Beijing and Kowloon (Hong Kong), was officially started in 1993 and was completed in November 1995 (one year ahead of schedule).[41] This line is 2536 kilometres long, with a total design capacity of 200 million tons. In parallel to Jing-Guang (Beijing-Guangzhou) and Jing-Hu (Beijing–Shanghai) lines, this is the third main railway line linking up the north and the south. Many foreign investors believe the areas along the line will become new focal points for investment in the next century.

After the rapid development during the eighth five year plan, the situation along the northwest and north-south corridors are greatly relieved; but in the southwest, northeast and Huadong (southeast), the situation remains inadequate, and so is the capacity for moving coal out of main coal production areas. In particular, demand increase for cargo has been extremely fast, and many bottlenecks cannot be eliminated in the short term; and the growth of passenger trains simply cannot keep up with demand. The transportation strategy in the nation's ninth five year plan (1996–2000) and in the long term plan for the year 2010 is to continue to develop railway as the most important transportation infrastructure, but road, water, air and pipelines will also be used to relieve the situation.[42]

In the last few years, rapid developments of other forms of transportation (road and air transportation in particular) have to some extent relieved the enormous pressure on the railway in certain areas. The inadequacy of the railway system in China also means it is losing market share quickly as market mechanisms are increasingly being introduced in China. Between 1985 and 1995, the market share of railway transportation in China reduced from 54.1 per cent (60.5 per cent in 1980) to 39.4 per cent for passengers, and from 71.3 per cent to 54.4 per cent for cargo. During the peak 50 days in the spring of 1996 (Chun Yun), while total transportation business volume in China increased by 1.6 per cent (4.5 per cent for road and 21.5 per cent for air), railway experienced a 4.7 per cent reduction. During the peak 50 days in the spring of 1997, while total transportation volume in China increased by 4.8 per cent, railway again experienced a 1.5 per cent reduction. Growing competition from road and air transportation forced the railway authority to adopt systematic measures to maintain its position in the market.

During the ninth five year plan, railway development will focus on eliminating bottlenecks, extending new lines, but most of all on increasing speed and capacity (faster and heavier trains). On 1 April 1997, the train speed on the four busiest railway trunk lines in China – Jing-Ha (Beijing–Haerbin), Jing-Guang (Beijing–Guangzhou), Jing-Hu (Beijing–Shanghai) and Long-Hai (Lianyungang–Lanzhou)

– was increased from 80–100 km per hour to 110–140 km per hour. At the same time, using Beijing, Shanghai, Guanzhou, Chengdu, Zhengzhou, Wuchang and Xi'an as focal points, 78 trains have been launched to travel to and from places 1000–1500 km apart (so people and cargo can arrive at various destinations overnight). This marked the beginning of the speed increase on China's busy railway networks. A series of other measures are also being adopted by the railway authority to compete effectively with other forms of transportation.[43] Nevertheless, the inadequate railway infrastructure – the most important form of transportation in China – will continue to restrict the operation and development of foreign invested enterprises.

Other transportation infrastructure

The high pressure on China's railway system is closely related to the under-development of other transportation infrastructures including road, air, water and pipelines. Since the early 1980s, numerous projects have been implemented to improve these infrastructures. Motorways and other high grade roads (together with electrified, high capacity railways) are being constructed along some of the main traffic axes to tackle major bottle-necks.[44] During the eighth five year plan (1991–95), China built a total of 112 000 kilometres of new roads, making a total road network of 1.14 million kilometres. The development of high grade road was particularly fast during this period, and a total of 7300 kilometres of first and second grade roads, and 1619 kilometres of motorways, were added onto China's road network (increasing China's total motorway to 2141 km).[45] By the end of 1995, all counties, 98 per cent of towns, and 80 per cent of villages in China were connected by road.

The rapid development of high speed roads between large cities has made it possible in many places to have day return trips between cities 400–500 km apart, and to reach cities 800–1000 km away on the same day. This has served to reduced the enormous pressure on the railway for short distance passenger transportation. In the next five years, China will need US$30 billion of foreign investment for its road construction programme, and by the year 2010, China's total road network will reach 1.35 million km. In the next twenty years, China's priority is to construct 35 000 km of new high grade roads to link Beijing and all provincial capitals.[46] To achieve China's road network development strategy, raising the enormous capital investment required is a key factor – which will undoubtedly open up attractive opportunities for foreign investors.

In China, the natural condition for developing water transportation is good, but it only accounts for less than 20 per cent of all cargo transportation in China. The potential for further development is enormous. During the seventh five year plan period (1986–90), the Chinese government funded 46 large and medium sized seaport related projects. Several modern large and medium scale new seaports were built, including Beilun Port in Ningbo, Shijiu Port in Rizhao, Bayuquan Port in Yingkou, and Fangcheng Port in Guangxi. The ports of Shanghai, Tianjin, Qinhuangdao, Dalian, Guangzhou and Lianyungang were modernized and their capacity was significantly expanded. The overall capacity of seaports increased by one hundred and twenty million tons. By 1990, the total capacity of seaports for the sixty one cities in the coastal region reached four hundred and eighty million tons – one and half times that in 1985.[47]

The rapid development of water transportation continued during the eighth five year plan (1991–95). During this period, China newly built or expanded 170 large and medium sized seaports, which added 138 million tons of new capacity. In main coastal sea ports, 283 new berths (container and coal berths in particular) were constructed, which added a new capacity of 120 million tons. By the end of 1995, China had a total of 412 deep water berths. It also improved 4200 kilometres of main river channels and built 92 new berths in main river ports, with newly increased capacity of 24 million tons. The total length of river channels reached 111 000 kilometres (5800 kilometres for ships over 1000 tons), and the total number of river berths reached 4500.[48]

Although they still lacked the high throughputs and efficiency of Hong Kong and Singapore, all China's ports became fairly efficient by the early 1990s, and the heavy port congestion and waiting time of the 1980s were mostly eliminated. A priority for all ports is to develop more berths for handling coal and grain. Coal is transported across the country to seaports by rail, and then loaded on freighters to move down the coast to southern ports in large quantities, which significantly relieves the pressure on railway for long distance transportation. In the ninth five year plan (1996–2000), China will focus particularly on coal, oil, iron ore, container, and rolling on/rolling off seaports that are linked to main transportation corridors. Major efforts will be devoted to improving inland water transportation systems along river and canal networks. Key measures include improving main channels, adopting new management techniques and increasing the level of mechanization.[49]

The improvement in air transportation has been the most significant among all modes of transportation in China. Among the 61 open cities in the coastal region, only 31 of them had established air travel services by 1990, with a total air freight of 200 000 ton kilometres, and a total air passenger turnover of 10 million person kilometres. By 1995, China already had a total of 139 airports in 133 cities.[50] Air cargo turnover reached 240 million ton kilometres; and air passenger turnover reached 65.2 billion person kilometres.[51] For over a decade, China has been the fastest growing aviation market in the world and will remain so in the foreseeable future.

Since 1980, China has imported on average over US$2 billion worth of aeroplanes each year. It has been projected that by the year 2000, total air passenger capacity in China will reach 170 million – with an annual growth of 18.8 per cent. 13 new airports will be built in provincial capitals including Shijiazhuang, Wuhan, Zhengzhou, Guiyang, Guilin, Fuzhou, Guangzhou, Shanghai, Nanjing, Haikou, Hangzhou, Nanchang and Yinchuan. The capacity of an additional 18 airports in major cities will be significantly expanded.[52] It is widely believed that between 1996 and 2010, China will need 800–1300 new aeroplanes, and by then China will become the third largest aviation market in the world after the USA and Japan.[53]

China has also been making every effort to improve related facilities, such as developing computerized booking systems, expanding existing airports and developing new ones, training pilots both in China and abroad. *The Financial Times* reported that China was unable to keep up with the rapidly growing demand, so that Russian planes as well as their crews were leased to relieve the pressure.[54] In the 1990s, China diversified its sources of supply by ordering 30 Airbus planes to reduce its over-reliance on Boeing for large aircraft. The joint development of a new 100 seater plane with foreign partners is currently underway,[55] and China will also participate in the development of the super jumbo with Airbus. Like the road network which reduced the pressure on the railway for short distance transportation, the rapid development of air transportation (for passengers in particular) has to some extent relieved the pressure on long distance passenger transportation by train.

During the eighth five year plan, China utilized US$3.4 billion in loans from foreign governments and other international financial sources in the transportation sector. The Chinese government has also increasingly encouraged foreign investors to invest solely or jointly with Chinese partners in the construction of motorways, bridges and tunnels and to invest solely in the construction of private docks and waterways for cargo shipping.[56] Over 590 joint ventures were formed in transportation services during this period. Different modes of transportation are increasingly co-ordinated, aiming to achieve a more balanced and more rational transportation structure and division of duties.

Further to the publication of China's energy policy, Chinese Premier Li Peng also published an important article on establishing an integrated transportation system in China.[57] He re-emphasized that transportation remains a priority area in China's ninth five year plan and in the ten-year long term plan. The development strategy for China's transportation system is to use the railway system as the main backbone, the road system as the basis, making full use of water transportation, whilst rapidly developing air transportation and appropriately developing pipeline transportation. By co-ordinating these different forms of transportation effectively, an integrated transportation system can be established in China. This policy will ensure steady and rapid development of transportation in China.

The transportation infrastructure is very unevenly developed in China, and because numerous new projects are underway, the geographical pattern of the transportation infrastructure is undergoing rapid changes. Some bottle-necks cannot be eliminated overnight, and they will remain a major constraint for foreign invested enterprises (as well as for China's domestic companies) in the future. The operational and management implications for foreign investors can be very significant. In particular, for industries where transportation is an essential element, the inadequacy of China's transportation infrastructure can significantly affect the delivery of raw materials and finished goods, and hence the production scheduling and business operations. Essential business travels can also be problematic. The problem can be particularly acute for foreign investors from developed economies where fairly adequate transportation systems for cargo and passengers have been taken for granted for decades. A convenient location is therefore essential for the success of a foreign invested enterprise in China. The ultimate resolution of transportation-related problems will take time and enormous investment, and China's transition from planning to market and the growing competition between different modes of transportation may speed up the process of improvement.

The poor quality and insecure supply of raw materials

The poor quality and insecure supply of raw materials and other inputs have been another serious problem encountered by some foreign investors. In particular, industrial supplies are frequently not up to the required standard, and items which are locally available may still need to be imported at higher cost as the quality of the local produce is often not good enough. This was especially the case in the 1980s. For example, the Shanghai Pilkington Glass unexpectedly found that it had to import the soda ash – an essential material in glass making – because the Chinese soda ash was unsuitable, which increased the company's operating costs.[58] The China Hotel in Guangzhou used local water pipes that burst when the water was turned on, so these pipes had to be replaced using pipes imported from Hong Kong.[59] In fact, the poor quality of local supply was so serious that it actually deterred many multinational companies from investing in China.

This problem has derived mainly from the overall low level of industrial development in China. China is still in the midst of a radical transformation from a centrally planned to a market economy, and the isolation of China from the international market for thirty years (see next chapter for more details) cannot be eliminated overnight. However, quality related problems are not insuperable. Once they have been recognized by the relevant authorities, most of them can be solved within a relatively short period of time, which has been demonstrated by, for example, the experience of Shanghai Volkswagen Automotive Co. Ltd.[60]

When the joint venture was first set up, most components (knocked down kits) were shipped in from other countries. Both the German and the Chinese partners wanted more local components to keep the cost down, but Volkswagen would not allow this unless the components locally supplied could reach its stringent standards. Neither did the Chinese partner wanted to undermine the quality of the finished car by using low quality local components. After decades of international isolation and the planning economic regime, most Chinese component suppliers were unfamiliar with foreign standards.[61] To supply Shanghai Volkswagen, Chinese suppliers from the very beginning tried very hard to improve the quality of components, and by 1992 the Volkswagen Santana model, produced in China, achieved 70 per cent local contents – including its key components such as the body, the engine, and the gear box – without affecting the quality of the finished car.[62] By 1993, the level of localization reached 80 per cent.[63] Similar evidence was found in other sectors.

The implications from this case are very complex for foreign investors, which goes beyond the issue of poor quality local supplies. The rapid improvement in the quality of components for Shanghai Volkswagen was achieved through investment and training made by the foreign partner, coupled with the collaboration and determination of the Chinese partner. The enormous market potential in China prompted Volkswagen to take some short term risks in order to achieve its long term strategic objectives. Indeed, Volkswagen could have assembled kits brought in from abroad. Instead, it became the only big foreign car producer to transfer management skills and technology (albeit outdated) from abroad. In 1993, Volkswagen made 100 000 cars in China, which accounted for about a third of the total car production in China.[64] That has certainly impressed the Chinese government, and on 11 April 1994 China decided that all foreign car makers wanting to drive into China should do the same; and moreover, no new joint ventures in the car industry would be allowed for three years, and after the three year ban, new car assembly plants will have to start with 40 per cent of local contents, improving to 60 per cent within three years.[65] This was a daunting blow to car makers still stuck outside the country.

In a panic, several leading car makers – including Ford, General Motors, Toyota, Nissan, and Renault – decided to invest heavily in components manufacturing in China in the hope that they would eventually be allowed to produce finished cars.[66] For example, Ford signed joint venture agreements worth $50m with two Chinese components makers, in what it intended to be the first substantive step towards assembling whole vehicles in China.[67] More significantly, what happened in the car industry was increasingly happening in other industries. Unlike much of the 1980s, when China welcomed any foreign investors with open arms, the Chinese government increasingly demanded long-term commitments from foreign investors in exchange for the enormous market potential in China. This issue has been discussed in detail in the last chapter.

It needs to be pointed out that quality related problems may exist in a whole spectrum of industries in China. Even McDonald, the fast food chain, delayed its first investment in China until 1992 because of the perceived difficulties in maintaining supply of quality inputs in China.[68] The situation has been improving steadily but some problems in the area may remain for a long time to come.

In addition to quality related problems, early foreign investors also faced the problem of insecure supply of raw materials – a problem still not fully resolved today. A survey[69] revealed that one of the most serious problems confronting joint ventures' operation during the 1980s was the shortage of materials. According to the theory of the Hungarian economist Janos Kornai, this problem is typical of the planned economy showing the symptoms of 'shortage economy'.[70] Between the early 1950s and the 1980s, China was primarily a centrally planned economy and, even today, central planning remains important in strategic industries. Although market mechanisms have been increasingly introduced since the mid-1980s, the transition from planning to market is still not completed and the market is still immature. Compared with the more mature markets, the price system in China is often 'irrational' because of heavy subsidies, price control and distortion and other government interventions. A new order of the market economy is still to be established and fine-tuned.

For many types of materials in China, there were two main channels of supply: planned allocation and market adjustment. Three types of prices – planned prices, state guidance prices, and market prices – co-existed at the same time. This has affected some foreign invested enterprises very badly, because many of them have no access to the planning sector. The supply of certain materials through the market channel was insecure, and the price tended to fluctuate by large margins and many foreign invested enterprises found it difficult to accommodate such price fluctuations. Although foreign investment law allows enterprises with foreign investment to purchase their materials in both the domestic and international markets, some of them rely on the domestic market due to lack of foreign currency (this will be discussed in Chapter 6).[71] The insecure supply of raw materials in some industries made it very difficult for some foreign invested enterprises to operate normally.

The situation has improved considerably over the past few years due to the increasing liberalization of the market and the improvement in local currency convertibility (see Chapter 6). Many interim measures were also adopted by various local authorities to ease the problem. For example, Jiangsu Province would rather stop production in domestic factories to guarantee supply to enterprises with foreign investment. Shanghai and Tianjin adopted similar measures.[72] Shanghai set up a special supply company for enterprises that used foreign investment.[73] Nevertheless, the insecure supply of certain raw materials for foreign invested enterprises perhaps will remain for some time to come, and resolving this problem will depend on the successful transition of China from a planning to a market economy and further liberalization of the market.

Telecommunications

The telecommunications infrastructure has been another major problem that restricted the smooth operation of foreign invested enterprises in China, which was particularly serious when the open door policy was first implemented. The domestic telecommunications infrastructure was terribly inadequate, and due to thirty years of international isolation of China, the infrastructure for international communications was even worse. Making a domestic long distance telephone call could take several hours, and very often this needed to be done via an operator, and the person making the call needed to do it in an official post office. In the early 1980s, even Shanghai – the largest and most advanced city in China – had only a total capacity of 210 000 telephone lines with very few automatic switches, which lagged behind the developed countries by almost half a century. The situation in other parts of China was even worse. This had caused some early foreign investors unimaginable communication problems both with their parent companies and with their business partners.[74]

However, the Chinese central and local governments have been taking serious steps to improve the situation. Ambitious strategic objectives were set for the Ministry of Post and Telecommunications (Now the Ministry of Information Industry). Since the early 1980s, telecommunications has also been one of the fastest growing industries in China, and the capacity growth has consistently surpassed the growth of the national economy.[75] By the end of 1994, China achieved both targets of total communications capacity and total service volume set for the year 2000 (six years ahead of plan). During the eighth five year plan (1991–95), China laid 100 000 kilometres of new fibre optic trunk lines, and added new switching capacity of 58.95 million lines, with an annual increase of 42 per cent! By the end of 1995, total telephone switching capacity reached 85 million lines, the number of telephones per 100 people reached 4.66; mobile telephones reached 4 million.[76] It was said that the scale of China's telecommunication development is the equivalent of 'one British Telecom (BT)' a year.

Technically, the telecommunications network in China has been significantly upgraded as well, with 86 per cent automatic switches for local calls and 98 per cent automatic switches for long distance and international calls by 1994.[77] Other advanced telecommunications services (for example, microwave communications, automated computer controlled telegraph exchanges) have also been installed for national communications between over one hundred cities and for international communications with Hong Kong, Macao, North America, Europe, Japan and Southeast Asian countries.[78] Cellular phones and pagers have been growing extremely rapidly, and have become increasingly common with business people in China. The number of mobile phone users increased from 4 million, in 1995, to 6.2 million in late 1996, and further to 10 million in 1997, and it was projected that the number will reach 20 million by the year 2000, covering 90 per cent of the east and middle regions and 50 per cent of western China.[79]

Telecommunications development has been particularly fast in the special economic zones and open cities in the coastal region. For example, Shenzhen only had five hundred telephones in 1979, but by the end of 1990, every two families had one telephone, communicating directly with over one hundred countries all over the world. In Xiamen, the Post and Telecommunications Bureau invested over 120 million yuan, increasing the number of local lines five times to 50 000 and the long distance lines six times to 2000 in 1992,[80] and by the end of 1994, the number of local lines doubled again. By the end of 1994, urban telephone coverage in China reached 15 per cent; and in cities such as Beijing, Guangzhou, Hangzhou, Haiko and many other open cities, the figure was over 30 per cent.[81]

China has also been engaged in close collaboration with world leading telecommunications companies, and because of the sheer size and the rapid pace of the development, the Chinese telecommunications market has been regarded by many as the 'land of dreams'.[82] Major deals have been made with companies such as AT&T, Siemens, Alcatel, and NEC to develop, supply and upgrade China's telecommunications systems.[83] In 1994, the State Council approved the establishment of a second basic telecommunications carrier, Lian Tong, in order to introduce competition into China's telecommunications market. Lian Tong acquired a respectable market share by 1997.[84] In mid-1997, China signed an agreement with the European Commission to strengthen co-operation in the field of information and telecommunications technologies (including the areas of regulations and policies).[85] All these will serve to speed up the development of the telecommunications industry in China.

In the foreseeable future, the rapid development in telecommunications will continue. By the year 2000, China intends to have a total telephone switching capacity of 174 million lines (more than double that in 1995).[86] All main cities will be connected by fibre optic networks, and telephone coverage will reach 10 per cent at national level, with urban telephone coverage reaching 30–40 per cent (one phone per household). All villages will also be connected by telephone.[87] By the year 2010, the figures will double again. New developments, such as the so called 'three gold project' which is currently underway, will require the support of advanced telecommunications networks to link up financial institutions, local and central governments and customs.[88] In fact, the improvements in telecommunications have been such that many serious problems encountered by early investors no longer exist today, although it will be some time before the level of services (for example, reliability, quality of services) in China can be improved to a comparable level with the developed economies.

SUMMARY

This chapter evaluated the quality and characteristics of China's hard environment for foreign investment, identified major problems that seriously restricted the operation and development of foreign invested enterprises, and speculated on their future prospects within the context of China's rapid economic development and socio-political transformation. Despite the inadequacy and serious problems with many types of basic infrastructure, China's hard investment environment has been improving steadily, and in some aspects, rapidly. Today, the enormous pressure on certain infrastructures (for example, telecommunications) has been significantly ameliorated, while problems with others (for example, transportation) remain unresolved. Although it would be unrealistic, impractical and indeed, unwise, to expect the general condition of China's hard environment to be improved to a comparable level with the developed economies in the short, or even medium, term (owing mainly to the level of China's economic development), the available evidence suggests that the future prospect is fairly positive.

Problems related to railway transportation and energy and raw materials supply may remain or even deteriorate in certain areas over the next few years because of the even faster growth in demand deriving from the extremely rapidly growth of the Chinese economy. For example, in the first six months of 1994, GDP growth, compared to the same period in 1993, was 11.6 per cent, while industrial growth was 15.8 per cent (which was only achieved after a wide range of actions by the central government to control economic overheating). However, the growth rate in energy production during the same period was only 4.7 per cent (coal, 5.5 per cent, crude oil, 1 per cent and electricity 11 per cent). The rail transportation capacity increased by merely 3 per cent, and the turnover increased by 5.5 per cent.[89] Equally, in 1995, industrial growth was 14 per cent; while growth in transportation (cargo) was 3.6 per cent for rail, 9 per cent for road, 8.4 per cent for water, 1.6 per cent for pipeline. Only air transportation grew by 26.3 per cent which was higher than the economic growth.[90] The situation is less serious in some places, but many elements of the hard investment environment will continue to restrict the operation and development of foreign invested enterprises in China.

China is a developing country, and its modernization requires huge capital investments in its infrastructure and industries. Capital shortage will continue to restrict the development of its infrastructure. Attracting foreign investment into China is, therefore, of strategic importance to its continued development. Strong pressure from foreign investors thus can play an important role in pushing the Chinese central and local governments to allocate more capital to improving its hard investment environment. More recently, China is extending the sources of capital supply for infrastructure development from financial allocation by the central government to including other channels – such as raising funds from the private sector, bank loans, and more recently, foreign investments in various forms (e.g. government loans, buyer's credit, and FDI).[91] Infrastructural projects including energy (oil, coal and electricity), transportation and some raw materials have become priority areas for attracting new foreign investments in China.[92] The World Bank estimated that China would need US$280 billion for its infrastructure development in the next five years, of which at least a proportion will have to come from foreign investment. The electricity industry plans to increase the proportion of foreign capital in its new development from less than 10 per cent to 20 per cent. Road transportation would need at least US$30 billion foreign capital, and telecommunications would need at least US$5 billion in the next five years. Several large infrastructural projects, such as the Sanxian Dam and the Jing-Hu motorway, are currently seeking over US$10 billion foreign capital injection.[93] All these will serve to speed up the improvement of China's hard investment environment. Moreover, the enormous potential for further development in these industries may provide some lucrative opportunities for foreign investors.

Notes

1. Geringer, J.M. (1991) 'Strategic determinants of partner selection criteria in international joint ventures', *Journal of International Business Studies* 20: 235–254.
2. De Bruijn, J.D. and Jia Xianfeng (1992) 'Transferring technology to China via joint ventures: Product selection perspective', paper presented at the conference on *Current Development of Joint Ventures in PRC*, Hong Kong, June 1992.
3. *Yue Gang Information Times (Yue Gang Xin Xi Shi Bao),* 1 March 1995, 'An eye-catching research about China's investment environment (*Yan Tao Zhong Guo Tou Zi Huan Jing, Yi Xiang Cheng Guo Bei Shou Zhu Mu*)', p. 1.
4. Jiang, Mingqing (1992) 'The economic development of China's coastal region (*Zhong Guo Yan Hai Di Qu De Jing Ji Fa Zhan*)', *Liaowang*, 27 January 1992.
5. Pomfret, Richard (1991) *Investing in China: Ten Years of the Open Door Policy,* page 127, Harvester Wheatsheaf, New York.
6. It needs to be pointed out that a large amount of coal has been consumed by urban and rural households for cooking and heating. Many organizations also need to provide their own heating during the winter. The most common solution for heating is to maintain their own coal fired boilers for central heating in workshops and offices. As such, coal shortage can seriously affect foreign invested enterprises in some areas. The situation has been improving rapidly in many large cities since the mid-1980s.
7. Yang, Qi (1997) 'China's coal resource' (*Zhong Guo De Mei Tan Zi Yuan*), *The Chinese Science Newspaper (Overseas edition),* 25 May 1997, p. 5. In this special article, Mr Yang Qi, a Fellow of the Chinese Science Academy, pointed out that coal accounts for over 70 per cent of the total energy consumption in China (75 per cent of industrial fuel and power generation, and 83 per cent of urban domestic fuel consumption!). Because of the uneven distribution of coal reserves, the general pattern of moving coal from the north to the south and from the west to the east will remain for a long time to come. Also

see Wu, Yuguang *et al.* (1984) *The Economic Geography of China (Zhong Guo Jing Ji Di Li)*, Beijing Normal University Press (*Bei Jing Shi Fan Da Xue Chu Ban She*), Beijing.

8. Yang (1997) *op. cit.*

9. *The Chinese Science Newspaper* (Overseas edition), 25 August 1995, p. 5, published an article written by Mr Fan Weitang, a Fellow of the Chinese Science Academy (*Zhong Guo Ke Xue Yuan Yuan Shi*), 'The development and future prospects of China's energy industries' (*Zhong Guo Neng Yuan Gong Ye De Fa Zhan Yu Zhan Wang*). Also see, Wu, Yuguang *et al.* (1984) *op. cit.;* Cannon, Terry and Alan Jenkins (1990) (eds) *The Geography of Contemporary China*, Routledge, London.

10. Qu, Guangmin (1997) 'China's oil and natural gas resources and their development strategy' (*Zhong Guo De You Qi Zi Yuan Ji Qi Kai Fa Zhan Lue*), in *The Chinese Science Newspaper (Overseas edition)* 25 May 1997, p. 5. Mr Qu is also a Fellow of the Chinese Science Academy.

11. Cannon and Jenkins (1990) *op. cit.*

12. Lee, Keun, Chung H. Lee, and Won Bae Kim (1990) 'Problems and profitability of direct foreign investment in China: An analysis of the survey data', *Journal of Northeast Asian Studies*, Vol. IX, No. 4, Winter 1990.

13. Thoburn, John T., H.M. Leung, Esther Chau and S.H. Tang (1990) *Foreign Investment in China under the Open Policy*, Avebury, Aldershot.

14. Christofferson, Gaye (1991) 'Plan and market in Shanxi province: The long "energy crisis" of the economic reforms', *China Information*, Documentation and Research Centre for Contemporary China, Arsenaalstraat 1, P.O. Box 9515, 2300 RA Leiden, Holland.

15. Thoburn *et al.* (1991) *op. cit.*

16. Jiang Mingqing (1992) *op. cit.*

17. *The Chinese Science Newspaper* (Overseas edition), 25 August 1995, *op. cit.; The People's Daily* (Overseas edition), 30 December 1995, 'The rapid development of the electricity industry during the "eighth five year plan" period' (*Dian Li Gong Ye "Ba Wu" Fa Zhan Xun Su*); 20 March 1996, front page, 'People's Republic of China National Economic and Social Development: Outline of the "Ninth five year plan" and long term targets for the year 2010' (*Zhong Hua Ren Min Gong He Guo Guo Min Jing Ji He She Hui Fa Zhan 'Jiu Wu' Ji Hua He 2010 Nian Yuan Jing Mu Biao Gang Yao*), approved by the Fourth Plenary Session of the Eighth People's Congress on 17 March 1996.

18. Nuclear electricity will develop rapidly over the next few decades. Between 2000 and 2020, China will need an estimated additional electricity generating capacity of 500 million kW, which would require 1.3 billion tons of coal each year. This is regarded as not acceptable because of the enormous pressure this would put on environment protection, transportation and the coal mining industry. Building more nuclear power stations is regarded as a more viable option. Apart from building stations using Chinese technologies, China has imported several more advanced stations from France, Russia and Canada. See *The People's Daily* (Overseas edition), 20 October 1995, 'Great prospect

for nuclear power development in China (*Zhong Guo He Dian Fa Zhan Qian Jing Kan Hao*)', p. 1.

19. *The People's Daily* (Overseas edition), 28 July 1997, 'China has enormous potential in developing nuclear electric power' (*Zhong Guo Kai Fa He Dian Qian Li Ju Da*), p. 1.

20. *The People's Daily* (Overseas edition), 5 March 1996, 'The People's Republic of China National Statistical Bureau Report on China's economic and social development' for 1995 (*Zhong Hua Ren Min Gong He Guo Guo Jia Tong Ji Ju Guan Yu 1995 Nian Guo Min Jing Ji He She Hui Fa Zhan De Tong Ji Gong Bao*), p. 5.

21. *The Financial Times*, 31 March 1993.

22. *The People's Daily* (Overseas edition), 20 August 1992.

23. *The People's Daily* (Overseas edition), 19 January 1994, *op. cit.*

24. *The People's Daily* (Overseas edition), 16 February 1994.

25. *The People's Daily* (Overseas edition), 26 July 1997, 'Another very large scale hydro-electric project starting next year' (*Wo Guo You Yi Te Da Xing Shui Dian Gong Cheng Ming Nian Dong Gong*), p. 1.

26. *The People's Daily* (Overseas edition), 28 July 1997, *op. cit.*

27. The World Bank (1990), *China: Between Plan and Market*. World Bank, Washington, D.C.

28. *The People's Daily* (Overseas edition), 30 December 1995, *op. cit*; 20 March 1996, *op. cit.*

29. *The People's Daily* (Overseas edition), 20 January 1997, 'National Electricity Corporation is established' (*Guo Jia Dian Li Gong Si Cheng Li*), p. 1.

30. *The People's Daily* (Overseas edition), 20 January 1997, 'China will increase its use of foreign investment in the electricity industry' (*Zhong Guo Jiang Kuo Da Li Yong Wai Zi Ban Dian*), p. 1.

31. Li, Peng (1997) 'China's Energy Policy', *The People's Daily* (Overseas edition), 30 May 1997, p. 2. First published in *Qiushi* magazine No. 11, 1997.

32. Thoburn *et al.* (1990) *op. cit.*

33. Sun, Yongfu (Vice Minister of the Ministry of Rail Transportation) gave these figures when talking about Jing-Jiu railway construction to *The People's Daily* (Overseas edition), 31 March 1994.

34. Liu, Zaixing *et al.* (1985) *The Allocation of Production Theory (Sheng Chan Bu Ju Yuan Li*), The People's University of China Press (*Zhong Guo Ren Min Da Xue Chu Ban She*), Beijing.

35. Cannon and Jenkins (1990) *op. cit.*; Liu *et al.* (1985) *op. cit.*

36. Christopher Howe (1990) 'Asia and the Pacific: Recent trends', *The Far East and Australasia* 1990, 2, Europa Publications Limited.

37. Zhang Wanqing, Yang Shuzhen, Gao Lianqing (1988), *Inter-Regional Co-operation and Economic Networks (Qu Yu He Zuo Yu Jing Ji Wang Luo)*, The Economic Science Press (*Jing Ji Ke Xue Chu Ban She*), Beijing.

38. *The People's Daily* (Overseas edition), 23 September 1995, 'Rapid railway construction in China, 5800km new lines in five years (*Zhong Guo Tie Lu Jian She Tu Fei Meng Jin, Wu Nian Pu Jiu Tie Lu Xin Xian 5800 Gong Li*)', p. 1.

39. *The People's Daily* (Overseas edition), 2 April 1996, 'The first fast passenger train in operation, top speed 140 km per hour' (*Wo Shou Lie Kuai Su Ke Che Ying Yun Zui Gao Shi Su Wei 140 Gong Li*), p. 1.
40. *The People's Daily* (Overseas edition), 7 February 1995, 'Modern times call for new trunk road' (*Shi Dai Hu Huan "Xin Gan Xian"*), p. 1.
41. *The People's Daily* (Overseas edition), 2 April 1996, 'Jing-Jiu railway becomes fully operational for cargo' (*Jing Jiu Tie Lu Quan Xian Tou Ru Huo Yun*), p. 1.
42. *The People's Daily* (Overseas edition), 20 March 1996, *op. cit.*
43. *The People's Daily* (Overseas edition), 2 April 1997, 'China's trains systematically increased speed' (*Zhong Guo Lie Che Quan Mian Shun Li Ti Su*), p. 1; 9 May 1997, 'Chinese railways significantly increase speed' (*Zhong Guo Tie Lu Da Ti Su*), p. 2.
44. Cheng, Jing (1992) 'A summary of the development of investment environment in the open region' (*Kai Fang Di Qu Tou Zi Huan Jing Gai Quang*). *The People's Daily* (overseas edition), 24 January 1992.
45. *The People's Daily* (Overseas edition), 23 January 1996, 'China's transportation infrastructure significantly improved during the eighth five year plan (*Ba Wu Hui Mou: Wo Jiao Tong She Shi Da Wei Gai Guan*)', p. 1.
46. *The People's Daily* (Overseas edition), 26 July 1997, 'China's road network enters capital market' (*Zhong Guo Gong Lu Wang Zou Zin Rong Zi Shi Chang*), p. 2.
47. *The People's Daily* (Overseas edition), 24 January 1992, *op. cit* .
48. *The People's Daily* (Overseas edition), 23 January 1996, *op. cit.*
49. *The People's Daily* (Overseas edition), 20 March 1996, *op. cit.*
50. *The People's Daily* (Overseas edition), 8 June 1996, 'Civil airports developments entered the fast lane in China (*Wo Guo Min Hang Ji Chang Jian She Jin Ru Kui Che Dao*)', p. 8.
51. *Ibid.*
52. *The People's Daily* (Overseas edition), 8 June 1996, *op. cit.*
53. *The People's Daily* (Overseas edition), 22 July 1995, 'Who can occupy China's "sky"? (*Shui Neng Qiang Zhan Zhong Guo "Tian Kong"?*)', p. 2; 6 November 1996, 'The enormous potential in China's aviation market' (*Zhong Guo Hang Kong Shi Chang Qian Li Ju Da*), The MD Chairman believed the demand in China over the next 20 years would exceed 1350 new planes, p. 4.
54. *The Financial Times*, 8 April 1993.
55. *The People's Daily* (Overseas edition), 6 November 1996, 'Airbus AE100 project, China, Singapore and Europe reached agreement on share ownership (*Kong Zhong Kuai Che AE100 Xiang Mu Zhong Xin Ou San Fang Gu Fen Que Ding*), p. 4.
56. *The Financial Times*, 26 January 1993.
57. Li, Peng (1997) 'Developing an integrated transportation system' (*Jian Li Tong Yi De Jiao Tong Yun Shu Ti Xi*), *The Economic Daily* (*Jing Ji Ri Bao*), 5 August 1997. Also reported in *The People's Daily* (Overseas edition), 6 August 1997, 'Establishing an integrated transportation system' (*Yao Jian Li Tong Yi De Jiao Tong Yun Shu Ti Xi*), p. 1.

58. *Asian Wall Street Journal*, 12 March 1985, 'Shanghai snags are worrying foreign firms'.
59. *Asian Wall Street Journal*, 7 January 1985, 'Chinese hotels testing foreign investors'.
60. For example, *The Financial Times Survey* on UK Relocation, 28 May 1993, 'Christopher Parkes on the German approach: China is new priority', p. xii; *Liaowang*, 6 April 1992, Vol. 14.
61. Harwit, Eric (1992) 'Foreign passenger car ventures and Chinese decision-making', *The Australian Journal of Chinese Affairs*, Issue 28, July 1992.
62. *Liaowang*, 6 April 1992, Vol. 14.
63. *The People's Daily* (Overseas edition), 29 March, 1994.
64. *The Economist*, 16–22 April 1994, 'Slow car to China'.
65. *Ibid.*
66. *Ibid.*
67. *The Financial Times*, 'Ford plans $50m China investment', 28 June 1994.
68. Pomfret, Richard (1991) *Investing in China: Ten Years of the Open Door Policy*, Harvester Wheatsheaf, New York; *The People's Daily* (Overseas edition), 23 April 1992.
69. Lee, Lee, and Kim (1990), *op. cit.*
70. This phrase was created by the Hungarian economist, Janos Kornai. Please see Rong, Jingben, Qui Shufang and Liu Jirui (1987) *Shortage and Reform (Duan Que Yu Gai Ge)*, Hei Long Jiang People's Publishing House (*Hei Long Jiang Ren Min Chu Ban She*), Haerbin. This book is a collection of Janos Kornai's major ideas and some of his latest papers (edited and translated by the authors into Chinese).
71. Sekiguchi, Sueo (1991), 'Direct foreign investment and the Yellow Sea Rim', *Journal of Northeast Asian Studies*, Spring 1991.
72. The United Nations (1992): *Foreign Investment, Trade and Economic Co-operation in the Asian and Pacific Region*, The Economic and Social Commission for Asia and the Pacific, The United Nations, New York.
73. Bucknall, Kevin (1989) *China and the Open Door Policy*, Allen and Unwin, North Sydney.
74. Sekiguchi (1991) *op. cit.*
75. *The People's Daily* (Overseas edition), 22 June 1995, 'Telecommunications services have been developing rapidly, consistently surpassed the speed of economic development in the past ten years (*Wo You Dian Tong Xin Shi Ye Fa Zhang Xun Su, Lian Xu Shi Nian Chao Guo Guo Min Jing Ji Zeng Zhang Su Du*)', p. 1.
76. *The People's Daily* (Overseas edition), 5 March 1996, 'The People's Republic of China National Statistical Bureau press release about national economic and social development in 1995 (*Zhong Hua Ren Min Gong He Guo Guo Jia Tong Ji Ju Guan Yu 1995 Nian Guo Min Jing Ji He She Hui Fa Zhan De Tong Ji Gong Bao*), p. 2; 22 September 1995, 'China has built advanced telecommunications networks (*Zhong Guo Tong Xin Shi Ye Kuo Bu Qian Jin, Jian Cheng Shi Jie Xian Jin Tong Xin Wang Luo*)', p. 1; 20 January 1996, 'China's telecommunications achieved great leap forward (*Zhong Guo You Dian Shi Xian Da Kua Yue*)', p. 1; 20 March 1996, *op. cit.*

77. *The People's Daily* (Overseas edition), 8 February 1994.
78. Cheng (1992) *op. cit.*
79. *The People's Daily* (Overseas edition), 20 January 1997, 'China's public mobile telephones leapfrog to the top ranks in the world' (*Zhong Guo Gong Yong Yi Dong Dian Hua Yue Ju Shi Jie Qian Lie*), p. 2.
80. *The Financial Times*, 4 November 1992.
81. *The People's Daily* (Overseas edition), 22 September 1995, *op. cit.*
82. *The Financial Times*, 2 June 1993, 'Investors move as Asia gets on phone'.
83. *The Financial Times*, 16 June 1992; 31 March 1993.
84. *The People's Daily* (Overseas edition), 25 July 1997, 'Lian Tong's development enters new stage' (*Lian Tong Fa Zhan Bu Ru Xin Jie Duan*), p. 1.
85. *The People's Daily* (Overseas edition), 5 June 1997, 'China and European Union sign joint statement on strengthening co-operation in the field of information and communications technologies' (*Zhong Guo Ou Meng Qian Shu Jia Qiang Xin Xi Yu Tong Xun Ling Yu He Zuo Lian He Sheng Min*), p. 4.
86. *The People's Daily* (Overseas edition), 15 May 1996, 'China intends to invest 90 billion yuan in telecommunications (*Guo Jia Ni Tou Zi You Dian Tong Xin Jiu Bai Yi Yuan*)', p. 2.
87. *The People's Daily* (Overseas edition), 22 September 1995, *op. cit.*; 20 March 1996, *op. cit.*; 24 January 1996, '"Ninth Five year plan" sets target for telecommunications' *(You Dian Tong Xin "Jiu Wu" Mu Biao Ni Ding)*, p. 1.
88. *The People's Daily* (Overseas edition), 20 April 1995, 'How big is the scale of the "three gold" project? (*"San Jin" Gong Cheng Gui Mo You Duo Da?*), p. 1; 15 April 1995, 'China speeds up national informatisation process' (*Wo Guo Jia Kuai Guo Jia Xin Xi Hua Bu Fa*), p. 2.
89. *The People's Daily* (Overseas edition), 12 July 1994; 19 July 1994.
90. *The People's Daily* (Overseas edition), 5 March 1996, *op. cit.*
91. *The People's Daily* (Overseas edition), 22 March 1994.
92. 'China's Economy in the 1990s', Premier Li Peng's speech at the annual meeting of the World Economic Forum in Davos, Switzerland on 30 January 1992. *Almanac of China's Foreign Economic Relations and Trade (1992/93)* pp. 9–12.
93. *The People's Daily* (Overseas edition), 21 July 1997, 'China will become the world's largest investment market for infrastructural facilities' (*Zhong Guo Jiang Cheng Shi Jie Zui Da Ji Chu She Shi Tou Zi Shi Chang*), p. 2.

5 The Foreign Investment Environment in China: The Soft Environment (I)

Compared with the hard environment for FDI, the soft environment is much more difficult to evaluate because it comprises a wide range of intangible factors. These factors are examined in detail in this and the next chapter. Since the opening up in 1978/79, China's soft environment has been particularly affected by problems such as insufficient foreign exchange facilities, inadequate legal frameworks, different labour relations, shortage of qualified managerial staff, the natural expectation of workers for a wide range of social services and welfare and high levels of job security, and the commonplace bureaucratism and corruption in local and central governments and their agencies. To a large extent, these problems have been derived from the unique historical, political, economic and social systems in China, and many of these problems are closely related to China's transition from planning to market.

The soft environment is extremely important to the operation and development of foreign invested enterprises in China, because even a high quality hard investment environment can be easily undermined by such soft factors.[1] Many soft factors are unique to China, and their characteristics are often profoundly different from those in the West and, indeed, from what have been commonly understood by people outside China. Failing to understand such differences will misguide (potential) foreign investors in their risk assessments and strategic decision-making. To reflect its complexity and importance, the soft environment is examined in two chapters in this book. This chapter focuses on the broad contexts for FDI in China, including the historical evolution of China's external relations, the political background of the reform and opening up, and the unique characteristics of Chinese society. The next chapter examines some more specific problems encountered by foreign investors.

As will be illustrated later in this chapter, central to the quality of the soft environment for FDI in China is the stability of China's political system, and in particular whether the reform and opening up will be reversed. For many foreign investors, the biggest attraction of China is its enormous market potential, which has existed for many years. What has made this market potential particularly attractive today is that the perceived risks of investing in China have plummeted with the reform and opening up. Foreign investors' confidence in, and their commitment to, the Chinese market to a large extent depend on the perceived political stability in China.

A stable political environment, however, would not guarantee success for foreign invested enterprises. The differences between China and the West in their history, social structure and culture are invariably reflected in the operation and management of foreign invested enterprises in China, the appropriate marketing approaches and sales techniques that should be adopted and, more generally, in the way business should be conducted. In fact, many well-tested management theories and techniques in the West may prove useless in China because of China's unique conditions.

One particularly significant factor to doing business in China is *guanxi*, or personal connections. This phenomenon has been derived from the unique history and the social, political and institutional systems in China, and it is deeply rooted in Chinese culture. *Guanxi* is extremely important to the operation and development of foreign invested enterprises in China. Handling it properly can make a seemingly difficult – even impossible – situation easy and free of problems, but mis-handling some key *guanxi* can make the life of a foreign investor extremely difficult, and in some cases can ruin the future of an otherwise sound and robust foreign invested enterprise. It has been found that building business relationships in Asia, and then keeping them, is much harder than many foreign companies have imagined.[2] This book examines the cultural and institutional roots of *guanxi*, which are especially relevant to foreign investors in contemporary China.

In the contexts of China's historical, political and social systems, there are a whole range of soft elements and problems. Some of the main problems encountered by foreign investors will be examined in the next chapter. It is emphasized that China is currently in the midst of a profound transformation in its political, economic and social systems, which means some of the problems discussed in this book may have already been resolved by the time it reaches the readers, and many others may have been relieved to such an extent that they should no longer be regarded as major problems.

In the meantime, new problems are bound to emerge. In addition, China is a massive country with enormous geographical differentiation, so many problems may vary significantly between regions. A geographical and time focus is clearly needed when assessing the quality of China's foreign investment environment.

'WAKING UP FROM THE PAST' – THE HISTORICAL BACKGROUND OF CHINA'S OPENING UP

Historically, China was one of a few countries actively involved in the development of international economic and cultural exchanges. As early as Xi Zhou (11th century BC to 771 BC), China had already developed economic relations with countries which were the forerunners of today's Japan and Vietnam.[3] By the time of the Han dynasty (206 BC–220 AD), the famous Silk Road was developed, which crossed the entire middle and southwest Asia to Europe. China also maintained important economic relations with countries around the southern China Sea via a number of sea routes. A variety of commodities was also exchanged regularly via sea or land with India and Europe.[4]

During the Sui (581–618 AD) and Tang (618–907 AD) dynasties, China's international trade developed significantly, and the situation reached its peak during the 400 years of the Song and Yuan dynasties (960–1368 AD). In fact, many government officials at that time were directly involved in international trade.[5] In the Ming Dynasty (1368–1644 AD), Zheng He and his fleet went to the eastern coast of Africa seven times, taking china, silk, metal products, gold and silver to trade with the local people. Such voyages were, however, fundamentally different from those of, say, Christopher Columbus, because the former were primarily intended for trade and cultural purposes, whereas the aim of Columbus was to find treasure and to discover new lands.[6]

This situation changed dramatically after the Ming Dynasty because the Chinese believed that the outside world was extremely backward, and China was the 'Central Kingdom' (*Zhong Guo*) of the world. In fact, the Chinese Government saw no need to maintain economic relations with other countries. The Chinese began to see themselves as the superior race, because the previous round of international relations showed them that while tribes of illiterate inhabitants still roamed the rest of the world, China was an empire of dazzling power and cultural achievement.[7] Isolation therefore characterized this entire period. This ethnocentric belief became an important part of Chinese culture. Even today, it is still reflected in many people's behaviours.

To make things worse, capitalism began to develop rapidly in a number of countries during this period, which increasingly demanded the internationalization of consumption and production. The progress of capitalization also gave some western countries the power to achieve that. The isolated China not only lagged behind these capitalist countries, but also was unaware of the situation until its closed door was forced open by the power of the Western guns in 1840 – the Opium War. Afterwards China was forced to submit to the commercial and political deputation of the western powers until 1945 (the end of the second world war).[8]

Throughout this period (1840–1945), the desire of the Chinese was to regain their status as a strong and independent nation; but the attainment of this aim was repeatedly frustrated by internal and external factors. Among these factors were the feudalistic rules of the Qing dynasty and the failure of several attempted reforms,[9] and after 1911, when the Qing government was overthrown, the civil wars between the warlords, the invasion of the Japanese, and the war between the Nationalist Party and the Communist Party.[10] Although the victory of the Communist Party in 1949 made China an independent nation, the desire of many Chinese people to restore its past glory and make China a strong and rich country remains unsatisfied even today.

Between 1949 and 1978, China was primarily regarded as an isolated or semi-isolated economy, particularly after the late 1950s when China broke its political and economic ties with the former Soviet Union and other Eastern European countries. This isolation was significantly deepened by western policies, which isolated the Communist government of China for several decades. During this period, China conducted a limited amount of trade with some third world and communist countries, and provided foreign aid to some of them. However, ideologically, capitalism was regarded as evil in China and something that should be overthrown. Foreign trade was not essential to the Chinese economy and self-reliance was the cornerstone of China's national economic development strategy. Foreign aid was mainly used as a political tool to win friends in the world. Although China won a series of diplomatic victories in the early 1970s (establishing diplomatic relations with the USA and Japan), it remained primarily an isolated country in terms of economic, technological, and cultural exchanges until the early 1980s.[11]

History repeatedly taught Chinese people the lesson that China's backwardness today was closely related to its international isolation and inward-looking mentality, and even during the period 1949 to 1978, the negative effects of being an isolated country were recognized by some government leaders. In late 1978, the adoption of the open door policy symbolized China's attempt to end the situation by participating in the world economy, so as to speed up its own economic growth and technological modernization. The rapid economic development achieved since 1978 demonstrated to the Chinese leadership the wisdom of the open door policy and the necessity for further opening up.

Information provided by the State Statistical Bureau (*Guo Jia Tong Ji Ju*) showed that since the reform and the opening up in late 1978, China's economic strength has increased markedly. The average annual national income growth was 8.4 per cent for the period 1978–90, compared with only 6 per cent for 1953–78. China's gross domestic product (GDP) was 1768.6 billion yuan in 1990 compared with 67.9 billion yuan in 1952. The average annual growth (GDP) between 1978 and 1990 was 9.7 per cent, significantly higher than the average annual growth rate of 6.4 per cent over the 26 years between 1952 and 1978. The country's financial revenues were 331.26 billion yuan in 1990, compared with only 6.25 billion yuan in 1952.

Since 1990, the growth of the Chinese economy has been even more impressive. Total GDP reached 5,760 billion yuan in 1995, which quadrupled that of 1980, five years ahead of the planned schedule. Annual GDP growth averaged 12 per cent during the eighth five year plan (1991–95), and the economic fluctuation during this period was the lowest in China's eight five year plans since 1950.[12]

China's impressive economic growth over the last 20 years has been achieved through implementing a comprehensive political and economic reform programme. Opening up to the outside world is a cornerstone of the programme, which represented a radical ideological change in China's political and economic thinking, and a shift of national economic development strategy from self-reliance to actively engaging in promoting foreign trade, attracting foreign investment and introducing advanced technologies, skills and management techniques (please see Chapter 1 for a more detailed discussion of the relationship between the reform and the opening up). Although it is often argued that reform in China has been an evolutionary rather than a revolutionary process,[13] the transformation in China since 1978 has been a bold and comprehensive undertaking. Some principles of the current reform were attempted in several initiatives in China during the 1950s, 1960s, and 1970s, but never in a consistent and comprehensive manner.

Before the reform and opening up, the central focus of China's economic policy was to increase the nation's capital accumulation, and the living standard of Chinese people only increased very slowly. In 1978, the average consumption level of Chinese people was 175 yuan, an increase of only 1.3 times over the 76 yuan level in 1952, giving an average annual increase of merely 3.3 per cent. In 1990, the average consumption level in China reached 714 yuan, 4.1 times that in 1978, yielding an average annual increase of 12.4 per cent. The improvements since 1990 have been even more impressive. By the end of the eighth five year plan, the average annual income for urban citizens reached 3893 yuan per person, and 1578 yuan for rural residents.[14]

Moreover, China's international trade has been increasing rapidly since 1978, making China the fifteenth largest trading nation in the world by the late 1980s, which was further improved to eleventh largest in 1992, and tenth largest in 1996. China also received billions of dollars of foreign investment and official development aid from foreign governments and other international organizations each year.[15] Although the negative impact of the 1989 Tiananmen Square tragedy was clearly felt in China, by 1991 the Chinese economy was running so strongly that its performance surpassed that of the 1980s, a decade when China had one of the world's fastest growing economies.[16] 1992 was an even more successful year than 1991, which was boosted particularly by the visit of Deng Xiaoping – China's supreme leader and ultimate decision-maker at that time – to southern China. The danger of economic over-heating and associated problems, such as high inflation, shortage of certain materials, growing pressure on basic infrastructures and utilities, and the loss-making state owned sector, to some extent overshadowed the optimism in 1993 and 1994. However, a series of indirect measures was adopted by central and local governments and by 1995 China successfully achieved a 'soft landing' without causing drastic disruptions. The economy has continued to run strongly and steadily since 1996, and new radical reforms are increasingly being introduced – such as reforming the banking system and the loss-making state owned sector.

In general, the reform and opening up in China has so far been very successful in spite of recurring problems and scepticism. Economic flexibility has increased, economic freedoms have been secured, and the living standard of Chinese people has been significantly improved. Most of all, since the necessity for opening up to the outside world has been demonstrated both negatively and positively from a historical perspective, the open door policy and the wider reform in China has become increasingly popular among Chinese people and their leaders. It will be very difficult and very unpopular to reverse it even if the central government chooses to do so. Just as Zhao Ziyang once said back in 1984:

> ... in view of the experience we have gained over the past thirty years or so, it is no longer a question among the Chinese people as to whether China should open up to the outside world. What we are exploring right now is how to proceed with it more actively, more fruitfully, and in bigger strides.[17]

Nevertheless, caution is still necessary because of the enormous obstacles on the road. Although ancient and contemporary history has indicated that China should have woken up from the past, it is not entirely impossible (however difficult) for China to reverse its current course. For the reform programme to proceed further, many extremely difficult and sensitive issues have to be handled properly (for example, how to absorb the enormous amount of surplus labour released from the state owned sector and from the rural areas?). In his book, Li Xiaojun used a comparative historical approach to compare the contemporary reform in China with the reform movements which have taken place at various points of Chinese history.[18] All such reform movements in the history of China failed, and in all cases, their failure was accompanied by the death of those who attempted to carry them through. Li's analysis concluded that the contemporary reform is surprisingly similar in many ways to those failed ones in history, and the important question is: will this reform be an exception?

Since 1978, the reform has suffered several set-backs, and from a historical point of view it is not entirely impossible that the open door policy will suffer the same fate as previous reform movements in Chinese history. However, as will be revealed in the next section, most available evidence to date suggests that the key question is not whether to continue the reform, but how to proceed steadily. The political events in Eastern Europe and the failure of the Soviet Coup also served to convince not only the Chinese people, but also foreign investors and western government leaders, that a reversal of the reform and opening up programme in China is very unlikely.

THE POLITICAL ENVIRONMENT IN CHINA – THE FLUCTUATION, STAGNATION AND CONTINUATION OF THE REFORM AND OPENING UP

Politics has dominated the central stage of China since 1949, and its decisive role in almost every aspect of Chinese society and the economy has been highly visible. Regarding the foreign investment environment, political fluctuations can easily jeopardize social and economic stability and the whole reform programme in China. Understanding the evolution of the Chinese political system is also essential for questions such as:

- How wide will China keep its door open?
- How and where will the reform and opening up proceed – and at what pace?
- Is there any chance that China will turn back to its old, rigid, central planning regime?

Answers to these questions are critical to the quality of China's investment environment, both at present and in the future.

The importance of politics in China has been clearly demonstrated by the tragic event in 1989. After China opened its economic doors in 1978, it quickly became one of the largest destinations for FDI in the world. By the end of 1989, about 20 000 projects, worth nearly US$34 billion, were approved, with US$15.4 billion of foreign investment actually utilized.[19] However, when in the spring of 1989 the sweeping student movement for political reform ended in the June fourth tragedy, there was almost an immediate end to this process. There was not only a sharp drop in the number of FDI applications, but also the stability of the domestic economy was significantly affected (though 1989 may have played an important role in cooling down the over-heated economy at that time). The psychological damage was probably even greater.

Despite the revival of foreign entrepreneurial interests in coastal provinces at the beginning of 1990, the number of projects approved in China during the first half of 1990 decreased by 8 per cent to 2784, and the total amount of contracted foreign investment was reduced to US$2.35 billion, 22 per cent less than the same period in 1989.[20] The repeated assurance from the Chinese government that economic reform and the open door policy would not be reversed did not remove the psychological deterrents, many fearing that the decade-long policy of liberalizing domestic and foreign economic activities in China had come to an end. Foreign investors in particular had to rethink their future commitments to the Chinese market. The key question was: would China keep its door open?

By late 1990, while the negative effects of the 1989 tragedy were still felt in China, a radical shift in the open door policy in China had not happened. In fact, foreign trade and investment in China continued to grow, and in the second half of 1990 the pace of FDI growth in China was faster than ever before. In 1990, despite a sharp drop during the first half of the year, the number of newly approved FDI projects reached 7276, with a total pledged foreign investment of US$6.57 billions, a rise of 25.9 per cent and 17.3 per cent respectively over 1989 (see Table 3.1).[21] Moreover, this was achieved whilst China was subjected to economic sanctions from all major Western countries. Between 1989 and the first half of 1991, China approved over 18 000 new FDI projects – more than the total number attracted to China during the entire period of 1978–88. In fact, 1991 and 1992 represented the third peak of FDI in China since 1978, following the first two peaks in 1984 and 1988 respectively.[22]

Overseas Chinese investors played a key role in restoring investment confidence after 1989, and in fact they have always been optimistic about the economic growth in China since 1978. Unlike most westerners, who pulled back after the 1989 tragedy, most overseas Chinese investors retained their faith and continued to invest. Even today, investors from Hong Kong, Taiwan and other south east Asian economies have bigger stakes than have American, European and Japanese multinationals.[23] The overseas Chinese have based their optimism on the belief that China is just the latest and largest in a series of Asian economic miracles, and they have experienced similar problems while their own economies were taking off. The experience from the Asian tigers (or dragons) suggests that China's rapid growth since 1978 will continue for many years to come (though the difficulties are enormous); and political fluctuations (even the 1989 sort of political turmoil) need not prevent economic growth. Indeed, political liberalization in China can, and should, only be implemented gradually as the market economy and rapid growth breed a more pluralistic society.

Information on other aspects of China's economic development showed a similar tendency. For example, the New York Times reported that 7000 Chinese students went to the USA between January 1989 and January 1990;[24] while thousands of American and other foreign experts continued to be invited to work in China.[25] This demonstrated that the June fourth tragedy in 1989 caused merely a slow-down or temporary hiccup in the reform and opening up, not a radical turn-back to old style isolationism. Although some Chinese leaders, after the Tiananmen Square tragedy, would evidently have liked to turn back the clock on the reform and the opening up, this did not happen – at least not in a major way, and nor is it likely to. The evidence since 1990 has generally confirmed this. We thus conclude that the reform and the opening up in China will continue. There are five major reasons for this conclusion.

First, the reform and the opening up have the support of a broad spectrum of Chinese people, who have already benefited enormously from these activities. It is highly unlikely that China would turn back to the Maoist style, self-reliant, semi-isolated economy, in which many people suffered so much. It is widely recognized that the Chinese economy cannot grow rapidly without close interactions with the rest of the world economy, and this perception is shared by the majority of Chinese leaders.

Second, some recent evidence shows that there are clear limits imposed by factors both inside and outside China that restrict the ability of Chinese leaders to adopt policies markedly different from the policies pursued in the recent past. In fact, China today is so closely integrated into the international community, and many Chinese people have learnt so much about democracy and economic development outside China, that Chinese leaders can no longer make decisions without considering the internal and external consequences. This is demonstrated by the fact that even after the 1989 tragic event, the framework of reform and open door policy remains largely intact.

The top priority of the current Chinese leadership is to promote China's wealth and economic power, because this development will determine their political success and failure. Since no one in China today has the prestige of Mao Zedong and Deng Xiaoping, the Chinese leaders cannot ignore development needs in pursuit of ideological or political goals. Most Chinese people are no longer as naive and enthusiastic as in the past, looking towards a Utopian future – they need to see some concrete results of development, today and tomorrow. Without continuous, rapid development, the current government may not even be able to remain in power for very long.

Third, China's leadership has always been divided and, after the Tiananmen Square tragedy, most senior officials were labelled either 'hard-liners' – the conservatives who want to retreat from the reform – or 'reformers' who want to maintain close ties with the West but on Chinese terms.[26] Immediately after the 1989 tragedy, the conservatives seemed to have regained considerable control, but the evidence since then has clearly indicated the resurgence of the reformers in strengthening their positions.

It is also important to note that, in China, making significant changes in policy is both politically sensitive and dangerous, because it draws attention to a leader, making him vulnerable to counter attacks by opponents in the leadership. The political system in China does not punish leaders without much achievement, but should anyone try something different and the result turns out to be not as good as expected, it more often than not spells trouble for them. This bias against change has become an important element of the 'Party culture', which has been dominating the behaviour of the majority of government leaders at almost all levels. The situation has changed considerably since the early 1990s. We will come back to this issue later in this chapter.

After the 1989 tragic event, the open door policy continued (albeit at the expense of some reformer leaders – most notably Hu Yaobang and Zhao Ziyang), and it is now the established policy. Those seeking to reverse it are likely to put themselves at risk. Today, most available evidence has indicated that the process of reform and opening up will continue. Even most so-called 'hard-liners' have proven records of following relatively moderate reform and open door policy, and few appear to favour a return to the rigid regime that cost China so dear in the past. The nightmares associated with the rigid Communist regime (particularly the Cultural Revolution) are still clearly remembered by most Chinese leaders as well as by a large proportion of the Chinese people.

Fourth, the contemporary international environment also serves to reinforce the tendencies of reform and opening up in China. All Chinese leaders seem to be aware of the need to develop the national economy quickly, and to achieve this goal it is necessary to pursue open interactions with the rest of the world. Of particular importance is the need to interact with the developed economies in order to obtain advanced technology and large scale investment. To do business with the West, Chinese leaders have learnt to compromise in many respects, but in the meantime, they also know that China has today become an indispensable player in the world economy and politics. Despite the symbolic sanctions enacted by the West and the Japanese after the 1989 tragedy, the Chinese leaders and the government leaders of other countries knew only too well of the potential negative effects on the world economic system if China were driven back into isolation. It is known to all that China – with its 1.2 billion population, its rapid pace of development and its enormous future development potential – is simply too big an opportunity for any country to ignore. It is also a recognized fact that the growth of mutually beneficial economic exchanges with China can only grow at a pace largely determined by China's willingness to remain open to the outside world. In order to get a slice of the pie, many Western countries have been competing with each other to maintain good relationships with China. Some commentators even suspect China has actively used this to get what it needs for its economic development (for example, advanced technologies).

In the meantime, it is also known to China that in order to obtain new technologies and foreign investment, it is necessary for China to satisfy some basic requirements of the international community, many of which the Chinese leaders have previously regarded as internal affairs. New technologies and investment from outside China are essential for China to continue its rapid economic development. Recent evidence suggests that for significant economic gains the Chinese Government is increasingly prepared to compromise in certain respects with other countries.

In addition, the collapse of the Eastern bloc in Europe has made China more isolated in an increasingly non-Communist world, so China will have to conduct itself more carefully in the new international community. The growing internal demand for not only rapid economic development but also democracy and political freedom means that Chinese leaders have to undertake radical changes in China's political and economic systems, although the critical importance of maintaining political and social stability has served to delay some radical changes.

Thus, no matter what happens, or does not happen, it is extremely unlikely that China will turn back to its old regime in the foreseeable future. Even though the current Chinese leaders have determined that China is to remain a socialist country (at least in name), they fully recognize the fact that improving China's economic power is essential to their survival in an increasingly non-Communist world. One key to achieving such a goal is to participate actively in international affairs. The question is, how fast can, and will, China change?

Fifth, the decentralization of economic and political power to the provincial levels from Beijing will continue to play a key role in China's future reform and opening up. Since 1978, considerable economic and political autonomy has been decentralized to lower levels. In particular, China's coastal provinces benefited enormously from the reform and opening up and they have developed extensive economic ties with the outside world. Provinces in middle and western China are eager to replicate the success of the coastal provinces. After the 1989 tragedy, the coastal provinces played an important role in restoring relations with the USA, Japan and other countries, with or without the blessing of the central government.

Although in time of crisis (such as economic over-heating), the central government tended to use familiar means of administrative measures to tighten up central control, it was also clear to all that recentralization was becoming increasingly difficult after two decades of reform and opening up. Recentralization inevitably cuts off established ties with the outside world. More importantly, many provincial leaders have strengthened their local support by promoting supporters at all levels, and recentralization or replacing the existing provincial leaders can often provoke strong resistance at all levels. It is even doubtful whether it is still possible for the central government to recentralize economic control without causing economic and political problems. A joke which has been told at parties in recent years is to the effect that the central government pretends to lead the country, and the local governments pretend to be led by the central government. This is, however, not to say that the central government can do little to manage the macro-economy. On the contrary, as the transition from planning to market in China continues, the central government has increasingly mastered indirect measures (such as fiscal policies and credit control) in managing the macro-economy – its successful handling of the 1993/1994 economic over-heating suggested that the Chinese central government has been learning quickly.

In sum, from the political perspective, the reform and opening up in China is set to continue. In spite of reoccurring fluctuations and one or two major set backs, the open door policy and the reform in general has continued to proceed steadily. The general atmosphere is one of cautious optimism, and the future of China will depend critically on continued stability in its domestic politics and international affairs.[27] Many economic and political parallels have been drawn between China and other Asian tigers, and it is widely believed that the rapid growth in China since 1978 will continue.

In the next few years, however, China will have to face a series of domestic political and social uncertainties and extremely challenging tasks, including reforming the loss-making state owned sector, restructuring the financial system (which is still not run on market lines) and, most of all, continuing the transition from planning to market and dealing with a wide range of destabilizing social problems (such as unemployment, high inflation, growing social disparity, and establishing new social security systems, to name but a few). How to maintain domestic social and political stability while undertaking such changes will be an extremely challenging task, which will inevitably be reflected in China's foreign investment environment.

In order to achieve rapid economic development and political and social stability, China will also need to maintain a stable international relationship with the outside world; and to speed up the process of modernization, advanced technologies and new investment from outside China are needed. In other words, to continue its rapid economic development, China has no option but to open up further. The end of the cold war has certainly brought new uncertainty to China, but the desire of Chinese people for rapid and concrete economic gains will continue to drive the policies and programmes in China. Thus, the open door policy and reform will continue, despite the possibility of temporary stagnation or set-backs. The detailed policies may change, the leadership may change, but the overall direction of the reform and opening up will be maintained. This conclusion is extremely relevant to foreign investors, because without the assurance of continued reform and opening up as the pre-condition, any other talks of China's foreign investment environment are meaningless.

THE SOCIAL ENVIRONMENT – THE CULTURAL AND STRUCTURAL TRANSFORMATION IN CONTEMPORARY CHINESE SOCIETY

Analyses from both the historical and political perspectives have suggested that, despite the possibilities of short term fluctuations and even major hiccups, the reform programme and the open door policy in China will continue. However, even under a stable political environment, the success of foreign invested enterprises in China can still be significantly affected by other forces, among which the unique Chinese culture and social structure stand out as two of the most important. The Chinese culture and tradition are deeply rooted. Although the history of China has been marked by periodic upheavals, its majority of Han people have experienced the longest span of homogeneous cultural development of any society in the world.[28] Over forty years of Communist rule (with the central planning economic regime) has also created a unique social structure in contemporary Chinese society. Radical changes in the social structure, accompanying the reform and opening up in recent years, are clearly reflected in changes in contemporary Chinese culture. Understanding Chinese culture and social structure, including their current transformation and future prospects, are extremely important to the success of any foreign invested enterprise in China, because they are clearly reflected in the values, attitudes, sense of priority and behaviour of Chinese people. Since the Chinese culture and social structure are very different from the western world, it is essential for potential investors in China to develop a comprehensive understanding of these differences.

Contemporary Chinese culture is a mixture of the traditional Chinese culture, the Communist party culture and elements of the modern western culture. The traditional Chinese culture has developed during the country's 5000 year history, and continues to have a very strong hold in Chinese society. However, today's Chinese culture is significantly different from the traditional culture because of over forty years of Communist rule. Through the creation of new social structures, many elements of the traditional culture were eliminated, weakened or distorted. New elements were also introduced or imposed on the Chinese people through propaganda and other measures. With the reform since the late 1970s, traditional culture has experienced a renaissance, particularly in rural areas. In urban areas, the strong influence of modern western culture has been increasingly felt. The changing balance between the traditional Chinese culture, the Communist party culture and the modern western culture is closely related to the structural transformation in Chinese society resulting from the reform and opening up.

Before 1949, traditional Chinese culture was the predominant culture in Chinese society, supplemented by some elements of western ideas. The ideology of many ancient Chinese philosophers, such as Kongzi (Confucius), Mengzi (Mencius), Muozi, Laozi, Xunzi, in combination with some religious thoughts, regulated most people's values, attitudes, priorities, and behaviours for thousands of years. From the perspective of management, Lockett identified four cultural values which are primarily derived from this stream, namely: respect for age and hierarchy; orientation towards groups; the preservation of 'face' (the recognition by others of one's moral character, social standing and position); and the importance of relationships or connections (*guanxi*).[29] These elements are still highly relevant today, and they remain the main roots of contemporary Chinese culture.

The Chinese culture is shame- rather than guilt-oriented.[30] What matters to people in China is how they are perceived by others, that is, their 'face'. Damaged relationships are almost impossible to repair. This factor can have profound implications to foreign investors when handling human resource issues and labour relations, as well as the relationship with joint venture partners, suppliers, buyers, and various local government agencies. To understand this, it is necessary to examine *guanxi*, a key concept that will be discussed in detail in the next section.

After the Chinese Communist Party came to power in 1949, some key elements of the traditional Chinese culture were largely abandoned. In the meantime, a series of new values, which have sometimes been termed the 'Communist Party culture', were superimposed on Chinese society. By imposing a Marxist-Leninist orientation in almost every aspect of Chinese lives, through the creation of new social structures, the Communist Party not only successfully overcame some elements of the traditional culture but also successfully used its other elements, such as loyalty, obedience, selflessness and diligence, for the Party's own purposes.[31]

In his book, Child expressed some doubts on whether the political ideology and associated values of the Chinese Communist Party have actually become part of the contemporary Chinese culture.[32] He argued that if the political ideology becomes established in people's mind and is handed on by them to succeeding generations, then one could consider that it has become part of the culture. He felt, however, that this is probably not the case in China, and that for decades people have been 'acting' as if they believed in the Party doctrines and propaganda. However, whilst recognizing his point, we feel that the political ideology has actually been passed to the new generation – even if some people do not genuinely believe in it.

Although the political freedom of Chinese people has improved markedly since the 1980s (compared with the previous three decades), and the Communist ideology in China itself has gone through several radical changes, political control remains tight today, and many people still have to 'act' in order to satisfy the ruling Communist Party. Even if people do not genuinely believe in the ideology (some people genuinely do!), at least ideas on how to 'act' (in ways as if one does) have been passed to the younger generation – which in fact has been a very important survival skill in contemporary China. This situation may remain so for many years to come.

Today, the Chinese Communist Party maintains absolute control over Chinese politics, despite radical economic and political reforms since 1978. Political loyalty (and being a party member) remains a key factor for promotion in the state owned sector and in central and local governments. Although the private sector has been growing rapidly, the dominance of the state owned sector has remained. In 1996, state owned enterprises still enjoy a monopoly in almost all strategic industries, with two-thirds of all urban workers employed in the state owned sector. While the state has full control of telecommunications, civil aviation and railway transportation, it holds majority shares in all other key industries – 91 per cent of the power industry, 90.9 per cent of the coal industry, 95 per cent of the petroleum industry, 79.2 per cent of the metallurgical industry and 77 per cent of the chemical industry. The state sector also plays a leading role in other industries such as electronics, machinery, textiles and foodstuffs. State owned enterprises make up 65 per cent of the total assets of all enterprises in China, employ 67 per cent of the labour force in urban areas and contribute 60 per cent of the state revenue.[33] That means a large proportion of Chinese people still depend on the Communist government for their (and their families') necessities and social security and welfare. In addition, the state often has considerable stakes in joint ventures and even the 'private' sectors. Therefore, the influence of the Communist Party culture will remain strong in many facets of Chinese society for the majority of Chinese people.

Indeed, even the level of freedom for private entrepreneurs and those working in foreign invested enterprises in China depends on the tolerance of the Communist government. In 1995, the Chinese Communist Party decided not to admit private business people as party members, because they are capitalists bent on exploiting the labour force.[34] The official reason for the decision (not to allow private entrepreneurs to join the Communist Party) was based on 'the nature of the party, its programme and its goals'. This is a very important move by the Chinese Communist Party to force some talented people in China to choose between being party members or private entrepreneurs. Party membership today remains an important 'qualification' in China, and being without it will rule out many potential options for one's career progress.

To put it in another way: although in the West some people do not genuinely believe there is a supernatural God up there governing the world (we have no intention to offend any readers with this example), the strong influence of religion and Christianity is clearly reflected in Western culture. From the authors' own personal experiences in the West, even some regular church goers are not genuine believers in God, but in church they behave in ways that indicate they believe in God no less than anyone else does. Similarly, although in China many people do not genuinely believe in Communism (indeed, some people perhaps do not even have the faintest clue what Communism actually means, and the meaning of Communism itself has evolved considerably even though the name has remained the same in China), many of them would claim to believe in 'it' under certain circumstances and often they behave as if they genuinely do. The younger generations need to learn the main ideas and techniques to survive and thrive in Chinese society. The point is, the strong influence of the Communist rule since 1949 is clearly reflected in contemporary Chinese culture – if it is not already an integral part of it – and it will continue to do so in the foreseeable future.

The Party culture is essential for the Communist Party to remain in power in China, because through culture creation, the Chinese

Communist Party can maintain effective control over almost every aspect of an individual's life in China. The main mechanisms through which the Party culture has been superimposed upon the Chinese people are the elimination of economic disparities throughout the society by force ('kill the rich and distribute the wealth to the poor', or more precisely, control of the wealth by the Communist Party), and the creation of the work unit and the household registration systems in urban areas. Through these systems, each individual becomes economically dependent on the state for essential needs and social welfare. Individuals' life styles and the overall structure of the society are therefore under the full control of the government – and the Communist Party. The situation has changed considerably in recent years, and the pace of change may well accelerate as more radical reforms are implemented, but the dependence of the majority of urban citizens on the state will remain for many years to come. The situation in rural areas is similar though the level of control is less tight.

Under the Party culture, most individuals in China have no choice other than to accept what is imposed on them. Under the planning regime, the Communist Party has adopted a low-salary system with high levels of social welfare (which are directly related to the job one does). Although the basic salary is very low (only enough for the essential necessities of survival for an individual and his/her family, such as food, clothes, basic homeware etc.), having a job in a state owned organization implies that the person is automatically entitled to free medical care, housing, a pension after retirement and many other benefits. His/her children may also be entitled to some benefits (for example, free medical care, free education) from the organization. Most jobs are permanent, and should an organization close down, the employees of the organization are automatically entitled to be transferred to another organization. However, if one resigns, or is sacked, the individual not only loses the basic salary, but also the job-related social welfare entitlement mentioned above. Regaining such a job after one has resigned or been sacked is almost impossible in China, although increasingly people have other options open to them.

Such a system has led to many unique behaviours in contemporary Chinese society. For example, people often have to accept whatever job is allocated to them. People are unlikely to express openly what is really on their mind – they have to say what the Party wants them to say and hide their real feelings deep inside if they wish to avoid any trouble. In addition, as has been discussed earlier in this chapter, this system does not punish those without achievements but those who have made mistakes. It follows that people are reluctant to accept new ideas and experiment with new things. Although in recent years the system has changed considerably, its profound influence in Chinese society will remain for many years to come.

The other system with which the government – and the Communist Party – maintains effective control over individuals in China is the household registration system, which significantly restricts labour mobility. This system was very tightly controlled before the 1980s, although it has now become looser. However, even today, it is still extremely difficult for rural residents to change their registration to urban areas. This means that even if they can find a job in town, they cannot bring their family with them. And were they to do so they would have to pay for schooling, for instance, which is free in the home village but costs 1000 yuan or more a term elsewhere. Urban citizens may also find it very difficult to move to other cities because of the system. This system is currently under reform and is much weaker today, but it is still very much a fact of life in China.

Since 1978, the private sector has been growing rapidly, and some people – private entrepreneurs and those working in foreign owned firms for example – have become economically independent from the state imposed jobs and the related social welfare entitlements. However, the number of such people is relatively small, and most workers still have permanent jobs in state owned organizations and are dependent upon the state and Communist Party for their essential necessities and social security and welfare. Many fear that should the government policy on the reform change someday, they will lose everything. Therefore, the majority of them choose not to risk losing everything related to their present job for temporary improvements in living standards and economic independence. In many families, people make conscious decisions to make sure at least one member remains in the state owned sector to protect their welfare while others make money outside the state owned sectors. As a result, although the Party culture is getting weaker and does not have the same power as in the past, it will continue to have profound influence on people's behaviour for some time to come.

As a result of the open door policy, particularly with the setting up of the 'special economic zones' in some coastal provinces, Western modernist culture is increasingly accepted by urban Chinese people. The experience of the last two decades has suggested that western culture can successfully co-exist with both traditional Chinese culture and the Communist Party culture. However, even in the special economic zones where the impact of the Western culture is the strongest and the Party culture the least influential, the influences of all three elements can still be clearly felt.

The contemporary Chinese culture can have significant impacts on the operation and management of foreign invested enterprises. For example, as mentioned earlier, Lockett reported that some elements of traditional Chinese culture can exert significant influences on the negotiation and management of foreign investment enterprises in Shenzhen, the first special economic zone opened in China.[35] Among these elements are respect for age and hierarchy, group consciousness, the recognition of one's social and economic status, and the importance of personal connections and family ties (that is, '*guanxi*') in getting around laws and regulations. These unique elements are to a great extent responsible for the differences in the negotiation techniques and styles, the decision-making processes, and the primary interests of Chinese partners in a project, compared with other countries.

Previous studies have also shown that due to cultural and other differences, some foreign firms have experienced difficult problems when negotiating a joint venture or other investment project, including differences in negotiation styles, the over-emphasis of long term relationships by the Chinese partner, a slow decision making process and lack of authority in making decisions by the Chinese negotiators.[36] Therefore, it is important for foreign investors to appreciate factors such as patience, preparation (being familiar with Chinese goals and constraints), resources, mutual benefits, relationship without over-involvement, and the nature of law and legal agreements in China.[37]

Party culture also exerts considerable influences on the decision making process in China and on workers' behaviours. Bureaucratism and corruption are still very commonplace throughout China, and any potential investors should be fully prepared for that. Re-allocation of jobs in a factory may provoke resistance, even if only passively, because, under the Communist Party culture, the only acceptable re-allocation of jobs is promotion [here age and working experience (not necessarily how good one's skills are, but how long one has been working in the organization) are the most important criteria]. Under that culture, only those who had made serious mistakes would be replaced or be moved to lower positions. Mis-handling of any of these factors may lead to resistance and unfavourable industrial relations.

Over forty years of Communist education has also convinced most Chinese workers that foreign investment in China is only intended for profit, and the only way to achieve high profit is to exploit or squeeze the workers (Karl Marx's theory). This ideology was particularly strong in the 1980s, but it will continue to have significant effects on the behaviour of workers. For example, work re-allocation on the production line for productivity purposes may lead to resistance or complaints from workers, suspecting that the foreign boss is trying to exploit them more; and the promotion of certain employees to higher levels may discourage or hurt the feelings of others with similar qualifications. For management staff, they may feel their foreign boss earns too much, which may make them reluctant to help with operational problems. Indeed, despite the growing influence of Western culture, its survival in China will depend critically on how well it fits in with other elements of culture in Chinese society. The experiences of Taiwan, Hong Kong, Singapore, South Korea and even Japan have demonstrated that tradition and new ideas may co-exist, but the unique features of Chinese culture and social structure do call for special caution when managing foreign invested enterprises, even at the level of handling minor problems.

Changes have accelerated in China in the 1990s, which will be reflected in the culture and social structure in Chinese society. In the ninth five year plan (1996–2000), China is determined to move from the experiments of the eighth five year plan to implementing radical reforms at large scales – such as reforming the loss-making state owned sectors, the employment system, the social security system, and the wage system.[38] Since the promulgation of the Labour Law (*Lao Dong Fa*) in July 1994, the reform of the employment system in China has achieved significant progress. By the end of 1995, 85 per cent of all employees in the state owned sector had become contracted workers, and employment contracts were to extend to the remaining 15 per cent of workers by the end of 1996.[39]

This reform was primarily intended to break the so-called 'iron rice bowl' employment policy involving job security and cradle-to-grave welfare coverage.[40] In the meantime, organizations are given more autonomy in managing their wage systems within the framework of national policies (such as the minimum wage).[41] With such changes, the social security system is being radically restructured – including unemployment benefits, the pension system and medical insurance, which were previously the responsibilities of the organizations but are now under the control of local governments.[42] Whereas such practices are introduced across the board in state owned enterprises, they are also becoming increasingly common in other forms of organization – such as township and village industries, joint ventures and private and foreign owned enterprises.[43] In particular, the All China Federation of Trade Unions (ACFTU) demanded that all foreign invested enterprises establish collective employment contracts.[44] The social implications of such reforms will be very profound – especially in the long term.

The unique features of contemporary Chinese culture and social structure can have profound implications for the operation and management of foreign invested enterprises. Although the private sector has been growing at a much faster pace than the state owned sector, the dominance of the state owned sector in the Chinese economy will not change in the short or even medium term, and will to a large extent determine the pace of social transformation in China. Despite changes in recent years, many features of the Chinese society – together with their profound management implications – discussed in this section will remain for a long time.[45] Foreign investors need to bear this in mind when assessing China's soft environment.

Many other social factors are equally important. For example, despite the fact that the overall educational attainment of the Chinese people in general is quite low, given the size of the country and the 1.2 billion population base, it is relatively easy to achieve the necessary scale of certain skills for a specific operation. High salary is only one factor that may attract high calibre employees, others factors such as housing, medical care, pension, sense of achievement, career progression route, and other arrangements (for example, what will happen to them if the investment fails and the factory closes down) may be equally attractive. Also, over-staffing is a common problem among state owned enterprises, and it is the responsibility of the Chinese partner and local labour bureau to find new jobs for the redundant workers. It is thus understandable that the local government often tries to persuade the foreign investors to employ more people than needed.

It is particularly worth noting that Chinese intellectuals may care much more for their reputation, working conditions (for example, autonomy), recognition of their work and so on than for other incentives such as money, an attitude which is closely related to traditional Chinese culture and values. All these call for special attention from foreign investors. In addition, China is still in the process of radical and rapid political, social, and economic transformations, and many factors of the investment environment in China are evolving rapidly. A dynamic view is therefore necessary when assessing the quality of the foreign investment environment in China.

GUANXI IN CHINESE SOCIETY

One issue that has been widely reported about doing business in China is the importance of *guanxi* (relationships, personal connections or networks in Chinese society). China insiders repeatedly remind people that *guanxi* is critical to doing business (and to many other things) in China, although they disagree on how critical it is. While some argue that in China it is not what you know that counts, but who you know,[46] the Economist Intelligence Unit's survey concluded that *guanxi* is valuable but overrated.[47] Numerous tips on how to build and maintain *guanxi* have been offered by academics, consultants and various 'China hands'.

Guanxi is an extremely complex and elusive concept, and it embraces a wide range of personal and business relationships and entails a sense of mutual trust or interdependence between individuals.[48] *Guanxi* is highly personalized, and it is an attribute one attains by demonstrating reliability, success, influence, etiquette and reciprocity in such relationships. A person's *guanxi* is measured by having access to and influence in various networks. It lies at the very heart of many business and other dealings in China.[49]

Guanxi can be developed through different means, but it is often initiated by establishing some sort of common interest or background between individuals (and/or their relatives) and strengthened and maintained by frequent social exchanges and by exchanging business and personal favours over time. For example, people who came (or whose ancestors did) from the same village, city or province (*Lao Xiang*), people who attended the same school or university (*Xiao You*), or people who share a common friend or hobby, are very common bases for initiating *guanxi* – and *guanxi* often extends to family members and close family friends. In Mainland China, *guanxi* has also developed unique features under the unique political, economic and, in particular, industrial governance structure. For example, people who previously worked for the same organization (*Lao Tong Shi*), or people from organizations under the authority of the same Ministry (*Tong Yi Ge Xi Tong*), are all bases for initiating *guanxi*. As people move (to a new place or a new job), established *guanxi* such as superior-subordinate relationships (*Lao Shang Ji – Lao Xia Ji*) can often be maintained. Business and personal relationships are often intertwined with each other. Over time, extremely complex and ever-evolving *guanxi* networks are developed. To understand the relevance of *guanxi* to doing business in China by foreign investors, it is necessary to examine the cultural and institutional roots of the phenomenon.

The cultural root

Guanxi is not a unique Chinese phenomenon, and even in the West, personal connections and informal business networks are very important to business success. However, Western and Eastern companies have very different approaches towards *guanxi*, and this phenomenon may be particularly significant in the Chinese community.[50] Schuster and Copeland argued that the necessity of establishing personal relationships as a prerequisite for entering the network and of maintaining those relationships as an essential part of continued success in business is a fundamental characteristic of Chinese culture, and it represents a significant departure from Western culture.[51] This point has been echoed by several other authors.[52]

Overseas Chinese businessmen are well known for their extensive and flexible use of business networks, a practice which has deep roots in Chinese tradition and culture (for example, group and family orientation, and the preservation of 'face').[53] Redding even argued that the success of overseas Chinese businesses is based on three factors, one of them being reliable and exclusive exchanges and contracts derived from personal connections or *guanxi* (the other two factors being stable leadership derived from Confucian paternalism and money as the safe support of insecurity).[54] The special industrial and governmental relations integral to the established networks enable people in these networks to have access to information (albeit imperfect), opportunities, decision makers and special expertise denied to others, which gives them a unique advantage over non-Chinese competitors.[55]

The Chinese culture is said to be a 'high context' environment, in which words and direct communications are not as important as in 'low context culture' (such as that in North America).[56] The fact that China is ruled more by men than by laws implies that personal relationships are vital to business (and many other) dealings, and relationships need to be established and maintained at many different levels.[57] Resolution of disputes, difficulties and new issues takes place through personal relationships, not by relying on a contract enforced or interpreted by a court (though the court is increasingly being used to settle disputes). Sometimes, if the two sides have difficulties overcoming disagreements, a third party can be brought in – often someone at a respectable or powerful position – to intervene and work out a compromise.

In Chinese society, a person's position is extremely important. Based on one's (extended) family, background, education, and personal achievements, each individual is accorded a particular position within society. The position involves mutual dependence with other individuals who may be family members or friends, schoolmates, colleagues, close friends and business associates. The type of networks one belongs to and one's position and influence within these networks are sometimes referred to as 'face'. Maintaining face is a fundamental concept of Chinese culture involving the ability to keep and enhance one's dignity, self-respect, and prestige; and it is essential for preserving and enhancing one's status and for increasing influence and power in society. Losing face makes it difficult for the individual to operate effectively in society, which can often bring shame to others in the network.

Therefore, the concept of giving, maintaining and saving face is an inherent part of functioning within a network. Such networks are highly personalised. The network begins with family relationships of giving and receiving assistance or opportunities and extends to specific working arrangements. In the business world, the network is a way of gaining access to information, opportunities, decision makers and special expertise. To maintain and increase one's *guanxi* in such networks, one has to prove to be a good business partner over time. An individual is often involved in more than one network, and such networks are inter-locked in complex ways and are evolving constantly. Keeping the ever increasing and flexible networks viable is a serious and time consuming responsibility, and it is vital to one's power and influence in society. However, such networks are not formal ties, contracts or legal arrangements, so they are extremely flexible, cost effective and responsive to changing demands of the environment. It allows the individual to have constant access to current business information from a variety of sources.

One's *guanxi* is therefore a complex mixture of personal and business relationships. Many good business relationships are based on close personal relationships; and good business relationships can often lead to close personal relationships. Maintaining strong personal relationships with family, friends, business partners and associates is a critical part of conducting business in China. Personal relationships are sometimes more important than other factors (such as higher specifications or lower price) when conducting business. One example here is the story of a Scottish businessman. His company specialized in supplying power generation facilities. After he successfully conducted a number of business deals in the northeast of China and developed comprehensive personal relationships in the region with governmental officials and business leaders, he was asked to supply a complete traffic signal control system for a large city in northeast China, a field in which his company had no expertise whatsoever. The fact that he had established himself as a good, reliable business partner in certain Chinese business networks and a personal friend to many people in these networks were the key for him to gain the trust of Chinese buyers and beat competitors with stronger expertise in the field. He is now also establishing himself in the Scottish Whisky business, with China being the major market.

Entering business networks is essential for doing business in China, and this can be done in two ways. One is the official route – the 'front door' – complete with all the bureaucratic guidelines. Going through the front door works, but it normally takes a long time. One needs to create relationships with government bureaucrats and business people in Chinese organizations who control access to permits, joint venture approvals, partnership sanctions, or other avenues for establishing a business.

However, to speed up the process, the 'back doors' are available to those with the right *guanxi*. Someone with the right connections to decision makers in a particular area can provide introductions to the decision makers, advice on how to approach the situation, or may be able to conduct informal discussions to determine the feasibility of a particular business proposal. Such assistance can significantly reduce the amount of time required, and enhance the success of business negotiations. Therefore, finding someone with the right *guanxi*, developing a good relationship with him/her and using his/her assistance to enter the network is one of the quickest and safest ways to business success in China.[58] In the process, one can also develop his/her own *guanxi*, which can be used for future businesses. This is also a main area where corruption occurs (for example, bribery – however, it would be quite wrong to simply equate *guanxi* to bribery[59]). We will discuss this issue in the next chapter.

As *guanxi* increases, an individual has access to a greater number of businesses, more diverse levels and areas of expertise, more positions within the bureaucracy and more knowledge of business affairs and opportunities. Access to networks does not guarantee a business deal, but it makes it possible for one to pursue opportunities. Without good personal relationships, business arrangements are simply not possible in many cases. As Tsun-yan Hsieh of McKinsey, a management consultancy, told *The Economist*: 'Relationship building is the essence of strategy, not the by-product of it'.[60] Also, because of the complexity of *guanxi* in China, choosing the people with whom to do business is also a critical decision. Some networks are mutually exclusive, and being associated with someone with a bad reputation may endanger one's own future prospect in China.

The institutional root

Personal and business relationships are often inter-locked, which is perhaps especially so in Mainland China where *guanxi* has developed many unique features. Some of these features have been derived from the political, economic, and social systems adopted in China since the early 1950s, which is referred to as the institutional root of *guanxi* in China. Officially, China is a socialist country and its constitution declares that all means of production are publicly owned and the state acts as the custodian of this public ownership. In spite of rapid development of the private sector in recent years and the rapid growth of FDI, the dominance of the state owned sector will not be affected in the near future.

Until recently, the concept of ownership (*Suo You Zhi*) in China was primarily a political and ideological consideration rather than an economic and legal one. It implies an overall system of governance based on ideological principles of socialism. Despite public ownership in China, the holders of industrial property rights vary from all managers and employees of the enterprise for collective enterprises, to various central and local authorities for state owned enterprises.[61] The functioning of the Chinese economic system is based on a complex web of administrative as well as other relationships.

In China, the government and the Party are inextricably linked, and together constitute the state. Consequently, the structure of China's industrial governance contains two parallel hierarchies, that of the administration and that of the Party. The administrative structure consists of two reporting lines for state owned enterprises: ministries and bureaux for industries and for specialized functions (for example, taxation, auditing, personnel, and investment finance). A specialized bureau in a particular locality has a reporting line in the relevant ministry, but its main line of accountability is to the local government. Party organs are embedded in each and every unit of the structure.

These administrative units have close relationships with the enterprise, and their involvement in the enterprise can extend to any aspect of the latter's work and operation, including appointing directors and approving contracts specifying enterprise performance targets. Child regards this relationship as similar to that in a holding company in the west.[62] These enterprises also have close ties with ministries and bureaux dealing with specialized functions such as taxation, auditing, pricing, investment finance, power supply, personnel matters and workers' employment. Some state owned enterprises are under the direct control of the State Council or industrial ministries, whilst others are controlled by various local authorities and industrial bureaux (sometimes called industrial corporations).

In parallel to this administrative structure is the political governance structure of the Chinese Communist Party. The Party has always played a formal role within the enterprise to promote ideological awareness, and to guarantee and supervise the implementation of party policies, although the role of managers has been strengthened considerably since the mid-1980s with enterprise reforms. One particular function of the Party is to monitor managers and employees, and in fact most managers are members of the Party (political loyalty is an important factor in personnel appointment) who are under the direct leadership of the Party Secretary in the organization. Some enterprise managers are also Deputy Party Secretaries in their enterprises, and sometimes the manager holds the position of the Party Secretary. During the 1980s, Deng Xiaoping promoted the system of management responsibility in enterprises, which weakened the position of the Party Secretary in the management of the enterprise, but after 1989, the policy was changed to the manager as the 'centre' but the Party Secretary as the 'core' in the enterprise.[63] The relationship between management and Party officials in the enterprise remains an unresolved issue today. Such complex relationships are inevitably reflected in the way business is conducted in China.

Another significant force in the Chinese enterprise system is the trade unions, which are a 'mass organisation of the working class led by the Party'. Apart from representing workers and defending their legitimate rights, the unions' role is also to assist the management in running the enterprise. Under the All China Federation of Trade Unions (ACFTU), there are fifteen industrial trade unions operating in China. The majority of China's workforces in state enterprises are members of these unions. Union representatives have the right to attend meetings of the board of directors as non-voting members to discuss labour issues as well as the enterprise's general operation. In addition, there is a whole range of other interested parties that are relevant to enterprise management in China – such as the Communist Youth League and the Women's Federation, all of them having close ties with the Communist Party.[64] Apart from achieving economic targets, Chinese enterprises are also responsible for the provision of a wide range of welfare and other benefits to their workers, and they are also obliged to support the local community. All these add to the complexity of enterprise management in China.

The intertwined political and industrial governance systems discussed above briefly outlined the institutionalized relations between various levels of government, ministries and bureaux, the party, the trade unions, the local community and the enterprises as well as their suppliers and customers. These complex, inter-locking and inter-dependent relationships form the institutional context for Chinese enterprises. Child regards this as a system of power, in which there is the potential for actors and their agencies to intervene in decisions from different levels and points of the system.[65] A key feature of the system is 'bargaining'. In the process of bargaining, personal connections are formed which allow interdependent actors to use the flexibility and loopholes existing in Chinese laws and regulations to (or not to) assist or sanction each other. In particular, many people may use their bargaining power in the system for personal gain, which forms part of the basis for corruption in Chinese society (which will be discussed in the next chapter).

The vertical relationships of the enterprise with the government bureaucracy are very important because their co-operation can play a key role in securing the future of the enterprise (for example, in allocating scarce resources, shortage supplies, new financial investment, and extra personnel, in setting production targets and assessment criteria, and in flexibly enforcing laws and regulations). Underlying this institutionalized relationship is the development personal relations (that is, *guanxi*). Established *guanxi* can often move with individuals as they transfer to new places or new jobs, and it often extends to family members and friends.

Institutionalized relationships or connections are only one type of *guanxi*, which always intertwines with *guanxi* developed through other means. The cultural root of *guanxi* has been discussed earlier in this chapter. The institutional and cultural contexts reinforce each other, which makes *guanxi* extremely complex.

Guanxi is extremely important to doing business in China. As will be discussed in the next chapter, the legal system in China is not complete and the terms of laws and regulations are often very 'flexible'. *Guanxi* thus becomes particularly important in determining how to interpret and enforce a particular clause, or how fast a requirement can be dealt with. Building and maintaining *guanxi* in China takes time, effort and resources, and Chinese people tend to mix business relations with social relations, so it is vital to reinforce *guanxi* through social activities during non-working hours. In order to do business successfully in China, foreign investors often need to tap into such networks, and more importantly, learn to nurture and maintain them.

In China, people often regard some *guanxi* as insurance policies, or a form of protection. You never know when you might need help. Developing *guanxi* with the right people may not only help to prevent problems, but also, when problems arise, some *guanxi* can be capitalized on. In China, many rules and regulations are either not written yet or not effectively enforced, and in many aspects the market is less transparent than in the West. *Guanxi* is often regarded as the safest or only form of commercial security. Tips on how to build and maintain *guanxi* have been given in numerous 'how to' books and consultancy reports on doing business in China.[66] However, understanding the rules of the game does not necessarily make one a good player of the game – and one's skills can only improve with practice and time. Many contemporary Western management ideas are in direct conflict with *guanxi* building.[67]

SUMMARY

In this chapter, the historical evolution of China's external relations, the political background of the reform and the open door policy, and the unique characteristics of Chinese culture and social structure have been examined. One critical factor for doing business in China – *guanxi* – is also highlighted in this context, and its cultural and institutional roots are analysed. These factors constitute the general context of China's soft environment for FDI.

From a historical perspective, we concluded that China should have woken up from the past, because both ancient and contemporary history has demonstrated that in order to achieve rapid economic development, China has no choice but to develop open exchanges – economic, technological, cultural and others – with the outside world. From a political perspective, we concluded that despite the possibility of short term stagnation and setbacks, the reform programme and the open door policy will continue. From a social perspective, some unique features of Chinese culture and social structure and their implications for foreign invested enterprises in China are highlighted. We also examined the cultural and institutional roots of *guanxi* in Chinese society, and the relevance of this phenomenon to doing business in China. In the next chapter, a wide range of operational problems encountered by foreign investors in China will be examined. These two chapters together outline the nature and key characteristics of the soft investment environment in China.

Notes

1. The Economist Intelligence Unit (EIU) and Andersen Consulting (1995) *Moving China Ventures out of the Red into the Black: Insights from Best and Worst Performers*, The Economist Intelligence Unit, London.
2. *The Economist*, 29 March–4 April 1997, 'Business: And never the twain shall meet . . . Building business relationships in Asia, and then keeping them, is proving far harder than foreign companies imagined', pp. 87–88.
3. Zhang, Youwen, Duan Xiping, Jin Bu (1986), *The Opening up of Our*

National Economy (Wuo Guo Jing Ji De Dui Wai Kai Fang), Shanghai Publishing House (*Shang Hai Chu Ban She*), Shanghai.

4. Fitzerald, C.P. (1961) *China: A Short Cultural History*, The Cressett Press, London.

5. Zhang *et al.* (1986) *op. cit.*

6. Fitzerald (1961) *op. cit*; Fairbank, John and Edwin Reischauer (1989) *China: Tradition and Transformation* (revised edition), Allen and Unwin, London; Fairband, J.K. (1992) *China: A New History*, The Belknap Press of Harvard University Press, London.

7. Wiethoff, Bodo (1975) *Introduction to Chinese History: From Ancient Times to 1912*, Thames and Hudson, London.

8. Fairband (1992) *op. cit.*

9. Such as the so-called 'Westernisation Movement' (*Yang Wu Yun Dong*) to introduce techniques of capitalist production initiated by the comprador bureaucrats in the second half of the 19th century; and in the early 20th century, the attempted reforms by Kang Youwei and Liang Qichou (*Kang Liang Bian Fa*).

10. Fairbank and Reischauer (1989) *op. cit.*; Fairband (1992) *op. cit.*

11. Zhang *et al.* (1986) *op. cit.*

12. Wang, Qingxian and Rong Huang (1996) 'We start from here' (*Wo Men Cong Zhe Li Qi Bu*); *The People's Daily* (Overseas edition), 7 March 1996, pp. 1 and 3.

13. For example, Child, J. (1994) *Management in China during the Age of Reform*, Cambridge University Press, Cambridge.

14. *The People's Daily* (Overseas edition), 5 March 1996, 'The People's Republic of China National Statistical Bureau Report on China's Economic and Social Development for 1995' *(Zhong Hua Ren Min Gong He Guo Guo Jia Tong Ji Ju Guan Yu 1995 Nian Guo Min Jing Ji He She Hui Fa Zhan De Tong Ji Gong Bao)*, p. 2.

15. Zagoria, Donald S. (1991) 'The end of the cold war in Asia: Its impact on China', in *Proceedings of the Academy of Political Science*, Vol. 38, No. 2; *The Economist*, 8–14 March 1997, 'The importance of foreign-devil money', *China Survey*, pp. 9–12; Lardy, Nicholas R. (1995) 'The role of foreign trade and investment in China's economic transformation', *China Quarterly*, No. 144, pp. 1065–82.

16. *The Economist,* 27 July – 2 Aug. 1991.

17. Zhao Ziyang (1984) 'The opening of China', in *Atlantic*, No. 6, Dec. 1984, p. 24.

18. Li, Xiao Jun and E.J. Griffiths (1989) *The Long March to the Fourth of June*, London: Duckworth.

19. The World Bank (1990) *China: Between Planning and Market,* Country Study, Washington D.C.: The World Bank.

20. *Ibid.*

21. *Beijing Review*, Vol. 34, No. 5, p. 30.

22. *The People's Daily* (Overseas edition), 18 October 1991; 'China's great leap forward', in *Union Bank of Switzerland (UBS) International Finance*, Issue 15, Spring 1993.

23. *The Economist*, 17–23 August 1996, 'China: A funny-looking tiger', pp. 17–19.

24. *New York Times*, 26 January 1990.
25. Sutter, Robert G. (1990) 'Changes in Eastern Europe and the Soviet Union: The Effect on China', *Journal of Northeast Asian Studies*, Summer, 1990.
26. *Ibid.*
27. *The Economist*, 17–23 August 1996, *op. cit.*
28. Child (1994), *op. cit.*
29. Lockett, M. (1988) 'Culture and the problems of Chinese management', *Organization Studies* 9: 475–96.
30. Martinsons, Maris and Paul Hempel (1995) 'Chinese management systems: Historical and cross-cultural perspectives', *Journal of Management Systems* 7(1): 1–11, special issue on *Management in Greater China*.
31. For example, Lin, Zhiling (1991) 'How China will modernise', *The American Enterprise*, July–August 1991.
32. Child (1994), *op. cit.*
33. *China News Digest*, 10 May 1996, 'State sector still strong in economy', p. 6.
34. According to the *Press Digest* published by the Party Central Committee's Organization Department. Also reported in the *China News Digest* (CND, News Global), Monday, 18 September 1995, 'CCP Says "No Admittance" to Private Business People'.
35. Lockett, Martin (1987) 'China's Special Economic Zones: The cultural and managerial challenges', *Journal of General Management*, Vol. 12 No. 3, Spring 1987.
36. For example, Child (1994) *op. cit.*
37. Che, B., J. Ki, Y.K. Mok and S. Stewart (1985) 'Investors' perception of the advantages and disadvantages of investing in an SEZ: Shenzhen', Department of Management Studies, University of Hong Kong; Child (1994) *op. cit.*
38. *China News Digest* (CND), 10 May 1996, *op. cit.*; *The People's Daily* (Overseas edition), 19 June 1996, 'China establishes new employment system' (*Zhong Guo Jian Li Xin Xing Lao Dong Yong Gong Zhi Du*), p. 4; *The People's Daily* (Overseas edition), 3 April 1996, 'China actively constructs new types of wage system, intensifies macro control of wages' (*Zhong Guo Ji Ji Gou Jian Xin Xing Gong Zi Guan Xi, Jia Qiang Lao Dong Gong Zi Hong Guan Tiao Kong Li Du*), p. 4; 14 December 1995, 'The reform and development of China's social security system' (*Zhong Guo She Hui Bao Zhang Zhi Du De Gai Ge He Fa Zhan*), p. 1.
39. *The People's Daily* (Overseas edition), 19 April 1996, 'China will implement employment contract system across the board within the year' (*Wo Nian Nei Quan Mian Jian Li Lao Dong He Tong Zhi*); *The People's Daily* (Overseas edition), 19 June 1996, *op. cit.*
40. Warner, Malcolm (1996) 'Managing China's enterprise reforms: A new agenda for the 1990s', *Journal of General Management* 21 (3) Spring 1996: 1–18.
41. *The People's Daily* (Overseas edition), 3 April 1996, *op. cit.*
42. *The People's Daily* (Overseas edition), 14 December 1995, *op. cit.*
43. Warner (1996) *op. cit.*

44. *The People's Daily* (Overseas edition), 20 May 1996 'China demands foreign invested enterprises sign collective employment contract' (*Zhong Guo Yao Qiu Wai Qi Qian Ding Yong Gong Ji Ti He Tong*), p. 2.
45. Child (1994) *op. cit.*
46. *The Economist*, 29 March–4 April 1997, *op. cit.*
47. The Economist Intelligence Unit and Andersen Consulting (1995) *op. cit.*
48. Schuster, Camille P. and Michael J. Copeland (1996) *Global Business: Planning for Sales and Negotiations*, The Dryden Press, Harcourt Brace College Publishers, Fort Worth, USA; Yan, Rick (1994) 'To reach China's consumers, adapt to *Guo Qing*', *Harvard Business Review*, September–October 1994: 66–74.
49. Bucknall, Kevin (1994) *Kevin B. Bucknall's Cultural Guide to Doing Business in China*, Butterworth Heinmann, Oxford.
50. *The Economist*, 29 March–4 April 1997, *op. cit.*
51. Schuster and Copeland (1996), *op. cit.*
52. For example, Bucknall (1994), *op. cit.*
53. Wong, Dorothy Suk Chee (1995) 'Understanding overseas Chinese businesses: Some barriers and traps', Paper presented at the *Association of Management (AoM) 13th International Conference*, 2–5 August 1995, Vancouver, Canada; Martinsons and Hampel (1995) *op. cit.*
54. Redding, Gordon (1995) 'Overseas Chinese networks: Understanding the enigma', *Long Range Planning* 28 (1): 61–69.
55. Schuster and Copeland (1996), *op. cit.*
56. Hall, Edward T. (1981) *Beyond Culture*, Doubleday, New York; Wong (1995) *op. cit.*
57. Frankenstein, John (1995) 'The Beijing rules: Contradictions, ambiguities and controls', *Long Range Planning* 28 (1): pp. 70–80; Bucknall (1994) *op. cit.* The Economist Intelligence Unit and Andersen Consulting (1995) *op. cit;* Child (1994) *op. cit.*
58. Dong, Jie Li (1994) 'In China, an understanding of *guanxi* can help open doors', *The Asian Wall Street Journal Weekly*, 16 May 1994, 7A–B.
59. *The Economist*, 29 March–4 April 1997, *op. cit.*
60. *Ibid.* p. 87.
61. Child (1994) *op. cit.*
62. *Ibid.*
63. Warner (1996) *op. cit.*
64. Nyaw, Mee Kau (1993) 'Managing international joint ventures in China', in Kelley, Lane and Oded Shenkar (eds.) *International Business in China*, Routledge, London.
65. Child (1994) *op. cit.*
66. For example, Bucknall (1994) *op. cit.*; The Economist Intelligence Unit and Andersen Consulting (1995) *op. cit.*
67. *The Economist*, 29 March–4 April 1997, *op. cit.*

6 The Foreign Investment Environment in China: The Soft Environment (II)

In the last chapter, the historical, political and social backgrounds of China's reform and opening up to the outside world were examined, and a key factor for doing business in China – *guanxi* (connections and networks) – was analysed. Within this broad context, this chapter examines some operational problems encountered by foreign investors in the aspects of foreign exchange, legal framework, labour relations, human resource supply, social security and welfare, and bureaucratism and corruption in local and central governments. After two decades of reform and opening up in China, problems in some of these areas have been greatly relieved today. In the meantime, new problems have emerged. A discussion of these evolving problems will give the readers some ideas about the main features of the rapidly changing soft environment for FDI in China.

INSUFFICIENT FOREIGN EXCHANGE FACILITIES

Insufficient foreign exchange facilities was one of the most widely reported problems encountered by foreign investors in China during the 1980s and early 1990s.[1] This problem caused many foreign investors a great deal of anxiety and disappointment, and in some cases foreign investors openly threatened to withdraw from China should the problem not be resolved quickly.[2] Today, the situation has been greatly improved, and from 1 December 1996 the Chinese yuan became freely convertible on the current account (see Chapter 3 for a more detailed discussion).[3] Nevertheless, it is interesting to see how this problem has evolved over the last two decades, and more importantly, what lessons can be learnt by foreign investors and by the Chinese government in dealing with similar problems.

The gradual improvement of this problem also vividly illustrated what is meant by a 'gradualist' approach to reform and opening up in China, which is in sharp contrast to the 'shock therapy' adopted by countries such as Russia.

The causes for foreign exchange shortage were very complex, with one of the most important being that the Chinese currency was not freely convertible and for many years the Chinese government maintained strict control over foreign exchange allocation in China. This was understandable because China is the largest developing country in the world. Importing high value-added goods and services from the developed economies is essential for its national economic development, and such goods and services have to be paid for with hard currencies earned through exports. Foreign currency shortage in China is, therefore, inevitable, especially during the early days of the reform and opening up. In fact, one original objective of attracting FDI in China was to gain an extra source of foreign currency supply, and all foreign invested enterprises were expected to be net suppliers to China's limited foreign exchange reserves at that time. This was demonstrated by the fact that China demanded that most foreign investors balance their own foreign exchange accounts by exporting at least a portion of their products.

However, as has been discussed in Chapter 2, one of the biggest attractions of China to many foreign investors is its potentially vast domestic market. Foreign investors selling to the domestic market, therefore, have to face the problems of a non-convertible local currency. All foreign investors in China need foreign exchange for importing supplies, payments to foreign shareholders' dividends and foreign employees' salaries, and for payments to foreign third parties (for example, for principal and interest on loans and royalties for technology).[4] This is true even for investors who have chosen to re-invest most initial profits in China, because they have to import machines, components and other materials for production. Foreign exchange shortages also caused some investors considerable anxiety with their long term prospects in China.[5]

Since the mid-1980s, the Chinese central and local authorities have taken a series of measures to relieve the pressure on foreign investors, largely due to the mounting pressure exerted by foreign investors on the Chinese government. The slowing down of new foreign investment between 1985 and 1986 (see Table 3.1.) prompted the Chinese government to promulgate the Joint Venture Foreign Exchange Balance Provisions on 15 January 1986, which allowed joint ventures to deal with foreign exchange deficits in a number of flexible ways. A more important solution was contained in the Provisions for Encouraging Foreign Investment promulgated in October 1986, which allowed foreign investors to swap foreign exchanges for yuan.[6] The transaction did not require the approval of the foreign exchange control authorities, although it must be conducted under their supervision. The buyers and sellers negotiated the rate at which the transaction took place, which in effect, brought foreign investors close to a free market for foreign exchange.

The first organized foreign exchange swap centre was set up in Shenzhen in 1985, and by 1988, over 90 such centres were established in large and medium-sized cities throughout China. By 1990, foreign exchange swap centres had been set up in all provinces, autonomous regions, municipal cities enjoying provincial status under the state plan, and in all special economic zones. In addition, open swap markets were established in Shanghai, Shenzhen, Fuzhou and Xiamen.

The foreign exchange swap markets to a large extent helped foreign investors maintain their foreign exchange balance, and the turnover of foreign exchange swapping grew steadily and rapidly from US$6.26 billion in 1988 to US$8.56 billion in 1989, and further to US$13.16 billion in 1990. The black market was also very active due to insufficient supply of hard currency in the domestic market and government control of the exchange rate.[7] Some local authorities also collaborated with joint ventures in solving the problem, for example, by providing opportunities for profitable unrelated exports in order to help foreign investors balance their foreign exchange accounts.[8]

In the early 1990s, government control over foreign exchange was greatly relaxed, mainly because of the continuing rapid growth of foreign exchange reserves in China. Figures released by the Chinese government showed that China's overall foreign exchange reserves increased from US$17 billion at the end of 1989, to US$26 billion at the end of 1990 and to US$30 billion by September 1991. The turnover of foreign exchange swap centres grew rapidly, and since the early 1990s the Bank of China has also showed interest in dealing foreign exchange at negotiated rates. In 1993, China took a new step towards liberalizing its economy by further loosening restrictions on its exchange rates in the officially controlled swap centres.[9]

In spite of the improvements, the foreign exchange mechanisms were still problematic, which continued to cause problems to foreign investors. Because multiple rates existed in different swap centres, resources had to be devoted to finding the best rate. The cost for urgently needed foreign currencies could be high. Most of all, the system also caused considerable uncertainty in terms of the relevant rate for calculating future financial flows, since no relevant forward markets existed in which to hedge against exchange rate risks. Nevertheless, by the early 1990s foreign exchange shortage ceased to be a dominant problem, and foreign currency could invariably be obtained when needed.

In 1994, a series of radical measures were devised by the Chinese authority to further improve foreign exchange facilities. As an important step to reform foreign trade and foreign currency control, the dual exchange rate for foreign currency was abolished and a unified exchange rate was adopted.[10] The China Foreign Exchange Trading Centre was set up in Shanghai in April 1994 to act as the foreign exchange trading and settlement market between banks. The members of the Centre included all major Chinese banks and a number of foreign financial institutions. A computerised trading network was set up to support the system. The Centre provided nation-wide foreign exchange trading and settlement services, which facilitated the free flow of foreign exchange capital between different regions within China. It provided the basis for creating a single exchange rate based on market supply and demand to replace the multiple exchange rates. This would eventually make the yuan a freely convertible currency.[11]

In November 1995 China announced, during the Asia Pacific Economic Co-operation (APEC) Forum in Osaka, Japan, that foreign exchange transactions by foreign invested enterprises in China would be incorporated into the banking system of foreign exchange procurement and sale, as part of China's ambitious plan to liberalize trade and foreign investment regulations.[12] Healthy trade balance and continued rapid increase in foreign exchange reserves[13] enabled China to announce in June 1996 that it would advance plans to allow foreign invested enterprises to buy and sell foreign exchange through the banking system throughout China by the end of 1996 (rather than the year 2000 as was originally intended) – making the yuan fully convertible on the current account.[14] From 1 December 1996, the Chinese yuan became convertible on the current account.[15] However, the timing for the full convertibility of the yuan on the capital account for purposes such as investment remains unknown and it will probably be some years before the yuan is freely tradable internationally.[16]

Although foreign exchange shortage has ceased to be a major problem today for foreign investors in China, a number of implications can be drawn from this issue. One is that the quality of China's investment environment has been evolving rapidly, thus in gathering information about China's investment environment, it is essential for the foreign investor to make sure that the information is up-to-date – figures can become outdated even before they are published. Secondly, because China intends to attract more and more high quality foreign investment, the Chinese government will have to address concerns of foreign investors quickly and sensibly. In improving the situation of foreign exchange shortage in China, foreign investors played a very important role in putting pressure on the Chinese government. Such pressure may be necessary in improving other aspects of China's investment environment.

PROBLEMS WITH FDI RELATED LEGISLATION AND THE QUALITY OF CHINA'S LEGAL ENVIRONMENT

Only a decade ago, many people would not have considered China as a country governed by the rule of law. There were few laws (especially in the area of international economic relations) and those that existed were often not effectively enforced. Having the right connections (*guanxi*) was the way to settle disputes and gain approvals. This situation has deep roots in ancient Chinese history and traditional Chinese culture (see Chapter 5). The unique political, economic and social systems adopted in China since 1949 also reinforced the situation.

Historically, the Chinese administrative tradition has been based heavily on the moral nature of people (*Li* – model behaviour). Many ancient Chinese philosophers [such as Kongzi (Confucius) and Mengzi (Mencius)] believed that people were inherently benevolent, righteous and wise, and such ideas have become deeply embedded in traditional Chinese culture. The basic goodness of both rulers and ruled in ancient China enabled a 'governance of man'. This is in sharp contrast to the Western premise of 'governance of law' which gives precedence to written regulations rather than the reciprocal rights and obligations of individuals. As Laozi, the ancient Chinese philosopher, once said: 'The greater the number of laws, the more law breakers there will be'. Many phenomena in contemporary Chinese society, such as the preservation of face, are clearly related to the *Li* philosophy.

Around the year 200 BC, Han Fei and his legalist contemporaries advocated safeguards against the arbitrary rule (*Fa* – written law), which perhaps marked the beginning of the *Fa* philosophy in China. Laws and rules were to regulate conduct. Punishments and rewards could be used to influence behaviour and preserve authority. Responsibilities and accountabilities provided means for maintaining order and control.[17] The influence of these two streams of philosophies is still clearly visible in contemporary China.

The Chinese legal tradition

The two ancient philosophies of *Li* and *Fa* have blended over centuries in China, with different levels of emphasis during various period of history, and today this continues to be an integral part of the Chinese legal system. The *Li* philosophy emphases virtue, relationships and social harmony, so laws should be flexible to accommodate the circumstances by use of mediation, education and reform. In contrast, the legalist tradition (*Fa*) uses written laws as a standard to impose order through strict enforcement and as a deterrent to inappropriate conduct through the use of severe punishment. Traditionally, *Li* has dominated over *Fa*, especially in the area of dispute resolution. Largely for this reason and the fact that law was typically applied to the people rather than applied by the people, many Chinese have come to regard the law as something to be avoided, and to be involved in the process is thought to reflect on them disharmony and absence of virtue.[18]

Before 1949, the Nationalist government emphasized the rule of law and utilized European codes (although the actual enforcement of the law was a very different matter). However, after 1949 when the Communist government took control of China, there was movement away from western influences, including moving away from the use of western legal codes. During the 1950s, new laws were established using the Soviet-style socialist model, but after the beginning of the Cultural Revolution in the mid-1960s, China was largely ruled by Mao's doctrine, as interpreted by the Red Guards.

In the late 1970s, with the death of Mao Zedong and the rise of Deng Xiaoping, China was once again placed on the track of legal development. In order to achieve economic development, China needed to rebuild a legal infrastructure and a commitment to the 'rule of law' rather than 'rule of man' system, which permits public and especially foreign confidence in new economic development. Since 1979, hundreds of new laws have been developed – initially to provide security to foreign investors, but gradually new laws were also developed for the domestic needs of Chinese enterprises and individuals. Along with these new developments came the rebuilding of a legal infrastructure to make the new laws work. By the end of the 1980s, an initial framework of foreign investment related legislation was established.[19]

The new development reflected the continuity of Chinese culture and its *Li* and *Fa* traditions while at the same time it borrowed some western approaches. The strong influence of both *Li* and *Fa* philosophies is clearly visible, and today, China emphasizes both moral education and the rule of law. The basis of government is a hybrid of legalization and personal authority, which is not only true in China, but also to some extent in other Chinese dominated societies such as Singapore.

The current Chinese legal tradition is a collection and reflection of ideas, Confucian and legalist theories, western and Soviet legal approaches and the strong influence of the Chinese Communist Party, all blended into what is called the Chinese law.[20] The 'rule of law' is increasingly being emphasized, and a fairly reliable and comprehensive legal framework has been established, especially in the aspect of international economic relations. Since the promulgation of the Law of the People's Republic of China on Joint Ventures Using Chinese and Foreign Investment on 8 July 1979, the Chinese central government alone promulgated well over one hundred new laws and regulations in the area of foreign trade and investment.[21] Numerous regulations have also been issued by various local authorities in order to attract FDI into their territories.

The Chinese Communist Party and the main sources of Chinese law

China is ruled by a single party, the Chinese Communist Party (CCP), so the Party and the Chinese government are intrinsically linked. The western notion of 'rule of law' is often subordinated to the will of the Party in China. Since the reform, the Chinese government and the Party have announced its intention to recede from direct involvement in the legal processes, but its real participation and influence in law making, the operation of the court and law enforcement remain very significant.[22]

Law is a very complex concept in China, and it encompasses a variety of laws (in the western sense), regulations and administrative decisions, issued by a variety of government bodies at different levels. Since 1979, there have been more than 300 laws promulgated by the National People's Congress, and the State Council issued over 400 regulations. The National People's Congress is perhaps the equivalent of a Parliament in the West, which is the highest organ of state power. The National Constitution provides that the National People's Congress can enact basic laws (*Falu*), and its Standing Committee can issue laws in the form of decrees (*Faling*), orders (*Mingling*), decisions (*Jueyi*) and instructions (*Zhishi*) under various circumstances.

The State Council is the executive branch of the government, and it is empowered by the National Constitution to enact administrative rules and regulations (*Guiding*) and orders (*Mingling*) that are in accordance with existing laws. In 1985, the National People's Congress also empowered the State Council to enact provisional rules and regulations regarding economic reforms and dealings with foreign investment. Ministries and Commissions of the State Council are empowered to issue directions and regulations. All these central government laws and regulations have the force of law and are applicable throughout China. Various regulations are also issued by local government bodies, including provinces, autonomous regions, municipalities of Beijing, Tianjin and Shanghai (and, since 1997, Chongqing as well) and special economic zones.

The administration of law is normally performed through the government bodies responsible for application at various levels, and many alternatives exist for resolving legal problems – such as the use of mediation, conciliation, arbitration, as well as ultimate enforcement through the use of the court. Since the Chinese Communist Party has strong influence at every level of the government, there is no clear governmental independence in the decision-making, administration or enforcement of the law. Understanding the complexity in the origin and enforcement of the law is becoming increasingly important to foreign investors in China.

As has been discussed in Chapter 3, this body of legislation (in the area of foreign investment and trade) has been formulated primarily through a process of 'reactive policy making'. It became increasingly clear to the Chinese authorities that in order to attract foreign investment, expand external trade and transfer advanced technologies, it was necessary for China to develop a relevant body of laws to protect the interests and rights of foreigners. In fact, many new laws had been formulated to resolve specific issues raised by foreign investors, and by the late 1980s, many western scholars believed that the body of Chinese laws in this area was sufficiently large.[23] However, because of the unique nature of the Chinese legal system, foreign investors need to live with several serious problems or realities, such as the 'flexibility' and ambiguities of some Chinese laws.

The 'flexibility' and ambiguities of Chinese laws

One of the major problems facing foreign lawyers and investors in China is the ambiguities of law in China and the frequent recourse by Chinese leaders to 'internal rules' held in strict confidence from outsiders.[24] Ambiguities in new laws are inevitable, and this is especially true of China because of its historical legal traditions (or the lack of them) and, more importantly, its so-called 'high context culture', in which words and direct communications are not as important as in a low context cultural environment (such as the USA).[25] Schuster and Copeland's study concluded that under the Chinese Confucian ethical system, the court is not a desirable last resort and historically has not been used for satisfying economic conflicts between business partners. A transparent legal system is not to be expected in societies dominated by Chinese culture (not just mainland China!). The resolution of disputes, difficulties and new issues takes place through personal relationships, not by relying on a contract enforced or interpreted by the court (see the section on *guanxi* in Chapter 5).[26]

The situation is further worsened, as some scholars have suspected, that from the very beginning of the opening up in 1979, the Chinese authorities have deliberately left plenty of room in foreign investment laws for administrative discretion in order to grant extra concessions to projects strongly desired by the state authorities.[27] These ambiguities have left plenty of flexibility in the negotiation process to make or withdraw concessions in particular cases, and provided both attractive points to advertise to foreign businessmen and bargaining chips for China.[28] Kleinberg summarized some discretionary concessions allowed by early Chinese foreign investment laws in a table (see Table 6.1), and he concluded that great flexibility was possible on almost every aspect of a contract.[29] The development of foreign investment laws has been used by the

Table 6.1 Discretionary Concessions Allowed by Chinese Foreign Investment Law

Preferential item	Ostensible criteria for preference	Extent of potential flexibility	Agency that decides
(1) Project approval	high-tech, large, export-oriented or project in preferred sectors	rejection or slow to rapid approval	state, provincial or local foreign investment agency
(2) Acceptance of equipment or technology as joint venture contribution	indispensability; import substitution, valuation does not exceed international price	acceptance or rejection of proposed capital contribution	state, provincial or local foreign investment agency
(3) Recruitment of labour outside locality	unsuitability of local candidates	no outside hiring, to open hiring subject to state employment rules	local labour management department
(4) Contract term extension (joint ventures and technology transfer)	large, high-tech, low profit margin, or high quality exportable product output	extension of contract to 30 years, 50 years or even more	state, provincial or local foreign investment agency; State Council for over 50 years
(5) Access to domestic market	advanced technology or equipment; or import substitute products	from zero access to unspecified proportion and period of domestic sales	Moftec
(6) Special currency conversion rights	hard currency earnings insufficient to cover expenditures; must be large, high-tech project and export unspecified proportion of goods, exceptional cases only	from strict RMB non-convertibility to state hard currency subsidies	Moftec and State Planning Commission
(7) Tax reduction	advanced technology project	up to two profitable years tax exemption; 50 per cent reduction in 3 subsequent years; 10–30 per cent in reduction up to 10 years after that	supervising foreign investment agency and Ministry of Finance
(8) Relief from provisions of subsequently enacted laws	'excessive burden or excessive losses'	possible permission for contract to supersede newly enacted laws	supervising foreign investment agency

Source: Adapted from Kleinberg, R (1990) *China's Opening to the Outside World*, Westview Press, Boulder

Chinese authorities as a powerful bargaining tool; and the substance of China's foreign investment laws has lagged far behind their quantity. In other words, the terms of these laws are not sufficiently specific.

The 1979 law was short and vague. Given that it would take time and experience to develop a complete legal framework, yet at the same time China wished to make progress with its foreign investment programme, it was understandable that China needed to adopt a pragmatic approach to developing its legal framework in the area of foreign investment. As a result, new laws and regulations were normally formulated in an incremental fashion, which allowed mistakes to be corrected and new items added when necessary. Many newly proposed laws and regulations were first tried out through internal guidelines and experimented with in special economic zones. Standard forms of foreign investment contracts were being used for many different types of foreign investment projects. Given the bureaucratic nature of the Chinese state sector industrial governance system, many internal guidelines and model forms of contract were treated by Chinese negotiators, local authorities and joint venture partners in much the same terms as the law. In fact, confining attention to China's published laws and regulations has misled some foreign investors into thinking there is more flexibility than there really is.[30]

The Economist Intelligence Unit and Andersen Consulting pointed out in their report that in a genuine effort to build a workable legal framework for businesses, the Chinese central government often creates confusions and uneven playing fields.[31] Part of the problem is the open-endedness of laws and regulations, which are often left open to interpretation. While this is done in the name of flexibility, it typically leads to inconsistent and contradictory enforcement. Also, with the central government writing the rules and the individual provincial or local bureaux enforcing them, interpretation is rarely the same from one region to another. The advantage of this vagueness is that a strong local relationship (*guanxi*) and intelligent negotiation skills can sometimes twist a seemingly damaging regulation to a foreign company's advantage, but this works with only some types of rules. Potential investors also need to bear in mind that this flexibility is a double-edged sword! It allows China to use this vagueness to protect specific domestic interests when necessary.

Two legal frameworks for foreign investors in China

Another problem for foreign investors in China is that there are two separate legal systems which govern foreign investment.[32] Most countries have special regulations which set out the procedures under which a foreign company can invest in the host country and specify the forms and types of investment, special incentives and so on. Once approved, however, the foreign invested enterprise will be regulated by the general laws of the host country which apply equally to domestic companies. In China, foreign investment laws not only set out the conditions and procedures under which foreign investment is permitted, they also lay down the forms of the enterprise so created and include special laws pertaining to foreign invested ventures on matters of foreign exchange, tax, accounting and labour related issues, for example.

The scope of laws and regulations specific to foreign invested enterprises is therefore greater than that found in most other countries. Domestic laws are applied when there are no specific regulations in China laying down how a foreign invested enterprise is to handle a legal problem. The result is that when a legal issue arises, the management of foreign invested enterprises must first ascertain whether there is a law or regulation on that issue which relates specially to foreign invested enterprises.

This problem will exist throughout China's transition from a planning to a market system. Although, since the mid-1990s, China has been talking about treating foreign invested enterprises in the same way as domestic enterprises (the so-called *Guo Min Dai Yu*), most existing domestic laws and regulations may not be suited for foreign invested enterprises. Domestic laws have mostly been designed to regulate transactions within a state-planned system, whereas those specific to FDI have been designed to approximate the legal relationships found in western market economies, often with foreign investors' expectations in mind. Laws and regulations specific to FDI in China often contain favourable clauses that do not apply to domestic enterprises (hence many Chinese companies form joint ventures with foreign investors not to obtain new technologies or foreign capital, but to gain particular concessions and preferential treatments that only apply to foreign invested enterprises![33]).

Since the mid-1990s, China has begun to change the situation by phasing out some of the favourable treatment of foreign invested enterprises. As has been discussed in Chapter 3, China announced in late 1995 that it would introduce a sweeping tax reform for foreign invested enterprises in China – the first step in a general overhaul of preferential tax policies for foreign investors. Under the old regime, foreign invested joint ventures pay 15 per cent corporate tax in special economic zones, 24 per cent in the 400 or so 'open areas', and 30 per cent elsewhere, compared with a 55 per cent tax for state owned enterprises. This tax system would gradually be replaced by a flat 30 per cent national corporate tax plus local taxes on top for everyone. Exemptions on equipment import by foreign invested enterprises would also be abolished.[34]

This tax reform would be accompanied by a series of other measures including tariff cuts; increased convertibility of the Chinese currency; the elimination of many import quotas and controls; and the easing of restrictions on operations by foreign invested enterprises in China.[35] These measures are part of China's effort to satisfy the conditions for its entry to the World Trade Organization (WTO), and it is also part of China's wider reform on the tax system to harmonize national corporate tax and to improve local taxation systems. Gradually, foreign investors will have to compete with Chinese companies on equal ground.[36] Eventually all companies will be treated in the same way in China no matter who owns them, although this objective will take time to achieve. As the body of laws concerning foreign investment continues to grow, as China obtains more experience in developing FDI-related legislation, as more pressure is put on the Chinese authorities by foreign investors to resolve various problems and, most of all, as China is gradually transformed from a planning to a market system, the vagueness of Chinese laws in the area of foreign investment will undoubtedly be reduced gradually. Nevertheless, the strong influence of Chinese historical tradition and culture in this area will remain, making China's legal environment distinctively different from that in the West.

It should be pointed out that the ambiguity in FDI-related laws in China is not necessarily a bad thing for foreign investors, because it allows various local authorities more room to formulate local regulations in order to address specific issues arising from particular foreign investment projects. Back in the mid-1980s, many problems associated with the vagueness of the joint venture legislation were addressed partially in the 1983–84 Regulations and more thoroughly in the October 1986 Provisions and some subsequently implemented laws and regulations,[37] but the most important steps were taken by various municipal and provincial governments, which produced detailed local regulations to guide the implementation of national laws and provisions in different localities (see Chapter 3).

China has been making other efforts to improve the transparency of the legal system. On 11 November 1988, the *China Daily* (pp. viii–ix) reported that the State Council would stop issuing regulations on the restricted official red letterhead (the 'internal rules'), and would have them publicly printed and distributed (although the time scale for enforcing this rule was not specified). In order to do that, the Chinese government clearly needed to improve its legal system in the area of foreign trade and investment. A series of new laws and regulations has since been promulgated, and by the mid-1990s major laws and regulations were enforced in all areas, including not only foreign investment, but also international trade and economic contract, intellectual property protection (trademarks, patents, computer software protection and so on), finance and banking, taxation, transportation, custom, public security, employment and many others.[38]

China also signed over 100 trade agreements with foreign countries, 72 investment protection agreements, and a whole series of multilateral treaties and agreements. Wu Yi, China's Trade Minister, reiterated that the Chinese government would do its utmost to protect the authority, impartiality and transparency of the law. In the area of foreign trade and investment, China would abolish all local rules and regulations issued by various local authorities and departments, and abandon all 'internal rules'. She said that in spite of the significant achievements in establishing a coherent and transparent legal framework in the area of foreign economic relations, problems do exist in enforcing these laws and regulations, which form a major obstacle to the further development of China's international economic relations. It was the intention of the Chinese central government to remove this obstacle.[39] Only time would tell to what extent such promises would be delivered.

The legal environment in China

It has been a great achievement by the Chinese authority to develop a large body of laws and a coherent legal framework within a relatively short period of time. Despite various problems, the available evidence suggests that the future of China's legal environment in the area of foreign investment is encouraging. The starting point of all laws in the area of foreign investment is to provide adequate protection of the interests and rights of foreigners in China through legalization and normalization, under the principle of equality and mutual benefits. Only so will China be able to attract more foreign investment and further its opening up policy. At the moment, considerable ambiguities still exist in many foreign investment laws in China. However, such ambiguities are double-edged swords which could be harmful to foreign investors but could also be used to their advantage.

HUMAN RESOURCE RELATED PROBLEMS

Human resource related problems for foreign invested enterprises have been widely reported in China in recent years.[40] Some of these problems are institutionally originated (that is, they have been primarily derived from the existing political regime and economic structure in China), while others are culturally rooted. Since culture tends to change at a slower pace than political and economic systems, culturally rooted problems are generally more difficult to resolve. In contrast, institutionally originated problems can be resolved quickly once the underpinning political and economic factors are removed.[41] In reality, institutional and cultural factors are often closely intertwined with each other. As the transformation from a planning to a market system in China accelerates, some existing problems will disappear but new problems will emerge.

According to the survey by the Economist Intelligence Unit and Andersen Consulting, the number one headache for many foreign invested enterprises in China in the 1990s is to find and to keep quality managerial and technical staff.[42] Similar concerns have been expressed in several other studies.[43] Since the Chinese partner of a joint venture is usually a state owned enterprise in the same industry, the most common source of labour for joint ventures is the local Chinese partner, and sometimes the Chinese partner insists that the joint venture should take on at least a portion of its workforce. Staff drawn from the local partner are relatively easy to recruit and are already skilled in the industry, and when the partnership is strong, the Chinese partner often selects good workers for the joint venture. However, there are also cases where the local Chinese partner is a strong competitor with its own brands, therefore the local partner is reluctant to release its best workers and instead views the joint venture as an opportunity to unload excess workers. Another problem is that the partner's employees rarely have any knowledge or experience of western management techniques, and sometimes there are difficulties with transferring employee loyalty to the joint venture from the Chinese parent. Also, if most employees are drawn from the Chinese partner, the joint venture may inherit the power and social structure of the Chinese partner, which may become a strong opposing force to creating a new organizational culture in the joint venture.

Today, foreign invested enterprises (including joint ventures) are allowed to recruit staff through other channels, including university recruitment, local labour bureaux, foreign service enterprise corporations, personnel exchange centres, job fairs, executive search firms (head-hunting) and personal contacts. These enterprises are free to advertise in local newspapers and conduct interviews, written examinations and psychological tests to select the most suitable candidates. However, finding the right people is not easy, and once they are found, transferring them from their old employers may not be straightforward if a recruit's work unit does not support the transfer. For example, the old employer may refuse to release the individual's personal file, which contains the employee's personal information such as official civil status, working identity, professional and salary ranks, educational and working history. Without the file, the employee faces the risk of being cut off from the state enterprise system and its lifetime welfare and other benefits. Therefore, failing to obtain the file deters the recruit from taking up the new job.

Transferring a new recruit from another city or locality is even more complicated, involving over 20 approvals from the labour bureau, the public security unit (police), the recruit's work unit, the employer of the recruit's spouse and other civil authorities controlling residence registration, housing and food supply allocation. Obtaining these approvals often depends on *guanxi* and a wide range of other factors (such as the political clout of the recruit's old employer, the political standing of the Chinese partner of the joint venture, the profile of the foreign investor, and the new recruit's own *guanxi*). Sometimes, the foreign investor may need to pay some compensation to the previous employer for the training and education provided to the recruit, which can range from 2000 to 10 000 yuan per worker.[44]

Once the right people are found and successfully employed, it is not always an easy task to keep them. Many investors are attracted to China by the low labour costs, but the whole remuneration package is often more expensive than many investors have expected. The complete wage package consists of basic wage plus bonuses as well as a wide range of subsidies including social security, housing benefits and so forth. As will be discussed in more detail later in this chapter, the provision of a wide range of subsidies to employees is a distinctive feature of the Chinese enterprise system. Under socialist principles, state and collective enterprises have to achieve a wide range of social welfare objectives in addition to meeting production quotas. A large state owned enterprise often has staff quarters, schools, hospitals as well as other social structures attached to it. Employees in the state owned sector, as well as their immediate family, are entitled to such subsidies. Therefore, in order to keep the best employees, foreign invested enterprises may have to consider other incentives, such as housing, medical insurance, overseas training opportunities, clear career progression route, and pleasant working conditions. Financial incentives alone will not be sufficient to keep skilled employees.

Annual wage increase has been very high for skilled workers, which in China averaged 35 per cent in 1993 and 1994, and no less than 25 per cent in 1995 and 1996. Even so there was no guarantee of keeping the best employees.[45] The labour market remains underdeveloped and wide disparities exist between similar jobs even in the same location. This problem is not unique to China, and rapid pay rise and frequent job hopping by managerial and technical staff were also found by foreign investors in other Far East economies such as Thailand.

Hiring the right employees and keeping them is not easy in China, and it is probably even more difficult to fire them. Although foreign investors possess the legal power to dismiss workers – either because the work quality is poor or because of the changing workload of production, in reality this can prove extremely difficult. China has been a society where life-long employment is the norm, and the dismissal of a worker is regarded as one of the most severe punishments of any Chinese person and his/her family. In fact, in the state owned sector, a worker was virtually immune from dismissal, and only those who made serious mistakes or committed crimes and were sentenced by the court would be dismissed.

Once a worker has been dismissed, it is quite unlikely that they will be able to obtain a proper job again in the state owned sector, because people will naturally believe they had made some unforgivable mistakes or committed crimes, so that the organization would rather employ someone else of inferior abilities. Therefore, the dismissal of a worker is an exceptional event, which destroys the worker's reputation and could possibly render them unemployable in the state sector for life. This situation has changed somewhat as the private sector continues to grow rapidly and as the state sector is being reformed. Since the early 1990s, the labour system in China has been moving away from permanent employment to a system of contract labour supplemented by unemployment and pension insurance, which may serve to speed up the development of the labour market in China.[46] This will be especially so with the implementation of radical reforms since the mid-1990s. However, people's perception of this issue and the permanent-employment mentality of socialism will only change slowly.

According to the joint venture regulations, a joint venture may dismiss employees who have become redundant as a result of changes in production and technical conditions, or who, after training, still fail to meet new work requirements and are not suitable for transfer to other types of work in the company. The management of joint ventures may also take disciplinary actions, which include dismissal, against workers who have violated the venture's rules and caused serious consequences. However, a joint venture is unable to dismiss workers entirely on its own and has to notify the relevant government department in charge of the venture and the local labour bureau. The venture's trade union must also be given advance notice and it has the right to protest against the dismissal.

Until the mid-1990s, a foreign invested enterprise could either sign individual labour contracts directly with their employees, or a collective labour contract with the venture's trade union. In 1996, the All-China Federation of Trade Unions (ACFTU), the top council of China's fifteen industrial trade unions, demanded that all foreign invested enterprises sign collective labour contracts.[47] Although trade unions are not mandatory in enterprises with foreign investment, the workers have the right to establish trade unions and carry out union activities in accordance with Chinese trade union laws.[48] Of all foreign invested enterprises in China, about 46 000 of them had established trade unions by the end of 1995. Only 2300 of them signed collective labour contracts in 1995, and ACFTU's target was a total of 13 800 by the end of 1996. The growing presence of trade unions in foreign invested enterprises makes the dismissal of workers more difficult.[49]

Also, when signing a contract with an existing Chinese firm to set up a joint venture, the foreign investor is often under pressure to agree that all existing workers will be kept on. Under Chinese law, the Chinese partner is responsible for making arrangements for all retrenched staff – which can be such a large expense that often the Chinese partner would rather live with the problems of over-staffing. For example, in the case of Chrysler and the Beijing Jeep Corporation (BJC), although the Chinese workers are on three-year renewable or non-renewable contracts to BJC, the firing of a worker is an exceptional event and the extent to which the management can direct their staff is limited.[50] Consequently, the labour discipline is poor, and labour productivity is much lower than in Chrysler's other ventures elsewhere. Moreover, just as Chrysler consistently pressed BJC for labour force reduction, Beijing Municipality consistently pressed BJC to hire more workers because of the large excess supply of local labour in Beijing (this is in fact a major nation-wide problem). The solution to this conflict is that BJC takes on fifty new workers each year but the decision on the allocation of these workers is BJC's.

As a result, if the foreign invested enterprise is dissatisfied with the workers' quality, the best option offered by Andersen Consulting is to institute training programmes.[51] Attempts to send them back to the Chinese partner or to fire workers are likely to create deep rifts in the partner relationship unless there is a specific agreement to do so. If dismissed workers came from the Chinese partner of a joint venture, they have to go back to their original work unit which may have a hard time in allocating them jobs – given the general situation of over-staffing in state owned enterprises in China. If the worker was hired through other channels, the worker may have to go back to their legal place of residence, register with the local labour bureau as unemployed and wait for another job. The resistance from the Chinese partner or the local labour bureau to dismissing workers is thus understandably strong.

The general implications from the above discussions are that foreign investors in China should be extremely careful about employing or dismissing workers. As the Chinese government gradually breaks the 'iron rice bowl' in state owned organizations, the perception of Chinese workers of this issue will change and the situation will gradually improve. However, even though a new employment system can be established quickly,[52] the mentality of the 'iron rice bowl' employment system will remain – especially when the social security system of the market economy is still not fully in place in China.[53] Our view is that the change will take considerable time to accomplish. Indeed, it is even doubtful whether China's labour market will eventually resemble that of the West. Similar views have been expressed by a number of other authors.[54]

It follows that, in the near future at least, all foreign investors should treat labour-related issues with great care, and appreciate the ideological differences between China and the West which are the roots of many difficulties facing foreign investors. Many well-tested theories and techniques in the West will simply not work in the same fashion in China. Firing some workers probably would improve labour productivity, but at the same time it might provoke passive resistance from the remaining workers, and the fact that the same could happen to them in the future could lead to short-termism in their attitude and behaviour, and the more talented employees may take their first opportunity to leave for more stable or better paid jobs.

Other human resource problems for foreign invested enterprises in China include frequent misunderstandings between foreign expatriates and Chinese employees, which can arise from a number of causes. In Chapter 5, we pointed out that over forty years of Communist education and the strong influence of the so-called 'Party culture' have genuinely convinced many Chinese workers that the foreign capitalists have only come to China to make profit by exploiting them through employment. Productivity improvements from re-allocation of jobs on production lines may be interpreted as tactics to squeeze more energy from the workers. The fact that most foreign expatriates earn several hundred times the annual salary and benefits of Chinese workers has confirmed their suspicion, and caused resentment, passive resistance and mistrust.[55] Also, due to the relative lack of understanding of Chinese traditions and culture by some expatriates, they have been known to damage well-established relations and hurt people's feelings without even realising it. In China, protecting one's 'face' is an extremely serious matter and damaged relationships are extremely hard to repair. Some related issues have been discussed in Chapter 5.

OTHER ISSUES

Apart from the aforementioned problems, there is a wide range of other issues concerning China's soft investment environment. Some of these problems are associated with China's transition from a planning to a market system, while others are related to the political regime (the one Party system), the economic system (industrial governance, resource allocation), social structure and culture (*guanxi* in particular) in China.

Social security and welfare

This issue has been mentioned briefly in the last section. Reforming China's social security and welfare system is essential for China's enterprise reform, and it also has profound implications for foreign invested enterprises. China has a tradition that large organizations supply a whole range of social security and welfare to their employees. Many large organizations have to serve all the needs of their employees and their families, including housing, medical care, pension, insurance, kindergartens and schools for employees' children, all sorts of stores and shops, staff canteens and many other services. Most such services are heavily subsidized by the organization and many of them are almost free of charge. Obtaining such services elsewhere can be very expensive. Such employee benefits not only add enormous costs to the organization but also demand considerable management attention. The level of such services provided is extremely important to people's perception and attitude towards the organization. Without reforming this system, the financial and social burdens on enterprises are simply too heavy for them to bear in a market system, and the transition from planning to market cannot proceed.[56]

The general implication is that if a foreign investor intends to obtain the best people available in China, it needs to either pay an exceptionally high salary (in Chinese terms, but which may still be very low compared with the salary levels in the West or even elsewhere in Asia), or provide them with some of these services, and make arrangements for their long-term security and welfare. In China, what 'salary' means is the net income (take-home pay) after the deduction for social security and welfare and tax. If a foreign investor does not intend to provide such services to its Chinese employees, the costs of obtaining such services elsewhere should be added on top of their salaries – which could be significantly higher than the perceived pay levels in China. A good understanding of such issues is extremely important to attracting and keeping good employees, setting realistic salary levels and, most of all, securing employee loyalty to the organization.

Bureaucratism and corruption

Bureaucratism has been a long-standing problem in the Chinese government and state owned enterprises, and this problem has been derived directly from the political and economic systems in China. Foreign investors are often not clear which department to turn to when there is a specific problem. In most places, the efficiency of government bodies is low, and the procedures for approving a contract or solving even the simplest problem can be extremely complicated and time-consuming.[57] This problem was particularly serious during the first half of the 1980s but has since been improving slowly.[58] Most places have now set up specialized units centrally responsible for the management of foreign investment and for providing relevant services to foreign investors.

In some localities, foreign investment laws and regulations are implemented in a way that was not intended by the central government, and local regulations are often insufficiently specified, all of which may add to the difficulties during the negotiation of a contract or in solving a specific problem. Bureaucratism and low efficiency are quite commonplace in many Chinese government bodies, and when there is a problem, many related authorities deny their responsibilities and push the problems around between different departments, which adds to the difficulties and time needed to solve the problem. This actually reinforces the importance of *guanxi* in China.

Closely related to bureaucratism is another serious problem – corruption. Because of the difficulties discussed above, personal connections and on-going relations (*guanxi*) are very often more important than laws and regulations in speeding up decision-making in the relevant authorities or in resolving a problem. This phenomenon is deeply rooted in the culture and political regime in China, which has been discussed in detail in Chapter 5. Bribery is an effective way to initiate and maintain *guanxi*, and some Chinese people seek personal gains or accept bribes by taking advantage of their power to grant a contract or solve a business-related problem. Cases of this kind have been widely reported.

This problem has, however, been recognized by the Chinese authorities at various levels, and a series of actions have been taken against bureaucratism and corruption. Through the decentralization of decision-making, the approval process for foreign investment has been simplified to reduce bureaucratism. Competition between local authorities for FDI has further eased the approval process, as complicated approval procedures and bureaucratism will reduce the flow of the much desired foreign investment into a region.

For example, Jiangsu Province, by simplifying the approval procedures and decentralizing decision-making, granted an average of three new foreign investment projects each day in 1991.[59] In the early 1990s, 'Pudong speed' became a popular phrase in Shanghai, owing to the high efficiency of Pudong local authority in resolving problems for foreign investors.[60] Today, the procedures of project approval and problem resolution in the area of FDI in China have been simplified in most regions, but bureaucratism and corruption have remained in this and many other areas. These problems are deeply rooted in the political and economic regimes of contemporary China and are closely related to contemporary Chinese culture – and as a result, they probably cannot be resolved in the short, or even the medium, term.

To sum up: in this chapter, we have examined several operational problems that have been encountered by foreign investors with China's soft environment, including their historical evolution, the current situation and future prospects. The list of problems is far from exhaustive and these problems themselves have been rapidly evolving. Today, some problems discussed in this chapter have been significantly improved (for example, foreign exchange shortage); some are in the process of being resolved (for example, the simplification of approval procedures for foreign investment); but some deeply rooted problems (for example, bureaucratism and corruption in local government) will probably remain for a long time. Many new problems are also emerging which need to be considered when assessing the quality of China's investment environment.

These problems have been derived from many sources. Some of them are integral to the transition of China from a centrally planned economy to a market system, and their ultimate improvement will depend on the wider economic and political reform in China as a whole. Other problems have their roots in Chinese culture and social structure, and some are closely related to China's level of development. To maintain its rapid growth of the past two decades, China needs to redouble its efforts in attracting high quality FDI, which in turn requires China to improve the investment environment for foreign investors and address their concerns. Nevertheless, some problems will probably remain for a long time to come, which foreign investors will have to learn to live with, or find ways to get around them. *Guanxi* may be particularly important in resolving operational problems with China's soft environment.

CONCLUSIONS: THE MAIN FEATURES OF THE INVESTMENT ENVIRONMENT FOR FDI IN CHINA

We have now examined China's investment environment for FDI in three chapters, and in particular many problems encountered by foreign investors in China were analysed, as well as their broad background, main sources, current situation and future prospects. Problems with China's foreign investment environment have been derived from several sources. The main ones include China's general level of economic development, the accumulated underdevelopment in certain aspects (for example, transportation) over the years, the extremely rapid growth in demand (which is often faster than new developments), the unique social structure and culture in Chinese society and, most of all, China's transition from planning to market economy. Our analyses suggested that China's hard environment will continue to improve in the foreseeable future. New investments from a wide variety of sources – including foreign direct investment – will serve to further speed up the process of development in energy supply, transportation, telecommunications, and other infrastructure. Although many problems with the hard environment discussed in the book will not go away overnight – indeed, the condition of some infrastructure in certain areas will probably deteriorate in the short term due to the even more rapid growth in demand – it will probably only be a matter of time before most problems are resolved. We are modestly optimistic about the medium- to long-term future of the hard environment.

The historical and political analyses suggested that the reform and opening up in China is going to continue, and the unique culture and social structure in Chinese society will continue to affect the operation and management of foreign invested enterprises. A critical factor for doing business in China – *guanxi* – was highlighted and its cultural and institutional roots were analysed. A series of evolving problems encountered by foreign investors with China's soft environment were also discussed. Although most tactical problems with the soft environment can be resolved relatively easily, many politically or socially sensitive problems cannot be resolved without further political and economic reform in China.

So far, China has benefited enormously from the reform and opening up, and the living standards of the Chinese people have been rising very rapidly. This is in sharp contrast with some Eastern European countries – in particular, the civil war and disintegration of Yugoslavia and the end of the Soviet Union. However, the next stage of China's reform will not be easy, because many difficult reforms have been deliberately delayed in the past in order to preserve political and social stability. China's transition from planning to market has now reached a stage such that many problems cannot be deferred any longer. Although China intends to carry out such reforms through a gradualist approach, it is increasingly doubtful whether some problems can be resolved this way. How to continue the reform and opening up programme whilst maintaining political and social stability remains the most difficult challenge facing the Chinese government: the way it handles these issues will significantly affect China's soft environment.

Since 1978, FDI has played a critical role in China's rapid economic development. To continue its success the Chinese authority will have to significantly improve the quality of its hard and soft investment environment. Whilst major capital injection from a wide variety of sources can speed up the construction of China's national infrastructure (that is, the hard environment), the 'reactive policy making' of the 1980s and early 1990s will certainly not attract enough high quality FDI to fuel China's rapid growth. Major new policy initiatives would be needed to further improve the soft environment and address the concerns of foreign investors – some of which call for radical reforms of the wider political, economic and social systems in China.

Notes

1. For example, Pearson, Margaret M. (1991b) 'The erosion of controls over foreign capital in China 1979–1988', *Modern China*, Vol. 17, No. 1, January 1991; Pomfret, Richard (1991) *Investing in China: Ten years of the open door policy*, Harvester Wheatsheaf, New York; Bucknall,

Kevin (1989) *China and the Open Door Policy*, Allen and Unwin, North Sydney.

2. Frisbie, John (1988) 'Balancing foreign exchange', *The China Business Review*, March–April 1988, p. 25.

3. *The People's Daily* (Overseas edition), 29 November 1996, '*Renminbi* will become convertible on the current account from next month' (*Xia Yue Qi Shi Xian Ren Min Bi Jing Chang Xiang Mu Ke Dui Huan*), p. 1; *The Financial Times*, 29 November 1996, 'China moves to Yuan convertibility', p. 4.

4. For example, Pearson, Margaret M. (1991a), *Joint Ventures in the People's Republic of China*, Princeton University Press, Princeton.

5. For example, Frisbie (1988) *op. cit.*

6. *Beijing Review*, 1986, Vol. 29, No. 43, p. 26.

7. *Ibid.*

8. Pomfret (1991) *op. cit.*

9. *The Financial Times*, 3 June 1993.

10. *The People's Daily* (Overseas edition), 24 Sept 1994, 'Constructing the basic framework for the new building: Past experience and future prospect in reforming China's economic regime this year' (*Gou Zhu "Xin Da Sha" De Ji Ben Kuan Jia – Jin Nian Jing Ji Ti Zhi Gai Ge De Hui Gu Yu Zhan Wang*), p. 1.

11. *The People's Daily* (Overseas edition), 4th April 1994; 20th April 1994.

12. *The Financial Times*, 20 November 1995, 'China plans reforms to break trade stalemate: Beijing to cut tariffs and ease investment rules in attempt to join WTO', p. 1.

13. Total foreign exchange reserves exceeded US$100 billion by November 1996. *The Financial Times*, 21 June 1996, 'China advances plans for convertible yuan', p. 4; *The People's Daily* (Overseas edition), 30 November 1996, 'China's foreign exchange reserve exceeded 100 billion US dollars' (*Zhong Guo Wai Hui Chu Bei Tu Puo Qiang Yi Mei Yuan*), p. 1.

14. *The Financial Times*, 21 June 1996, *op. cit.*; *The People's Daily* (Overseas edition), 21 June 1996, 'Foreign invested enterprises will buy and sell foreign exchange through the banking system, making yuan fully convertible on the current account before the end of the year' (*Wai Zi Qi Yie Jiang Shi Xian Yin Hang Jie Shou Hui, Jin Nian Nian Di Qian Shi Xian Ren Min Bi Jing Chang Xiang Mu Ke Dui Huan*), p. 1.

15. *The People's Daily* (Overseas edition), 29 November 1996, *op. cit.*; *The Financial Times*, 29 November 1996, *op. cit.*

16. *The Financial Times*, 21 June 1996, *op. cit.*

17. Martinsons, Maris and Paul Hempel (1995) 'Chinese management systems: Historical and cross-cultural perspectives', *Journal of Management Systems* 7(1): 1–11, special issue on *Management in Greater China*.

18. Brown, Ronald C. (1993) 'The role of the legal environment in doing business in the People's Republic of China' in Kelley, Lane and Oded Shenkar (eds) *International Business in China*, Routledge, London: pp. 63–87.

19. Kenworthy, James L. (1989) *A Guide to the Laws, Regulations and*

Policies of the People's Republic of China on Foreign Trade and Investment, William S. Hein and Co, Buffalo, New York.

20. Martinsons and Hempel (1995), *op. cit.*; Brown (1993) *op. cit.*
21. Cheng, Jing (1992) 'A summary of the development of the investment environment in open areas' (*Kai Fang Di Qu Tou Zi Huan Jing Fa Zhan Gai Shu*). *The People's Daily* (Overseas edition), 24 January 1992.
22. Brown (1993) *op. cit.*
23. Cohen, J. (1988) 'Legal framework for investment' in Lawson, E. (ed.) *US-China Trade: Problems and Prospects*, Praeger, New York; Kenworthy (1989) *op. cit.*
24. Kenworthy (1989) *op. cit.*
25. Hall, Edward T. (1981) *Beyond Culture*, Doubleday, New York; Schuster, Camille P. and Michael J. Copeland (1996) *Global Business: Planning for sales and negotiations*, The Dryden Press, Harcourt Brace College Publishers, Fort Worth.
26. *Ibid.*
27. For example, Kleinberg, Robert (1990) *China's Opening to the Outside World*, Westview Press, Boulder; Child, J. (1994) *Management in China during the Age of Reform*, Cambridge University Press, Cambridge.
28. The Economist Intelligence Unit (EIU) and Andersen Consulting (1995) *Moving China Ventures out of the Red into the Black: Insights from best and worst performers*, The Economist Intelligence Unit, London.
29. Kleinberg (1990) *op. cit.*
30. Child (1994) *op. cit.*
31. The Economist Intelligence Unit (EIU) and Andersen Consulting (1995) *op. cit.*
32. Child (1994) *op. cit.*
33. *Ibid*; Andersen Consulting and the Economist Intelligence Unit (1995) *op. cit.*
34. *The People's Daily* (Overseas edition), 29 December 1995, 'China adjusts preferential tax policy for foreign invested enterprises: Creating better investment environment for foreign investors' (*Zhong Guo Tiao Zheng Wai Qi Shui Shou You Hui Zheng Ce Jiang Wei Wai Shang Chuang Zao Geng Hao Tou Zi Huan Jing*), p. 1.
35. *The Financial Times*, 20 November 1995, *op. cit.*
36. *The People's Daily* (Overseas edition), 29 December 1995, *op. cit.*
37. Pomfret (1991) *op. cit.*
38. *The People's Daily* (Overseas edition), 15 June 1996, 'A summary of Chinese laws in the area of foreign relations' (*Zhong Guo She Wei Fa Lu Gai Kuang*), by Zhang Shijin, p. 4.
39. *The People's Daily* (Overseas edition), 10 November 1995, 'China will intensify the construction of legal systems in the area of foreign trade and investment, improve the transparency and impartiality of laws' (*Zhong Guo Jiang Qiang Hua Wei Mao Fa Zhi Jian She Ti Gao Fa Lu Tong Yi Xing He Tou Ming Du*), p. 1.
40. For example, Tsang, Eric (1994) 'Human resource management problems in Sino-foreign joint ventures', *International Journal of Manpower* 15 (9/10): 4–21; Easterby-Smith, Mark, Danusia Malina and Lu Yuan (1995) 'How culture-sensitive is HRM? A comparative analysis of practice in

Chinese and UK companies', *The International Journal of Human Resource Management* 6(1): 31–59, February 1995; Warner, Malcolm (1996) 'Managing China's enterprise reforms: A new agenda for the 1990s', *Journal of General Management*, 21(3) Spring 1996: 1–18; The Economist Intelligence Unit and Andersen Consulting (1995) *op. cit.*; Child (1994) *op. cit.*; Tsang (1994) *op. cit.*

41. Tsang (1994) *op. cit.*; Child (1994) *op. cit.*
42. The Economist Intelligence Unit and Andersen consulting (1995) *op. cit.*
43. For example, Child (1994) *op. cit.*; Tsang (1994) *op. cit.;* Warner (1996) *op. cit.*
44. Tsang (1994) *op. cit.*
45. The Economist Intelligence Unit and Andersen Consulting (1995) *op. cit.*
46. Warner (1996) *op. cit.*, Sun, Jiuping (1996) 'Reforming China's social security system', *China Opening Herald*, 25 (7): 18–21.
47. *The People's Daily* (Overseas edition), 20 May 1996 'China demands foreign invested enterprises to sign collective labour contracts' (*Zhong Guo Yao Qiu Wai Qi Qian Ding Yong Gong Ji Ti He Tong*), p. 2.
48. Tsang (1995) *op. cit.*
49. *The People's Daily* (Overseas edition), 20 May 1996, *op. cit.*
50. Aiello, Paul (1991) 'Building a joint venture in China: The case of Chrysler and the Beijing Jeep Corporation', *Journal of General Management*, Vol. 17(2), Winter 1991.
51. The Economist Intelligence Unit and Andersen Consulting (1995) *op. cit.*
52. *The People's Daily* (Overseas edition), 19 April 1996, 'The labour contract employment system will be established throughout China before the end of the year' (*Wo Nian Nei Quan Mian Jian Li Lao Dong He Tong Zhi*), p. 1. *The People's Daily* (Overseas edition), 19 June 1996, 'China establishes new labour deployment system' (*Zhong Guo Jian Li Xin Xin Yong Gong Zhi Du*), p. 4.
53. *The People's Daily* (Overseas edition), 14 December 1995, 'The reform and development of China's social security system' (*Zhong Guo She Hui Bao Zhang Zhi Du De Gai Ge He Fa Zhan*), p. 1.
54. For example, Child (1994), *op. cit.*; Pomfret (1991) *op. cit.*; Chan, J.C.M., N.Y. Li and D. Sculli (1989) 'Labour relations and foreign investors in the Shenzhen special economic zone of China', *Journal of General Management*, Vol. 14(4), Summer 1989.
55. Aiello (1991) *op. cit.*; Chan *et al.* (1989) *op. cit.*; The Economist Intelligence Unit and Andersen Consulting (1995) *op. cit.*; Tsang (1994) *op. cit.*
56. *The People's Daily* (Overseas edition), 14 December 1995, *op. cit.*
57. Ji, Chongwei (1988) *op. cit.*
58. The Economist Intelligence Unit and Andersen Consulting (1995) *op. cit.*
59. *The People's Daily* (Overseas edition), 17 January 1992, p. 1.
60. *The People's Daily* (Overseas edition), 10 March 1992, p. 1.

7 Distribution, Marketing and Consumer Behaviour in China

For many foreign investors, one of the main attractions of China is its enormous market size and the even greater potential for future growth (See Chapter 2). With the Chinese economy growing at about 10 per cent a year for nearly two decades, a new market roughly the size of Hong Kong, Taiwan and Singapore combined has been created annually.[1] However, as some foreign investors have found out, getting products to consumers is a daunting task in China, and special marketing approaches are often needed to meet the unique Chinese consumer behaviour.

Since China is still in the midst of the transition from a centrally planned economy to a market system, the newly established consumer market has been characterized by dramatic fluctuations and rapid changes. China in area is almost as large as the continent of Europe, with enormous regional differences in income levels and consumer preferences. The poor transportation infrastructure, the rigid and unreliable state distribution systems, and the fragmented and rapidly evolving retail systems, have together made it very difficult for producers to get products to customers efficiently and in the right condition. The economy has been growing very rapidly, and as people get rich they develop new tastes, new preferences, and new desires for purchases. So, a fashionable item in high demand today could become out of fashion tomorrow.[2] Many foreign investors failed to anticipate the enormous difficulties with distribution, marketing and the volatile market fluctuations in China, which has resulted in the failure of an increasing number of foreign invested enterprises.[3]

This chapter will briefly outline the main characteristics in distribution, marketing and consumer behaviour in China, and highlight their implications for foreign invested enterprises. In particular, it will examine some practical problems which foreign investors encountered in China and shed some light on how they should go about dealing with such problems.

DISTRIBUTION AND SALES IN CHINA

Before the reform in China in the late 1970s, the distribution and sale of industrial and consumer goods were monopolized by the state. The Ministry of Commerce held overall responsibility for regulating the supply of consumer goods, while the Ministry of Materials and Equipment controlled the supply of industrial goods. Under these Ministries, there were specialized corporations divided along product lines to handle different categories of goods. The distribution of consumer goods had three main tiers.[4] The first tier consisted of three offices in Tianjin, Shanghai and Guangzhou, reporting to the Ministry of Commerce in Beijing and their respective local bureaux of commerce. These offices purchased goods from all over China and accepted imported goods, and then distributed the goods to the second tier – the provincial offices, normally located in the provincial capitals. These second tier offices then distributed goods purchased from the three main offices to the third tier wholesalers located in different cities and counties. These wholesalers then distributed the goods to local retailers (mostly state owned). The supply and distribution of goods in rural areas was under the control of the Supply and Sale Co-operatives (*Gong Xiao She*). The distribution system for industrial goods was very similar, although the control by the state was often even tighter.

Since the reform, the Chinese economy has moved some way from a centrally planned to a more market oriented and more decentralized economy. As this transition continues, the old distribution system in China is increasingly unable to cater for the market demands both in trade volume and commodity variety. A number of changes have thus been introduced. The state monopoly for the distribution of industrial and consumer goods (with some exceptions) has been relaxed; and alongside the multi-tiered state distribution system, private individuals, collectives, producers and other government units are increasingly allowed to buy and sell certain products freely. Foreign invested enterprises (as well as domestic companies) no longer have to rely on the state-controlled wholesale channels to market their products, and they are increasingly allowed to seek customers directly. In March 1993, the Ministry of Materials and Equipment and the Ministry of Commerce were merged to form the Ministry of Domestic Trade, and since then the state distribution system has been radically restructured. The members of the state distribution system have been allowed more freedom in choosing their suppliers, and more importantly they are also allowed to own and use self-raised funds and to determine the prices of their commodities within the range set by the state.

Today, the distribution system in China is extremely complex, and the options available to manufacturers vary from product to product, and from locality to locality. Child used some examples to explain the extremely complex distribution channels for industrial goods (for example, chemicals), branded goods (for example, food, alcohol) and non-branded consumables (for example, milk, vegetables), and highlighted some of the major changes introduced since the reform started.[5] For many products, the state distribution channel is still the most important, but numerous other channels have been opened up since the early 1980s through decentralization and relaxation of control. In particular, control over the distribution of many branded goods and non-branded consumables has been greatly relaxed.

For example, since the early 1990s, there has been virtually no restriction on the direct marketing within China of branded consumer goods by manufacturers, so long as they secure a licence from the relevant local authority. The manufacturers can choose which goods are to be sold where, what promotions to undertake and how payment is to be made. State owned enterprises still face restrictions on export marketing but they can choose any foreign trade organization in China to import and export for them. Joint ventures can export directly without having to go through a foreign trade organization in China.

The retail system has also been reformed. Most state owned retail outlets are now managed under the so-called 'contract responsibility system' (*Cheng Bao Zhi*), and they are allowed to select their sources of supplies and are responsible for their own profits and losses. The fixed price on most commodities has been abolished and now suppliers and retailers are free to vary their prices within a certain range. The wholesale industry also boomed because of the increasing demand from retailers, although most non-state wholesalers are small. In the 1990s, foreign investors are allowed to set up their own marketing and distribution channels, and in particular, they are allowed to enter joint ventures in the retail industry to sell products directly to consumers.[6] The wholesale trade is not open to foreign investors, but control over this is likely to be relaxed soon.

Despite the reforms and the relaxation of state control over distribution and sales in China, foreign invested enterprises still have to face serious challenges. As has been discussed in Chapter 4, China's transportation infrastructure is both underdeveloped and inefficient, and this makes the movement of goods in a country as large as China very difficult. The highway system is underdeveloped and fragmented, and most distributors have to rely on the railway for long-distance transport. The main capacity of the railway system has been allocated to passenger traffic and strategic commodities such as coal and agricultural products that are still under state control, which leaves the distributors of other goods to fight for the remaining capacity. Those maintaining good *guanxi* with the local railway authorities can often receive better services, but maintaining such *guanxi* requires time, effort and money, and the favours from the railway authorities must be repaid by various means. Moreover, the slow and unreliable rail and road systems can often cause companies, particularly those producing fragile or easily perishable products, serious problems.

Just as in most other markets, having an efficient distribution system is essential for the success of foreign invested enterprises in China. Because the state owned distribution system is not capable of moving consumer and industrial goods either efficiently or according to demand, many companies – particularly foreign invested enterprises – are often left with the job of constructing their own distribution systems. The Chinese economy has until recently been production rather than market driven, so few people in China are experienced with establishing such a system in a market environment. Foreign investors often have to work closely with Chinese partners to build sales forces to interface with distributors and customers, ensure the wholesalers are properly selected and managed, and work with the media to develop an effective brand image.[7]

The challenge of getting products to a large number of customers across the huge territory of China is made even more difficult by the highly dispersed and informal nature of China's retail and distribution systems. Companies often do not know where their goods are, when they will turn up, and in what condition. Some foreign invested enterprises do not even know how their products have reached certain areas in China![8] Direct sales to retail stores in China are not easy because of their large numbers and frequent changes of management and product lines, so most companies have to live with the multi-tiered distribution system. The problem is very often that the company has little control over who receives the goods, and in what condition. The enormous difficulties involved in developing one's own distribution system mean that this option is only suitable for very large companies or those operating in a limited geographical area. Other companies may have to learn to live with the existing systems. Constructing one's own distribution can also put a severe strain on management, because for each product and in each geographical area, the company must deal with a different set of distributors!

Today, the transition from a centrally planned to a regulated market system in China is only partially accomplished. Child pointed out that the duality of bureaucratic and market governance structures has created a context, combining institutionalized power and market forces, within which enterprises have to conduct their transactions.[9] Although market forces have developed in many areas, administrative agencies of the central and local governments still have considerable power in regulating prices and distribution channels, and they are also directly involved in the process of allocating the more strategic categories of supply and demand. Many foreign invested enterprises will have to develop their distribution strategy in this context, because the Chinese partners of most joint ventures in China are state owned enterprises, and even wholly foreign owned enterprises have to deal with state owned enterprises (suppliers and buyers) and other government agencies in China.

Since the mid-1990s, there have been some significant new developments which may ease the situation in distribution and sales for foreign invested enterprises in the future – such as the rapid development of large hypermarkets and 'cash and carries' in major metropolitan areas. This was made possible by the promulgation of the National Chain Stores Business Development Plan on 26 June 1995.[10] Several foreign investors have already responded to the new opportunities, such as the Dutch chain, Makro stores, and the Hong Kong based Districentre. Some foreign producers in China believed that the proliferation of such developments will change the way that retailing operates in China (as has happened in Taiwan and elsewhere around the world). At the moment, such developments have been confined to some large metropolitan areas in the coastal region, but as these hypermarkets and 'cash and carries' start to develop into chains nationally, they will be able to help manufacturers on more than just the local scale. This will provide a new option to foreign producers for getting their products to consumers around China.[11]

Today, most consumer goods manufacturers in China have set up comprehensive sales teams to work with wholesalers. The sales teams typically make the primary sales to the local wholesalers and distributors in each geographical area in China. The wholesalers then make the secondary sales and deliveries to the retail outlets.[12] In the big cities which are linked by highways, it is feasible for companies to distribute their products to the wholesalers by road. In other parts of China, where the highway network is not well developed, it is probably better for companies to use the state controlled distribution system. Some companies are actually using a combination of different channels for different regions.[13] The state controlled distribution system is inefficient and crumbling, but often has extensive networks and can ensure the products are carried in a wide range of retail outlets. Private wholesalers are booming and are often more efficient, but they tend to lack the range and scope of contacts possessed by large state owned wholesalers. For certain products, some foreign invested enterprises have used rather primitive but innovative sales methods. Avon, a cosmetics group, recruited 40 000 women in southern and eastern China to sell beauty products directly to their neighbours, friends and colleagues. These ladies often cycle for miles to pick up the products from various depots.[14]

To sum up, getting products to consumers is one of the greatest problems that producers face in China. The poor transportation infrastructure has created physical problems which are made worse by the slow, inefficient distribution systems and the small, fragmented retail systems. Regulations restricting foreign involvement in distribution have made it very hard for foreign invested enterprises to solve these problems by themselves. The state distribution systems which most manufacturers use are slow, inefficient and confusing. Other distribution channels are often more efficient but they tend to be small and fragmented. Although companies today have a series of options open to them, products often stay in the distribution pipeline for a long time. Unilever claimed that it can take as long as six weeks for its products to get to consumers.[15] The implications are very profound. On the one hand, getting a product out of the factory gate does not necessarily mean that the product is selling well. It takes time to fill up China's long and slow distribution pipeline, and constant low levels of stock could simply mean the product is sitting somewhere (rather than being sold)! On the other hand, a company has to anticipate market changes and plan production a long time in advance.

CONSUMER BEHAVIOUR AND MARKETING IN CHINA

The term *consumer* describes two different kinds of consuming entities – the personal consumer and the organizational consumer. Personal consumers buy goods and services for their own use, for the use of the household, or as a gift for a friend. Such goods and services are normally for final use by individuals. The organizational consumer (including business organizations, government agencies and institutions, and charities) buys products, services and equipment in order to run the organization.[16]

In China, the behaviours of both individual and organizational consumers are very different from those in the West, so foreign invested enterprises often need to adopt different marketing approaches if they intend to make their products appeal to Chinese consumers. Unlike much of the developed western world where consumption is a matter of routine, for many Chinese people consumption is a novel, pleasurable and important part of the day; and in pursuing this pleasure, they do not hesitate to spend as much as 80 per cent of their total income.[17] Chinese consumers have time to browse and will usually visit several shops before making a purchase, so choosing the right retailers and pricing the product properly are very complex tasks. The Chinese consumer market has been transformed from a seller's to a buyer's market since the reform.[18] However, the new market is still immature and fragile, and sometimes, very 'strange' consumer behaviours have been observed.

For example, in the early 1980s just before the Government relaxation of price control on a wide range of consumer goods, many people rushed out to various stores (most of them state owned) before the expected price increase. One couple we knew bought a variety of white goods (including a television, a washing machine, a bicycle, a sewing machine and an electric fan) for their three-year-old daughter as her dowry – marriage in China normally happens in people's twenties! Another family bought hundreds of bottles of soy sauce and vinegar and fifty kilograms of cooking salt for their own consumption! In fact, for a short period, the shelves in some stores became empty again for the first time since the reform. In the meantime, some early entrepreneurs, with their newly found 'wealth', purchased foreign-made products outrageously priced to demonstrate their wealth (they probably would not have bought them were the products priced cheaply, and similar behaviour was reported in the 1990s in Russia[19]). Many urban young people became brand crazy (and most of them still are), and they paid exceptionally high prices for fashionable western brands, often at the expense of sacrificing other basic consumption.

Today, the Chinese consumers have become more sophisticated and they are less impressed by brands, and many people are determined to find reliable supplies of high quality, good value products.[20] However, major differences in consumer behaviour still exist between China and the West, and those who try to apply well tested practices in product differentiation, shelf-space management and other techniques in China are likely to be disappointed (we will come back to this issue later in the chapter).[21] Any company wishing to deliver a product with the value, quality and convenience that will appeal to Chinese consumers needs to consider the unique characteristics of the Chinese market.[22] An increasing number of studies have been published in recent years on this topic.

Compared with individual consumers, organizational consumer behaviour in China is even more different from that in the West. Because China has been a socialist economy, people are used to receiving a wide range of services and welfare from the state via their employers. Many organizations regularly purchase a variety of products and services for their employees as part of the welfare or as bonuses, and such products can range from clothes and shoes to food and household appliances. Many organizations also regularly purchase various products and services to maintain *guanxi* with useful people, and the purchases for such purposes can include cars, furniture, electronic appliances, entertainment, health care, and even houses in some cases. Many such purchases are not reported, and some of them are even illegal. The exact amount of this type of organizational consumption is almost impossible to know, but one estimate puts the figure at US$16.6 billion per year, and it is rapidly growing.[23] Also, because of the nature and special purposes of such consumption, the products and services tend to be luxurious, expensive (even extravagant), and high quality.

Many legitimate purchases by organizations are also regularly used for private purposes. In 1993, China imported around 100 000 cars (officially), and 99 per cent of them were paid for by organizations. Many of these cars are regularly used for private purposes. Because cars are mainly purchased by organizations and the car is an important symbol of status, small hatchbacks or three-door cars are often not considered proper cars in China, which forced

Volkswagen to quietly shelve its Volkswagen Golf project.[24] The individual consumer behaviour has certainly been affected by this situation. Also, because the main car buyers are state owned organizations and government agencies, the car market in China is not as price sensitive as in many other markets. Shanghai Volkswagen sold its Santana saloon car at nearly twice the price it charged in the more open market of Brazil, and Santana is the most popular model in China and Volkswagen has over 50 per cent of the Chinese car market![25] The car market in China is probably more influenced by government regulations and restrictions on car usage in state organizations than by prices. The situation has been changing as the number of private car buyers increases, so foreign investors need to be aware of some of the unique features of Chinese consumer behaviour when entering the Chinese market.

How big is the Chinese consumer market?

Although China has a population of 1.2 billion, it has been increasingly recognized that China is also a poor country where the official per capita GDP was just over US$600 in 1995/1996. Even using methods such as purchasing power parity (PPP), the figure is still only US$2000–3000 (because the Chinese consumers pay low prices for most basic goods and services).[26] Over 70 per cent of China's population are rural farmers with tiny incomes, and the Economist Intelligence Unit (EIU) and Andersen Consulting report regarded '1.2 billion consumers' as the first myth about the Chinese market.[27]

The size of the Chinese consumer market is difficult to estimate. Reliable market information is extremely difficult to obtain – if available at all in China. The State Statistical Bureau alone employs 60 000 people to collect and analyse various economic data for central planning purposes, but market information is difficult to extract because it is scattered in various government agencies, commissions, ministries, national corporations and industrial councils. As a result, foreign investors often need to gather primary data by themselves or by using specialized consulting companies.[28] However, such studies tend to focus on specific geographical areas such as the largest cities, the special economic zones or certain parts of the coastal region. The first foreign-sponsored nation-wide survey of consumer behaviour and attitudes in China was conducted by the Gallup Organization in 1994 (data released in 1995).[29]

The Hong Kong Office of McKinsey, a management consultancy, estimated that in 1994 China had about 100 million people with an annual income of over US$1000, and this would increase to 270 million at the turn of the century. The figures suggested that China was not yet a market of 1.2 billion consumers, but in a few years time, the number of people who could afford basic foreign brand name products (for example, shampoo or toothpaste) would exceed the population of the USA![30] Similarly, the report of the Economist Intelligence Unit (EIU) and Andersen Consulting estimated that about 5 per cent of the 102 million Chinese urban households earn more 14 000 yuan a year (US$1683), permitting moderate to high consumption of durable and semi-durable goods. The London-based Henley Centre for Forecasting reckons that of the 220 million households in China, 45 million households (180–200 million people) will have enough income to buy mass market consumer goods by 2000.[31]

However, it should be noted that although the average income of Chinese people is exceptionally low, the proportion of their disposable income is high, because the state supplies, or at least subsidies, life's essentials and provides a wide range of social security and welfare free of charge. Yan estimated that Chinese people spend over 80 per cent of their income on various consumer goods, which together represent a huge market, although the per capita expenditure is low.[32] When housing is subsidized and cars and real estate prices are out of the reach of most people, they turn to products such as home electronics, clothes and foreign branded shampoos and detergents. Some people would save for years for such items as a good TV. Sometimes, they sacrifice other consumption in order to make a certain purchase. Also, many Chinese consumers are obsessed with the latest technology, and as will be discussed later in this section, to win the battle in the Chinese market, foreign investors increasingly have to use technology's cutting edge.

Chinese people like quality brand names, and many people are prepared to pay a 30–50 per cent premium over other popular brands – even if that means they have to delay their desired purchase for some time. Locally brewed and imported Carlsberg beer are sold side by side, but the imported ones command a 20–50 per cent premium. Many foreign products such as washing powder and shampoos have become best sellers in China. The profit margin for many high quality foreign brand products is also high compared with more mature markets, and most fast moving consumer goods command a gross margin of 18–25 per cent, compared with less than 10 per cent in the USA.[33]

Another factor which needs to be born in mind is that the Chinese market is fragmented and it has been said that China is really a collection of 30 or so economic entities, each with its own characteristics (which is partly responsible for the difficulties in distribution). A country-wide approach to the Chinese market is thus far too ambitious for most foreign investors. Most foreign consumer product companies are currently targeting 30–70 million consumers. The lower figure represents the population of the 3–5 largest cities in China, while the higher figure represents the 15–20 cities with over one million people. These people are relatively easy to reach, and the proportion of them with above-average income is higher than in medium and small cities and rural areas. These people also tend to be more open minded to new ideas and more willing to try out new products.

The ownership of consumer durables in China gives some idea of the real size of the Chinese market. The Gallup national survey in 1994[34] found that the proportion of households that own basic articles were as follows: bicycle (81 per cent); electric fan (63 per cent); black & white TV (54 per cent); colour TV (40 per cent); and washing machine (36 per cent). Also, 25 per cent of Chinese households own a refrigerator, 24 per cent own a hair dryer and 22 per cent own a steam iron. Other items include: camera (14 per cent); stereo (13 per cent); VCR (12 per cent); vacuum cleaner (6 per cent); food blender (4 per cent); air conditioner (4 per cent); dishwasher (3 per cent); clothes dryer (3 per cent); automobile (3 per cent); video camera (3 per cent); mobile phone (3 per cent); and microwave oven (3 per cent). For many items, the ownership is considerably higher among urban households. For example, compared with the national average of 25 per cent for refrigerators, the figure for urban households is 67 per cent, and for the nine largest cities it is 90 per cent. For colour TV, the national average figure was 40 per cent as compared with 83 per cent for urban households and 94 per cent for the nine largest cities. Similar tendencies were found for items such as cameras, vacuum cleaners, and air conditioners. Moreover, the purchase intention for many items was high. The proportion of households that made plans to buy in the next one or two years was (including replacing old ones): colour TV (31 per cent), washing machine (22 per cent), refrigerator (21 per cent), VCR (16 per cent) and stereo system (15 per cent).

So the ownership of household durables is likely to increase very rapidly.

These figures are considerably higher than for most other countries in the world when they had a per capita GDP of US$400 or even US$2000–3000! In fact, the ownership of certain items in the nine largest cities in China is already comparable with figures in the USA and Europe, although the income levels of these cities are considerably lower than the latter. For colour TV, the figure for the nine largest cities in China is 94 per cent compared with 97 per cent in the USA (national average) and 91 per cent in Europe; and for refrigerators, the figures are 90 per cent for the nine cities in China compared with 98 per cent (USA) and 97 per cent (Europe).

This represents a unique characteristic of the Chinese consumer market. Although the average income of Chinese people is low, they tend to have a high proportion of disposable income, and this income has been increasing rapidly. Also, the official or reported salaries of most people do not represent their total income, because many people get bonuses (often more than the basic salary!) regularly; and considerable individual consumption is hidden in organizational consumption accounts. The correlation between personal income level and desired purchases observed elsewhere may not apply in China. A product represents a better living standard and is affordable will quickly become a necessity in China, even if that means people have to suppress other consumption temporarily.

For example, the TV market in China was negligible before 1980, because few individuals could afford one. Since 1980, people's income has been increasing rapidly, and many people made purchasing a TV their households' first priority. To save for a good TV, some households even retrenched from other consumption. During most of the 1980s, the demand for TVs was overwhelming, so over one hundred TV manufacturers were set up (many of them joint ventures), which resulted in an over-capacity towards the end of the 1980s. Since 1990, the TV market has been characterized by strong competition, and consumer demand is changing from 'having a TV' to 'having a top brand TV with high specifications'. From the authors' own experience, most of our relatives bought their first 12 inch black and white TVs in the early 1980s, replaced them with 18 inch colour TVs in the mid-1980s (imported Japanese brands preferred), and in the early 1990s several families have changed to 28–32 inch flat screen colour TVs (imported or locally produced). People in rural areas tend to lag behind those in towns and cities for some five years with such demands, but their demands have also been upgrading rapidly.

The focus of consumer attention has also been changing as people get rich. Before 1980, the focus was on 'three big items' (*San Da Jian*), namely, bicycle, wrist watch, and sewing machine. After 1980, the focus shifted to 'six big items' (*Liu Da Jian*): TV, washing machine, refrigerator, VCR, camera and electric fan. Since the late 1980s and early 1990s, items such as an air conditioner, motorcycle, hi-fi system, telephone (mobile phone), home computer (PC), keyboard and piano also came onto people's buying lists. A small proportion of rich people began to look at items such as a house or car, investment and financial services (stock), occupational education, leisure and overseas travel, which probably will become the focus of urban citizens' desired purchase/consumption before the turn of the century.[35]

Euromonitor drew some parallels between the consumer markets in contemporary China and Japan in the 1950s.[36] It used an interesting figure to illustrate why consumption patterns tend to change dramatically (Figure 7.1). As people's purchasing power grows, demand tends to follow a certain pattern. However, demand does not rise in proportion to income gains but in a step-wise fashion. This means the growth of per capita income tends to trigger a disproportionately large increase in the sale of a particular set of products. Subsequent increases in income may bring only marginal gains in demand for the original set of products but have a larger impact on demand for an entirely different set of products. This to some extent explains the dramatic changes in consumer demand for certain products in the Chinese market. The implications for foreign investors targeting the Chinese market can be extremely profound.

Market segmentation and consumer behaviour in China

The Chinese market is highly segmented. Geographically China is an immense country with 30 provinces and autonomous regions, riddled with cultural differences, variations in natural conditions and levels of economic development. Because of the government's emphasis on self-sufficiency at the local level (especially before the reform), the poor transportation infrastructure, and the protection of local industries by their respective local governments, many people regard the Chinese market as really a collection of 30 economic

Figure 7.1 The Relationship between Growth in Income
and Product Demand

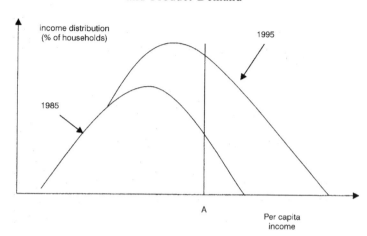

Source: Euromonitor (1994) China: A Directory and Source Book 1994,
Euromonitor Plc, London

entities with different characteristics. The purchasing power of people
in the coastal region is much higher than in the interior, whilst
major differences also exist between the south and the north. What
sells in Shanghai could flop in Beijing, Guangzhou or Xi'an.

For example, there are clear similarities and differences between
consumers in Beijing, Shanghai and Guangzhou – three of the most
developed cities in China. Most people in these cities prefer imported foreign brands to those produced by joint ventures in China,
which in turn are preferred to local brands. However, Guangzhou
consumers are more selective and more prepared to accept new
products; Shanghai consumers are more cautious and 'calculating'
in making a purchase (so price is very important); whilst Beijing
consumers are more emotional and more receptive to advertising
messages.[37]

The price level for identical products also varies significantly
between places. In 1996, the National Statistical Bureau investigated the prices of 170 commodities in eight large cities (Beijing,
Tianjin, Shanghai, Guangzhou, Shenyang, Wuhan, Chongqing and
Xi'an), and concluded that for each unit of money, the purchasing
power is the highest in Chongqing and the lowest in Guangzhou.[34]
These eight cities can be classified into three categories. The first

Figure 7.2 The Average Income in Eight Cities (August, 1996, yuan)

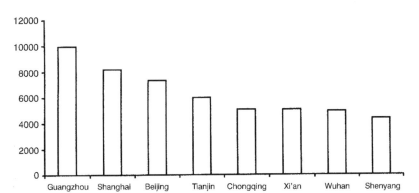

Source: *The People's Daily* (Overseas edition), 2 June 1997, p. 2. 'The purchasing power per unit money in eight cities in China' (*Zhong Guo Ba Cheng Shi Dan Wei Huo Bi Gou Mai Li Pai Xu*).

category, where the purchasing power per unit of money is the lowest, only consists of Guangzhou, where one needs to spend 120.3 yuan for products which only cost 100 yuan in Beijing and 89.7 yuan in Chongqing. The second category only consists of Shanghai, where the purchasing power per unit of money is 8.2 per cent lower than Beijing but 10.5 per cent higher than Guangzhou. The remaining six cities make the third category where the purchasing power per unit of money is similar.

The survey also identified major differences in the spending structure (on different types of products and services) and income levels between the eight cities. Income levels can be classified into two categories (Figure 7.2). The first category consists of Guangzhou, Shanghai and Beijing, and the second category consists of the remaining five cities. It was predicted that it would take six to seven years for cities in the second category to reach the 1996 income level in Shanghai.[39]

An even more significant market segmentation in China is perhaps between urban and rural consumers. This is more of a social segmentation than a geographical one, because the social status of these two groups of people, as well as their income levels and the state welfare they are entitled to, are very different. Urban populations are generally more wealthy and more prepared to accept new products and new ideas. Most foreign investors in China are currently targeting the urban populations although the rural populations are quickly catching up. This segmentation is clearly shown in the result of the Gallup survey. For example, given a choice between statements describing quality products versus inexpensive ones, people in urban areas are more likely to opt for quality than are those in rural areas. Urban residents choose 'will pay for high quality' over 'will buy inexpensive products regardless of quality' at the ratio of 53 per cent to 12 per cent, compared with 34 per cent to 38 per cent for rural residents. In spite of the Chinese government's efforts to reduce differences between urban and rural areas (such as reforming the household registration system), this market segmentation will perhaps remain for a long time to come.[40]

Numerous other criteria have also caused market segmentation in China. Key factors include age (the old and the young), employment status (who is the employer – state owned organizations, joint ventures, foreign companies, self-employed, or others – which determine their income levels and job security), income levels, education, gender and many others. Children are always important in Chinese families, and one particular factor worth mentioning is the one child policy. One estimate indicated that about half of the premium goods that are purchased in China are for the so called 'little emperors'.[41] Also, the Gallup survey indicated that the most important goal for savings (among a list of eight) for the national population was 'financing a child or children's education' (64 per cent), and followed by 'paying off a child's or children's wedding' (39 per cent) as the fifth most important goal for savings.

Competition and marketing in China

Although difficult to estimate, the Chinese market is big and the future prospect is optimistic.[42] However, this by no means implies that there is room for all foreign players in China. As the consumer market evolves, competition is also getting stronger and maintaining market share is as important in China as in anywhere else in the world. This is further complicated by the fact that increased average income may not increase the demand for an existing category of products but may suddenly increase the demand for a new category of products (Figure 7.1). Since China has been perceived as the last great untapped market, top companies from all over the world, including the USA, Europe, Japan and other Asian economies, have been drawn in to do battle on its turf. Chinese domestic companies are also quickly catching up.

For many foreign investors, the main competitors are often not local companies, but other foreign investors in China. The survey by the Economist Intelligence Unit and Andersen Consulting indicated that 64 per cent of survey respondents (foreign investors in China) reported fierce competition from other foreign ventures and 35 per cent encountered strong competition from domestic companies.[43] Similar tendencies were reported by *The Economist*.[44]

Today, the Chinese consumers have become much more sophisticated and discriminating than they were only a few years ago. Even in the early 1990s, foreign brand products easily beat Chinese products for the former's perceived quality; and higher price tended to encourage (rather than repel) purchase because it was treated as a signal of high quality. However, as the quality of local brands improves rapidly, and as people gradually get used to foreign brands (and the novelty factors fade), the situation is changing dramatically. In particular, Chinese consumers are rejecting foreign cast-offs that have failed to sell elsewhere and are demanding the latest products. Today, China has a very clear agenda driven by technology transfer, and it does not want to become a dumping ground for the world's obsolete technologies. Jim Bercaw of AT&T told *The Economist* that western firms can command high margins in China only if they sell up-to-date products, rather than using China to unload obsolete goods. Because France's Alcatel gave China its state-of-the-art telephone switching technology, it now commands a 50 per cent market share. Even AT&T have found it difficult to break the strong hold of Alcatel on the Chinese market for telephone switching, unless it competes with even more advanced technologies.[45]

Another interesting example is Volkswagen, the German car maker, in China. The two Volkswagen models produced in China are the 1970s-designed Santana and Jetta (which are both obsolete outside China). These technologies matched Chinese automakers' abilities to supply components and to service the car in the 1980s, and Volkswagen made profit from the first year it invested in China. Although Volkswagen today still occupies considerable market share (50 per cent), customers often compare Volkswagen cars made in China with other imported models and asked why Volkswagen technologies are so old. Martin Posth, the Chairman of Volkswagen Asia Pacific, was worried about Volkswagen's reputation for old-fashioned machinery in China and the long term implications of this perception.[46]

The Chinese authorities also recognized that Volkswagen failed to transfer new technologies and research and development capabilities to China. Other car manufacturers intending to enter the Chinese market have used technology transfer and latest models as bargaining chips and competitive weapons. In 1995, Ford and its Shanghai joint venture partner applied for permission to produce cars in 1997 in China, and the proposed model was so modern that it would not even be launched in the USA until late 1996. For various reasons, the deal was offered to General Motors in March 1997 during US Vice President Al Gore's visit to China, which involved two joint ventures (one making cars and the other an automobile technology research and development centre), with a total investment of US$1.57 billion (50 per cent by each partner) and a production capacity of 100 000 cars per year.[47] Although Volkswagen has upgraded its models for the Chinese market in recent years (such as the Santana 2000), the Shanghai General Motor joint venture will produce some of General Motors' latest models, which would certainly have the edge in style and sophistication over the outmoded Volkswagen Santana.

Product image is extremely important in China, which requires foreign invested enterprises to devise their marketing strategy carefully. It has been said that one of the main ingredients of some companies' success in China is their advanced marketing techniques. Foreign companies, such as Unilever and Procter and Gamble, are leagues ahead of Chinese companies in marketing techniques, so that they are now market leaders for washing powers and shampoos in China. In addition to aggressive advertisement through various media and high quality packaging, Procter and Gamble also innovatively used the 'neighbourhood committees' to hand out detergent samples, which ensured that Procter and Gamble products reached every corner of Chinese cities. In the meantime, Tsingtao (*Qingdao*), the leading beer brand in China, is likely to be overtaken by foreign brewers (such as Heineken) through the latter's aggressive marketing campaigns.[48] Consumers' limited experience with modern marketing has made them depend on reputable brands and track records for assurance. The security that brands afford is said to account for one-third to one-half of all consumer expressions of intent to purchase.[49]

In China, the trusted media are those used for official purposes, including TV, radio, newspapers and magazines. The penetration of such media is high, and the Gallup survey revealed that, of all the people they interviewed, 92 per cent watch televisions, 80 per cent listen to radios, 70 per cent read newspapers and 66 per cent read magazines. These media are tightly controlled by regulatory bodies, and sometimes the public tend to believe that the regulators have verified all advertising claims. In the Gallup survey 48 per cent of respondents said they look at advertisements before making a purchase. Other marketing approaches, such as deep discounts or free trials, can be ineffective if not executed properly. Such promotions can cheapen a product, and cheap products cannot be good. However, modesty has been regarded as a good virtue in China, and blowing one's own trumpet is generally disliked. Such promotions tend to make people suspicious and they might think something is wrong with the product. Similarly, it was found that because Chinese people plan their purchases carefully, it is often not important to position one's product in a fancy display or prime shelf space. Chinese consumers will look for them if they have heard about them and want to buy.[50]

Consumer buying habits

Chinese consumers have some distinct buying habits. These habits are difficult to generalize because they tend to change over time and differ between places. However, some common features revealed by the Gallup survey are that people prefer to buy high quality, long lasting products (63 per cent), and many people are prepared to pay high prices for high quality (38 per cent). People tend to look at advertisements carefully before making a purchase (48 per cent), and in many cases they want to see complete information about product specifications. Thirty per cent of respondents preferred to buy leading brands even if they are more expensive, and 19 per cent preferred foreign-made products. These features are particularly evident in urban areas.

When making a major purchase, Chinese people tend to plan it carefully, and there is a disinclination for convenience or impulse buying. Window shopping and browsing are favourite evening and weekend pastimes. They listen to others (neighbours, colleagues, shop assistants and other shoppers) carefully before buying and people tend to buy for usefulness rather than for design. They prefer to buy at stores they can trust. Some people decide which product to buy before they visit stores, and others will usually visit two or three stores before they decide on the product. Typically, expensive items are perceived to be of higher quality, and consumers are suspicious of cheap goods. At the same time, Chinese consumers are also known to spend time searching for price mark-downs. So one successful pricing strategy is to price the product high initially and then lower it gradually, which gives the consumers a sense of getting a quality product at a bargain price.

A distinctive aspect of the Chinese culture that influences consumer behaviour is that some Chinese people are reluctant to be pioneers. Many people do not want to be the first to try a new product. However, another important aspect of Chinese culture, the preservation of 'face', means they are equally reluctant to be left behind by their neighbours, colleagues and friends. So once a new product is tried by some people, others tend to follow and 'referral is the most powerful way of expanding trials to the first wave of consumers'.[51] However, this buying habit also means that market demand tends to fluctuate dramatically. After a successful trial, demand may jump dramatically, but this may not last long and may drop quickly as people move to their next target. So companies should be sceptical of strong initial sales.

SUMMARY

This chapter briefly examined the distribution and sales systems in China and identified their potential problems for foreign invested enterprises. It also explored the nature of the Chinese market and highlighted some key features of Chinese consumer behaviours. In the foreseeable future, distribution and sales will continue to pose serious challenges to foreign invested enterprises. These problems are related to the fact that China is a developing country, and it is in the midst of a profound transition from planning to market, so administrative and market forces will continue to affect the operation of Chinese and foreign companies in China. Today, the state distribution system has crumbled, but the new systems have not been formed. The poor transportation infrastructure, and various government regulations and restrictions, will continue to restrict the development of fast, reliable, integrated and efficient distribution systems. However, improvements since 1990 have been very significant, and foreign invested enterprises now have a wide variety of options open to them in formulating a distribution and sales strategy.

The Chinese market is huge and rapidly growing, but the exact size of the market is difficult to estimate. The ownership of consumables in Chinese households is considerably higher than in most other countries when they were at China's current level of economic development. As the general income level increases, people's desired purchases tend to change rapidly. The behaviour of Chinese consumers is in many aspects different from people in the West, and such characteristics should be taken into account when formulating a marketing strategy. Many well-tested marketing and sales techniques elsewhere may simply not work – in fact, some of them could be potentially damaging – in China.

As the last great untapped market in the world, China has drawn in numerous world-leading companies. Some of the bloodiest battles in the Chinese market have been fought between familiar rivals in other markets. Local companies are also quickly catching up in terms of product quality and marketing techniques. The Chinese market is big, the potential is great, but so is the number of powerful players. To win a slice of the market, one has to be able to distribute products efficiently and quickly to consumers – and in the right condition. Since the market has been transformed from a seller's to a buyer's market, consumers are increasingly spoilt for choice, so making one's product appeal to the Chinese consumers is essential to the development, and indeed, survival of a foreign invested company in China.

Notes

1. *World Executive Digest*, May 1994.
2. Euromonitor (1994) *China: A Directory and Source Book 1994*, Euromonitor Plc, London; Brahm, Lawrence and Li Daoran (1996) *The Business Guide to China*, Butterworth-Heinemann Asia, Singapore.
3. Tseng, Choo-sin, Paula Kwan and Fanny Cheung (1995) 'Distribution in China: A guide through the maze', *Long Range Planning*, 28 (1): 81–91.
4. *Ibid*.
5. Child, J (1994) *Management in China during the Age of Reform*, Cambridge University Press, Cambridge.
6. Brahm and Li (1996) *op. cit.*
7. The Economist Intelligence Unit and Andersen Consulting (1995) *Moving China Ventures out of the Red into the Black: Insights from Best and Worst Performers*, The Economist Intelligence Unit, London.
8. Tseng, *et al.* (1995) *op. cit.*
9. Child (1994) *op. cit.*
10. McLaughlin, Bruce (1996) 'The way to market', *Chinese Business Impact*

(*Ying Zhong Jing Ji Dong Xiang*), June 1996, Issue 19, p. 7 and p. 26, published by *Si Yu* Chinese Times Publication, Manchester.

11. Brahm and Li (1996) *op. cit.*
12. The Economist Intelligence Unit (EIU) and Andersen Consulting (1995) *op. cit.*
13. Tseng *et al.* (1995) *op. cit.*
14. *The Economist*, 3–9 December 1994, 'How not to sell 1.2 billion tubes of toothpaste', pp. 95–96.
15. *Ibid.*
16. Schiffman, Leon and Leslie Kanuk (1994) *Consumer Behaviour* (Fifth Edition), Prentice Hall International, Englewood Cliffs, N.J.; Ward, Scott and Frederick E. Webster, Jr (1991) 'Organizational buying behaviour', in Robertson, Thomas S. and Harold H. Kassarjian (eds.) *Handbook of Consumer Behaviour*, Prentice Hall International, Englewood Cliffs, N.J., pp. 419–459.
17. Yan, Rick (1994) 'To reach China's consumers, adapt *to Guo Qing'*, *Harvard Business Review*, September–October 1994, 66–74.
18. Tseng, *et al.* (1995) *op. cit.*
19. *The Financial Times*, 31 July 1996, 'Consumerism's new citadel: Western companies are pouring into Russia to meet the rapidly increasing demand for consumer goods', reported by Roderick Oram. p. 19.
20. *Gallup Survey* (1995) the first foreign sponsored national study of consumer attitudes and lifestyle trends of the People's Republic of China, conducted during May–September 1994 and results released by Gallup Organization on 15 February 1995 in New York.
21. Euromonitor (1994) *op. cit.*; Brahm and Li (1996) *op. cit.*
22. Yan (1994) *op. cit.*
23. *Ibid.*
24. The Economist Intelligence Unit (EIU) and Andersen Consulting (1995) *op. cit.*
25. *Ibid.*
26. Yan (1994) *op. cit.*; China Statistical Yearbook, 1996.
27. The Economist Intelligence Unit (EIU) and Andersen Consulting (1995) *op. cit.*
28. Tseng *et al.* (1995) *op. cit.*
29. *Gallup Survey* (1995) *op. cit.*
30. *The Economist*, 3–9 December 1994, *op. cit.*
31. The Henley Centre (1997) 'From Marxism to the market', *Global Futures*, Summer 1997: 12–16.
32. Yan (1994) *op. cit.*
33. The Economist Intelligence Unit (EIU) and Andersen Consulting (1995) *op. cit.*
34. *Gallup Survey* (1995) *op. cit.*
35. Yan (1994) *op. cit.*; Guo, J.H. and N. Macpherson (1996) 'Marketing practices in the People's Republic of China – The way ahead for the next millennium', *MEG'96 Conference*, Glasgow; Fang, Minsheng (1996) 'The prospect of China's consumer market at the turn of the century', *China Opening Herald*, Vol. 20 No. 2/3. pp. 31–33.
36. Euromonitor (1994) *op. cit.*

37. Tseng *et al*. (1995) *op. cit*.
38. *The People's Daily* (Overseas edition), 2 June 1997, 'The purchasing power per unit of money in eight cities in China' (*Zhong Guo Ba Cheng Shi Dan Wei Huo Bi Gou Mai Li Pai Xu*), p. 2.
39. *Ibid*.
40. Fang (1996) *op. cit*.; Pan, Xipan (1996) 'Will it cause great confusion if we abolish the household register system?', *China Opening Herald*, Vol. 30 No. 12: pp. 50–52.
41. Yan (1994) *op. cit*.
42. Fang (1996) *op. cit*.
43. The Economist Intelligence Unit (EIU) and Andersen Consulting (1995) *op. cit*.
44. *The Economist*, 2–8 December 1995, *op. cit*.
45. *Ibid*.
46. The Economist Intelligence Unit (EIU) and Andersen Consulting (1995) *op. cit*.
47. *The People's Daily* (Overseas edition), 27 March 1997, 'The largest Sino-US joint venture signed, two automobile companies established in Shanghai' (*Zhong Mei Zui Da He Zi Xiang Mu Qian Yue, Liang Jia Qi Che You Xian Gong Si Zai Hu Cheng Li*), p. 1; *Chinese Science Newspaper* (Overseas edition), 25 April 1997, 'The largest Sino-US joint venture will be set up in Pudong' (*Zhong Mei Zui Da He Zi Xiang Mu Jiang Luo Hu Pu Dong*), p. 3.
48. The Economist, 2–8 December 1995, *op. cit*.
49. Yan (1994) *op. cit*.
50. *Ibid.*
51. Yan (1994) *op. cit*. p. 71.

8 The Economic and Social Influences of FDI in China

China's opening up has three key objectives: attracting foreign investment, promoting foreign trade, and introducing advanced technologies, skills and management techniques.[1] Of these, attracting FDI is probably the most dramatic manifestation of China's opening up, and it also significantly affects the other two objectives. FDI brings new technologies, new management techniques, foreign people with different values and cultural backgrounds, and foreign ways of doing business, into China. It increasingly exposes the Chinese economy to international competition. More importantly, as China opens its door to foreign capital and people, the Chinese society is increasingly influenced by foreign values, ideologies and cultures. The economic and social influences of FDI, and the perception and selective acceptance (or rejection) by the Chinese people and Chinese leaders of such influences, will inevitably be reflected in the future policies and regulations for FDI in China, and in the quality of China's soft environment for FDI in general.

Since the 1980s, the enormous contribution of FDI to China's rapid economic development has been widely recognized. The most obvious contributions include relieving capital supply bottlenecks, promoting economic growth and creating new employment opportunities. FDI has also contributed significantly to government revenue, foreign trade, technological progress, and enterprise management in China.[2] By the end of 1996, China had attracted over 280 000 foreign invested enterprises, with a total accumulated FDI (utilized) of US$176.59 billion (US$469.39 billion contracted). In the eighth five year plan (1991–95), FDI (utilized) accounted for about 11.8 per cent of total fixed assets in China, which further increased to 13 per cent in 1996. The proportion of China's total industrial output accounted for by foreign invested enterprises rose from nothing in 1978 to 2.1 per cent in 1990, and further to 7.2 per cent in 1995.[3] FDI also played a key role in China's phenomenal export success, which in less than two decades lifted China into the ranks of the world's ten biggest exporters of manufactured goods!⁴

However, until recently, most studies of FDI in China have focused on its economic influences, particularly the positive contributions of FDI to the Chinese economy. The negative economic influences and the less tangible social influences of FDI have rarely been studied, and these can be even more profound in the long term. As will be discussed later in the chapter, people working in foreign invested enterprises can earn several times more than those with similar skills but working in state owned organizations. This serves to exacerbate income disparities both within and between regions, which challenges the basic principles of socialism and destabilizes the Chinese society if not handled properly. In fact, the rapid growth of FDI is facilitating a radical social transformation in China, and the profound cultural and structural changes are leading to a radical re-orientation in people's values and ideologies, which are increasingly reflected in people's new life styles and behaviours.

This chapter examines some of the most significant economic and social influences of FDI in China. However, several practical difficulties for the study need to be emphasized. First, since the opening up is only one part (however important) of China's broader economic and political reform, the influence of FDI has always been interwoven with that of the reform in general. It is difficult to say whether a particular change was brought about by FDI or by other factors. Second, evaluating the influences of FDI is a complex task: they cannot be simply classified into positive and negative categories. For example, FDI has contributed to the rapid economic development of the coastal provinces, but at the same time it facilitated growing regional economic disparities – which is potentially destabilizing in Chinese society.

Third, the accuracy of figures obtained from various sources is difficulty to verify. Even the official figure about the total amount of FDI attracted to China could be inaccurate. It has been suspected that some township enterprises and government departments have shifted money secretly out of China and then brought it back in as foreign investment. By doing so, the enterprises can enjoy various tax breaks and other privileges granted only to foreign invested enterprises (perhaps this has contributed to the fact that nearly 70 per cent of total FDI attracted to China between 1979 and 1995 originated from Hong Kong, Macao and Taiwan, and nearly 60 per cent from Hong Kong alone!).⁵ Equally, some successful foreign invested enterprises in China simply claimed to be doing badly in order not to attract attention from state owned enterprises in the same sector or to avoid taxes – making it impossible to tell how well, or how badly, foreign invested enterprises are actually doing in China.[6]

Fourth, different approaches are required to examine the economic and social influences of FDI. While the economic influences of FDI can be examined by analysing the relevant economic data (albeit inaccurate sometimes), the less tangible social influences of FDI can only be investigated indirectly by observing emergent social phenomena. Since many of the social changes in Chinese society are still not fully emerged, this chapter will only speculate on some relevant issues.

THE MAJOR ECONOMIC INFLUENCES OF FDI IN CHINA

A systematic evaluation of FDI's economic influences is a complex task. For example, China's export of manufactured goods has been increasing very rapidly – from a mere US$9.8 billion in 1978 to US$121 billion in 1994, and 30 per cent of these exports were accounted for by foreign invested enterprises in China. However, these enterprises produced only 2 per cent of China's total manufactured goods,[7] and China's over-dependence on foreign investors for exports has clearly cast a shadow over the country's future prospects in export growth. This could also mean that gains in efficiency, management techniques and new technology that are enjoyed by foreign invested enterprises have failed (or at least been slow) to spill over to the state owned enterprises. Moreover, the enormous difficulties faced by state owned enterprises are, at least to some extent, the result of growing competition from foreign invested enterprises in the Chinese domestic market. Reactions from the Chinese authorities and state owned enterprises to this situation will inevitably affect future policies and regulations for FDI in China. This section examines the major economic influences of FDI in China, and both the positive and negative influences are highlighted.

FDI has been playing an increasingly important role in China's rapid economic development. It has made significant contributions to China in relieving capital supply bottlenecks, increasing government revenue, promoting foreign trade and regional development, facilitating technological progress, improving enterprise management and marketing techniques, and creating local employment.[8] Without FDI, the economic wonders of the special economic zones in China – and the east coastal region as a whole – perhaps would not have been possible. Shenzhen, the first special economic zone in China, has grown from an underdeveloped rural fishing village of 50 000 people in 1980 to a still rapidly expanding modern city of over two million inhabitants;[9] and since the late 1980s, it has been the richest city in terms of per capita income in China! Valuable lessons have been learnt from the success of Shenzhen for China's reform in general. In the meantime, some negative economic influences of FDI are increasingly recognized.

Relieving capital supply bottlenecks

Since the early 1980s, FDI has been playing an important role in meeting the country's increasing demand for capital derived from its rapid economic development.[10] During the 1980s alone, China attracted a total FDI worth over 300 billion yuan, roughly the equivalent of China's total investment in capital construction for 1989 and 1990![11] By the end of 1995, the total number of foreign invested enterprises in China reached 258 903, with a total utilized FDI of US$133.37 billion (US$176.59 billion by the end of 1996!).[12] A large proportion (88.1 per cent of total FDI between 1983 and 1995) of these investments have been concentrated in the east coastal region. In Beijing, total utilized FDI between 1980 and 1986 amounted to US$850 millions, the equivalent of two years' total investment in fixed assets by the city under the state plan and 1.25 times the total amount of foreign exchange the city was allowed to retain from its export earnings for the same period.[13] By the end of 1996, Beijing approved a total of 12,621 foreign invested enterprises, with a total pledged FDI of US$33.19 billion (US$19.73 billion utilized), including investments from 279 well known multinationals, with 132 of them in the ranks of the 500 largest corporations in the world.[14]

Similarly in Tianjin, the largest industrial city in the north, total utilized FDI exceeded US$16 billion and, by the mid 1990s, the 10 000 plus foreign invested enterprises accounted for over 40 per cent of the urban economy, employing over 320 000 people. About two-thirds of all FDI projects in Tianjin are in industrial sectors, and total industrial outputs from these enterprises accounted for 41 per cent of the city's total.[15] The role of FDI in the largest city in China, Shanghai, has been even more crucial, and Shanghai's share of FDI in China has risen from 3.3 per cent in 1991 to 7.8 per cent in 1995 with the establishment of the Pudong Development Zone.[16] The annual growth rate of the Shanghai economy averaged 14 per cent between 1992 and 1996, and its GNP per capita increased rapidly from about US$1000 in 1992 to over US$3000 in 1996![17]

The role of FDI in China has further increased substantially since the early 1990s and it has now become crucial to the development of the Chinese economy. Between 1989 and the first half of 1991, over 18 000 new foreign invested enterprises were approved by China, which was more than the total number approved during the entire preceding decade (1979–88).[18] This was achieved under economic sanctions by all major industrial powers in the world after the Tiananmen Square tragedy in 1989. In 1992, total FDI attracted to China was about two and half times that in 1991,[19] and in 1993 the figure equalled that for the entire period of 1978–92 (fourteen years). A total of 83 265 new foreign investment projects were approved in 1993, with pledged and utilized foreign capital of US$110.52 billion and US$25.759 billion – an increase of 70.6 per cent, 90.7 per cent and 134 per cent respectively from 1992! [20] Although the total contractual FDI (pledged) reduced to around US$85 billions in 1994 and 1995, and further to US$70 billion in 1996, utilized FDI (actual inflow) has been growing steadily from US $25.76 billion in 1993 to US$42.35 billion in 1996.[21]

Some commentators suspected that FDI in China perhaps peaked in 1996, because of various difficulties encountered by foreign investors. Others, however, argued that many of China's attractions – its potentially huge domestic market and its abundant supplies of cheap labour – will continue to exist for a long time, and with the increasing relaxation of government restrictions in sectors ranging from air transportation and retailing to banking and insurance, China will continue to be a favourite destination for FDI in the foreseeable future.[22] According to Mr Yao Zhenyan, the Governor of China Development Bank, China intends to utilize at least US$30 billion of FDI each year in the next five years according to China's ninth five year plan.[23] FDI in China during the period 1983 to 1996 is provided in Figure 8.1.[24]

It should be pointed out that FDI has not only provided an important supplement to the limited domestic capital supply in China, but also, more importantly, the capital provided by foreign

Figure 8.1 Foreign Direct Investment in China
(Utilized, 1983–1996; US$bn)

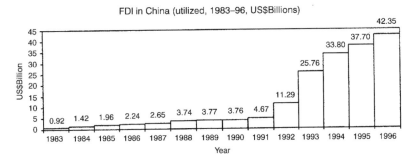

Sources: 'The People's Republic of China National Statistical Bureau Report on China's Economic and Social Development' for 1983–1996 [*Zhong Hua Ren Min Gong He Guo Guo Jia Tong Ji Ju Guan Yu 1983 (–1996) Nian Guo Min Jing Ji He She Hui Fa Zhan De Tong Ji Gong Bao*]. Released annually in *The People's Daily* (Overseas Edition) in March or April

investors is often in hard currency, which was particularly needed in China during the early days of the reform. The rapid growth of FDI also enabled China to put more money into the construction of ports, railway lines, power plants and oilfields, thereby greatly strengthening China's economic power. Since the early 1990s, foreign investors have increasingly been encouraged to participate directly in the construction of China's infrastructure. The tax income collected from foreign invested enterprises has also become an important source of government revenues.

Since the mid-1990s, with over US$100 billion foreign exchange reserves and continuous rapid economic growth, China has become increasingly selective with foreign investors in order to attract FDI into desirable sectors and/or locations. On 1 July 1995, the Chinese government published the Regulation on Guiding the Direction of Foreign Investment (*Zhi Dao Wai Shang Tou Zi Fang Xiang Zan Xing Gui Ding*) and The Index of Foreign Investment Industrial Guide (*Wai Shang Tou Zi Chan Ye Zhi Dao Mu Lu*), which provided a list of industries in which FDI is encouraged, restricted or prohibited.[25] The main aim of the new regulation and the index is to channel FDI into certain sectors, including agriculture, energy, transportation, and new materials. Foreign investors are also encouraged to use advanced technologies to make products needed by the domestic market and for export,[26] and to invest in the middle and west of China.[27]

In the future, China will need to redouble its effort in attracting high quality FDI. Without new foreign investment, China will not be able to maintain the high speed economic growth achieved over the last two decades. A World Bank report estimated that in the next five years, China would need US$280 billion for its infrastructure development alone, and between 1995 and 2005, US$744 billion would be needed for its public facilities and infrastructure. Such massive demand for new investment simply cannot be met by China alone. Between 1983 and 1995, 88.1 per cent of total FDI was concentrated in the eastern region. Since 1993, the ratio of per capita FDI attracted to the east region and that attracted to the rest of China (the middle and western regions) was 10.4 to 1. The middle and western regions would need US$170 billion of new foreign investment to reach the same level of FDI (per capita) achieved in the east in 1993.[28] All these suggest that the potential for FDI growth is enormous, and FDI will become increasingly crucial to China's economic development in the future.

Technological progress

FDI has contributed significantly to China's technological progress, which has been clearly demonstrated in a series of industries, such as colour televisions, washing machines, refrigerators, and cars. These and many other industries developed very rapidly in the 1980s and early 1990s through joint ventures and other forms of technological transfer. The successful adaptation of a new technology in a new socio-economic context often requires intensive human interactions, such as the transfer of suitable management techniques and on-the-spot co-operation between foreign experts and Chinese engineers, technicians and workers. Foreign invested enterprises are clearly in a favourable position in providing such conditions. These enterprises have to provide the essential training for their Chinese employees, which contributes to the proliferation of new skills in China in the long run. In joint ventures, interests shared between the Chinese and foreign partners often ensure the smooth transfer of suitable technologies to China.[29]

During the 1980s, some joint ventures experienced considerable difficulties in the area of technology transfer. The Chinese government was criticized (and it still is today!) for being biased towards the most advanced technologies – preferably the most advanced designs incorporated in large factories – rather than the older but more appropriate technologies for China. Examples included joint ventures such as Shanghai Bell, Beijing Jeep and Alcatel, all involving costly mistakes in introducing technologies beyond China's absorptive capacity in the 1980s.[30] However, by the early 1990s, considerable experience had been gained in the area of technology transfer in China. Some emerging problems, such as the effective protection of proprietary technologies and intellectual property rights, have also been dealt with at both the inter-governmental level and the corporate level.[31]

Numerous examples have shown that China has successfully absorbed new technologies and associated skills and techniques through FDI. When Volkswagen first invested in China through a joint venture in Shanghai in the mid-1980s, the automobile industry in China lagged behind that of the developed world by several decades. Although the Volkswagen Santana (a medium sized saloon car) introduced in China was an old, obsolete model in the developed world (a 1970s design), it still posed considerable technical challenge to Shanghai Volkswagen. Through close co-operation between the Chinese and German partners, however, most technical problems were overcome, and by 1990 Shanghai Volkswagen was able to produce 70.73 per cent of all parts used for the Volkswagen Santana – including its five key components such as engine, body and gear box – without affecting the quality of the vehicle, and the figure rose to 75 per cent in 1992[32] and further to over 80 per cent in 1993.[33] For over a decade, Santana has been the most popular car in China, and the annual production of the model increased rapidly from 35 000 in 1991 to 65 000 in 1992, and further to over 200 000 in 1996![34] The design of the Volkswagen Santana was revised in the early 1990s, and today it remains the most popular car in the Chinese market – with a market share of over 50 per cent!

Volkswagen was particularly satisfied with the result, and in 1992 it also began to produce the Volkswagen Jetta model in China with another partner – the First Automobile Corporation in Changchun (in the North East), and in 1993, the Golf model as well (although the Golf was not as successful due to consumer preferences in the Chinese car market – see Chapter 7).[35] The production capacity for the Volkswagen Jetta reached 150 000 by the mid-1990s, with 84.02 per cent local contents by the end of 1996.[36]

A similar situation was experienced by Chrysler–Beijing Jeep. When the joint venture was negotiated, the Chinese partner insisted on a contract with the American partner that provided for continuous technology transfer to enable the joint venture to update its products in line with new developments in the auto industry abroad. In spite of various problems it experienced during the early days, however, the joint venture successfully changed its main product from an old model (CJ Jeep) to a 1983 AMC model (XJ Jeep) in 1985.[37] More importantly, the successful transfer of technologies in these enterprises during the 1980s contributed to the rapid development of the motor industry in China. Since the early 1990s when China negotiated new joint ventures in the motor industry with enterprises such as Ford, General Motors, and Mercedes Benz, the proposed models are in line with the latest models for the developed world![38]

In other sectors, such as the production of elevators, the Chinese partner successfully absorbed new technologies through joint ventures with partners from Switzerland and Hong Kong. This enabled these enterprises to upgrade their products from that of the average level of the industrialized economies in the 1950s and 1960s to that of the mid-1980s in only a few years time.[39] Similar experience has been found in industries ranging from colour televisions, video recorders (VCR), VCDs, refrigerators, washing machines, microwaves, air conditioners, and cameras, to motor cycles and bicycles.

Today, China has a very clear agenda driven by technology transfer, and it does not want to become a dumping ground for the world's obsolete technologies.[40] In car manufacturing, the Chinese authorities are conscious of the fact that the technologies transferred to China by Volkswagen were mostly obsolete in developed countries, and Chinese consumers are also increasingly concerned that Volkswagen cars in China are very 'out-dated' compared with technologies used in imported cars. Several other car manufacturers – such as Ford and General Motors – have used their latest designs and technology transfer as important bargaining chips and competitive weapons to break the strong hold by Volkswagen in the Chinese car market. In the telecommunications sector, such as telephone switching, China is rejecting foreign cast-offs that have failed to sell elsewhere and is demanding the latest products. Enterprises such as Alcatel and AT&T have been working hard to transfer their latest technologies in order to maintain their positions in the Chinese market. To be successful in the Chinese market, foreign investors increasingly have to use cutting-edge technologies to beat other foreign as well as domestic competitors.[41]

So far, China has successfully absorbed many new technologies, and it is now able to design and produce many high-tech products, ranging from telephone switches to colour television tubes, by introducing and absorbing the technologies and techniques of leading multinational enterprises. Before the opening up in 1978, China could not even make many of these products, and now many joint ventures have become the primary production base in China. Their products have not only become the leading brands in the Chinese market, competing directly with imported brands, but also have increasingly entered the international market.[42] Despite problems such as lack of new product development capacity in joint ventures, there is no doubt that, without FDI, technological progress in a wide range of Chinese industries would have been much slower!

In the ninth five year plan, China extended its plan to transfer and absorb new technologies in order to speed up technological progress and national economic restructuring.[43] The plan focuses particularly on market demand, and emphasizes the role of enterprises in the transfer, absorbence and development of new technologies. The role of FDI in China's technological progress would certainly be further enhanced through the implementation of this plan.

Enterprise management

FDI has also contributed significantly to enterprise management in China. In addition to capital and new technologies, foreign investors often bring with them new forms of work organization and new organizational culture, new management styles and new marketing techniques.[44] Such soft skills are particularly valuable for China after decades of international isolation and centrally planned economy.

Before the reform and opening up in the late 1970s, the Chinese economy was predominantly a state or collectively-owned, centrally planned economy in which the primary objective of all productive organizations was to fulfil the requirements of the economic planning authorities. In contrast to a market economy in which all enterprises try to produce what is demanded by the market, all productive organizations in China produced what they were ordered or instructed to produce by the planning authorities. Whether these products were of high quality and required by the consumers, and whether the organization was efficient and innovative that are critical to the success of any enterprise in a market economy, were only of secondary concern. Some of the similarities and differences between Chinese and western approaches to management have been sum-marized by Child and Lu (Table 8.1).[45]

As a result, when China decided to transform its planned economy to a market system in the early 1980s, most managers in China were not well positioned to adapt to the new situation. Many or-ganizations' leaders had been promoted from a political, rural and military background, and they had little industrial and commercial experience, and lacked managerial qualifications. Today, the lack of qualified managerial staff remains one of the most serious problems facing both foreign invested enterprises and Chinese do-mestic companies.[46]

Through direct and indirect means, foreign investment has contributed to the improvement of enterprise management in China in the market environment.[47] Many joint ventures adopted partially or entirely the management systems introduced by their foreign partners, and the differences between Chinese and western ap-proaches to management often required partners to find ways to reconcile such differences – an extremely valuable learning experi-ence for Chinese managers (as well as for foreign investors). Wholly foreign owned ventures also provided essential training for their Chinese managers. Moreover, the Chinese suppliers and clients of foreign invested enterprises can gain considerable experience through business dealings with foreign invested enterprises. As the number of foreign enterprises grow, many Chinese enterprises have more chance to do business with foreign invested enterprises in China than dealing directly with foreign enterprises outside China. The experience that many Chinese enterprises gain from such activities is an invaluable preparation for them to enter the international market. The high turnover of managerial staff in foreign invested enterprises in China also contributed to the diffusion of relevant managerial skills.

Today, China has attracted numerous top enterprises from all over the world, and the competition between these enterprises them-selves, as well as between these enterprises and Chinese domestic enterprises, is very strong.[48] The battles between them have not only intensified direct competition in the Chinese market and provided the Chinese managers with the opportunity to develop

Table 8.1   A Comparison between Chinese and Western Approaches
to Management

Concepts and Practices	Chinese management under a centrally planned economy	Western management and market economy
Corporate governance	Planning authorities acting on behalf of state ownership	Boards of directors acting on behalf of shareholders
Decision-making authorities	Industrial bureaux or ministries	Boards of directors and CEOs
Managerial autonomy	Little before reform, much improved now	CEOs enjoy autonomy under the board
Organizational performance criteria	Multiple rationality – economic, political, and social obligations	Economic rationality, tampered by social responsibility
Degree of procedural formalisation	Low formalization, but highly personalized processes	Highly formalized and relatively impersonal
Information communication	Mainly vertical; little horizontal flow	Multi-directional
Management training and development	Not emphasized before mid-1980s	Highly emphasized
Reward policies and incentive systems	Rewards dependent on age and long service; incentives not closely related to performance	Performance related

Source: Reproduced from Child, John and Yuan Lu (1996) 'Introduction: China and international enterprise', in Child, John and Yuan Lu (eds) *Management Issues in China: Volume II*, International Enterprises, Routledge, London, p. 3

and practise their skills. They also provided the Chinese corporate audience in general with most spectacular shows at their door step, which they would otherwise only have a limited chance of viewing. The lessons that Chinese managers learn by participating in and by watching these battles have contributed significantly to the development of management skills and techniques in China, which increases the chance for Chinese enterprises to succeed in the international market.

Foreign trade

As has been discussed earlier in this book, FDI has contributed significantly to foreign trade in China. One of the original objectives of the Chinese Government in allowing FDI in China was to facilitate export and earn hard currency. During the early days, the net effect of FDI on foreign trade was understandably negative as imports exceeded exports. This was perhaps why all foreign invested enterprises were required to balance their own foreign currency accounts.[49] However, as more and more of them become operational and competitive, an overall balance of import and export by foreign invested enterprises was achieved by the early 1990s.

Since the mid-1980s, the contribution of FDI to Chinese exports has been increasing very rapidly. Taking joint ventures, for example, direct exports in 1985 amounted to US$320 millions, increasing to US$480 millions in 1986, US$960 millions in 1987 and US$2.1 billions in 1988. Their proportion in China's total exports also grew from 1 per cent in 1985 to 5 per cent in 1988.[50] In 1991, the total exports by foreign invested enterprises reached US$12 billion (16.7 per cent of China's total exports in 1991), although they also imported US$16.9 billion.[51] In 1993, foreign invested enterprises accounted for as much as 37 per cent of China's foreign trade.[52]

China's economic dynamism has been particularly linked to its success in manufactured exports, and foreign invested enterprises have played a key role in the process. In 1978, China's total export of manufactured goods was a mere US$9.8 billion, which increased to US$121 billion in 1994, making China the eighth largest exporter of manufactured goods in the world. While foreign invested enterprises in China accounted for just 2 per cent of China's total manufactured outputs, they accounted for 30 per cent of its exports, and this proportion is still growing![53] In addition, FDI also contributed to China's trade balance by selling products in the Chinese domestic market, so the need for import was reduced.

The contribution of FDI to China's foreign trade is not evenly distributed between regions, however. In the eleven coastal provinces and cities, total exports by foreign invested enterprises were US$11.65 billions in 1991, about 96.7 per cent of the national total (exports by foreign invested enterprises). Those from the five special economic zones were US$4.29 billion, about 35.6 per cent of the national total.[54] In sharp contrast, exports by foreign invested enterprises in the middle and western regions in China only accounted for 3.3 per cent of the national total. Although FDI is increasingly penetrating into the middle and west of China in recent years, the overall geographical pattern has remained, and it is unlikely to change in significant ways in the near future. This has contributed to the growing regional disparity in China (which will be discussed later in this section).

Employment opportunities

Although China's transition from a planned to a market system resulted in an extremely rapidly growing economy, a major problem facing the Chinese government is growing unemployment. Not only is this happening in urban areas as state owned enterprises and government agencies strive to improve efficiency and cut down labour costs (which is becoming increasingly serious with the reform of the state owned enterprises since the mid-1990s), an increasing number of the rural population are also being released from the land each year. Official estimates in 1995 indicated that about 100 million Chinese in rural areas did not have enough to do, therefore some of them decided to try their luck in the city. In 1995, about 70 million Chinese lived outside their home registration areas.[55] How to provide job opportunities to these people is a key challenge to the Chinese government – a sensitive and potentially destabilizing force in Chinese society.

As one of the fastest growing sectors of the Chinese economy, foreign invested enterprises are playing an increasingly important role in providing employment opportunities in China. In 1992, the total number of Chinese people working in foreign invested enterprises reached three millions,[56] and this figure has been growing very rapidly since then. Although three million is a rather modest figure in China, the role of FDI in providing local employment opportunities in FDI-concentrated areas (such as the east coastal provinces and cities) has been very significant. For example, in Tianjin, the 10 000 or so foreign invested enterprises employed over 320 000 people in 1995.

It should be pointed out that not all jobs in foreign invested enterprises are new jobs. Where FDI creates totally new enterprises, they tend to draw skilled workers and managers from existing state owned enterprises. Where FDI enterprises are formed in conjunction with existing state owned enterprises, the total number of employees may even decrease as the productivity of the new venture increases (unless the total output increases faster than that of productivity).[57] Moreover, not all new jobs will be filled by the local labour supply, as people move in from other areas. Nevertheless, as FDI in China continues to grow and foreign invested enterprises continue to expand, its contribution to local employment in China will increase. Some relevant issues have been discussed in Chapter 6.

Uneven regional development

FDI has contributed to China's growing regional disparity because foreign invested enterprises are highly concentrated in the east coastal region (88.1 per cent of total FDI in China between 1983 and 1995). Although, historically, uneven regional development has been an important feature of the Chinese economy, the situation has been significantly exacerbated since the early 1980s with the reform and opening up.[58]

To a certain extent, regional disparities and uneven economic development are unavoidable, and in fact the Chinese government's economic development strategy is to let some individuals and regions get rich first, and then the country will have more resources to help the less developed regions and the less well-off individuals. However, growing regional disparities inevitably cause dissatisfaction among people in less developed regions, and hence it is potentially a destabilizing factor in Chinese society and a major barrier to China's further economic development. As the Chinese government has repeatedly emphasized, maintaining social and political stability is of paramount importance, and the Chinese government is prepared to do absolutely anything to maintain it (take the response to the 1989 student demonstration, for example). Uneven regional development and people's perception of and reaction towards it are already affecting China's reform and further opening up. This has been clearly reflected in the new open door policies since the mid-1990s – fortunately not by holding back the development of the coastal region but by encouraging more foreign investors to invest in the middle and western regions in China.

Historically, the coastal region has been more prosperous, and its economic development has been faster than the rest of the country. This pattern has been enhanced since the reform and the opening up. In 1992, there were only seven provinces and municipal cities with a development speed higher than the national average, and all of them were in the east coast.[59] Although many factors have contributed to their above-average growth, these seven provinces and cities have been among the most successful in attracting FDI.

China attracted a total of 167 500 foreign invested enterprises by the end of 1993, but these enterprises were very unevenly distributed in China. According to the number of foreign invested enterprises in the region, the top ten provinces and cities are Guangdong (44 705), Jiangsu (18 082), Shandong (12 561), Fujian (11 990), Zhejiang (8085), Shanghai (8056), Hainan (7390), Liaoning (7365), Beijing (6516), and Tianjin (6004). These provinces and cities are all located in the coastal belt. In contrast, all of the provinces with less than 1000 foreign invested enterprises, including Xizang (Tibet, 27), Qinghai (63), Ningxia (216), Xinjiang (508), Gansu (723), Neimenggu (Inner Mongolia, 734), Guizhou (740), and Yunnan (750)[60] are in the west and middle regions of the country. A similar geographical pattern was found in the total exports by foreign invested enterprises, which has been discussed earlier in this section (with foreign trade). Since foreign invested enterprises have been developing much faster than the rest of the Chinese economy, the geographical distribution of FDI has certainly contributed to the uneven regional development in China.

Growing regional disparities have been recognized by the Chinese government, and a series of measures have been taken to reduce them. Since the early 1990s, China's opening up has been extended from the east coast to all regions in China.[61] In the ninth five year plan (1996–2000), new preferential policies have been designed by the Chinese government to encourage more foreign investors to invest in the middle and western parts of China. However, even with such measures, the existing patterns of economic development may not change in significant ways in the near future.

Income distribution

Closely related to uneven regional development, FDI has also contributed to the uneven distribution of personal incomes both within and between regions.[62] The salary level in foreign invested enterprises can be several times higher than that in state owned companies for the same type of work. A study by the People's (Renmin) University of China suggested that before the reform in 1978, personal income was very evenly distributed in China (that is, income differentiation was among the lowest in the whole world).

However, in 1994, the poorest 20 per cent of families in China only earned about 4.27 per cent of total income, compared with the richest 20 per cent with 50.24 per cent. The comparable figures for the USA in 1990 were 4.6 per cent for the poorest 20 per cent versus 44.3 per cent for the richest 20 per cent. This means that income is even more unevenly distributed in communist China than in the capitalist USA in the 1990s! If the situation is allowed to continue, there could be serious social and political consequences, which the Chinese government cannot afford not to address. Although FDI is only one of many factors contributing to this problem in China, the Chinese government's responses to this problem will inevitably affect foreign invested enterprises.

The influences of FDI in the Chinese economy

In this section, we discussed FDI's influence on various aspects of the Chinese economy, and both the positive contributions and negative influences were highlighted. FDI has contributed significantly to China's rapid economic development by relieving capital supply bottlenecks, facilitating technological progress and improving enterprise management, but it also contributed to problems such as growing regional disparities and uneven distribution of personal incomes. Some other important economic issues were not discussed in this section – such as that the rapid growth of foreign invested enterprises may have contributed to the enormous difficulties faced by state owned enterprises in China. Moreover, the strong social influences of FDI in China have also emerged in recent years. These issues are the focus of the next section.

FDI AND THE SOCIAL TRANSFORMATION IN CONTEMPORARY CHINA

Today, the economic influences of FDI in China have been widely recognized. At a deeper level, FDI is also facilitating profound changes in Chinese society, which have not been systematically studied so far.[63] The reasons for that are complex, partly because FDI is still a relatively new phenomenon in China and its long term social influences have not yet fully emerged. Some social influences of FDI are politically sensitive, particularly in the aspects of ideological and cultural changes, which may have prevented some Chinese researchers in China from getting involved in such studies.

Understanding the social influences of FDI is extremely important to both the Chinese government and foreign investors, because
the perception of, and the reactions to, the social influences of
FDI by Chinese people (particularly by Chinese leaders) will inevitably be reflected in the policies and regulations for FDI in China
in the future and in the quality of China's soft environment. As
will be discussed later in this section, almost all employees of state
owned organizations are entitled to a wide range of social welfare,
mostly provided through their employers. However, until the early
1990s, many foreign invested enterprises did not provide any such
benefits. As the number of Chinese people working in non-state
owned enterprises (including foreign invested enterprises) increases,
the Chinese government has recently demanded that all foreign
invested enterprises pay into five government funds (pension, medical care, maternity, unemployment and disability) in order to provide adequate social security for their Chinese employees.[64] This
certainly affects the costs of doing business in China for foreign
investors. Other measures have also increasingly been introduced
to protect the interests of Chinese employees in foreign invested
enterprises.

This section focuses on the following issues. First, the role of
FDI in the clash between Chinese and foreign culture and the
associated changes in people's ideologies and values. Second, how
the rapid growth of FDI has facilitated the structural re-fabrication
of the Chinese society. Third, how these social changes are reflected
in the rapid improvements of FDI-related legal systems and government
services in China.

FDI and changes in the mainstream ideologies and values in Chinese society

Since China's opening up in the late 1970s, the clash between Chinese and foreign culture has facilitated significant changes in people's
ideologies and values, which are clearly reflected in a wide range
of new phenomena that are in sharp contrast to the basic elements
of Chinese society before the reform and opening up. For example,
the flood of advertisements in various media versus the political
slogans and propaganda; the elegant fashion shows versus the dull,
grey- or blue-coloured, Chinese tunic suit (*Maoist style Zhong Shan
Zhuang*); the fanatic desires for foreign-made home electronics

versus the self-satisfied nationalistic patriotism; the pursuit of materialistic well-being versus the much praised self-sacrifice and resistance to 'capitalistic decadence'; and the conscious stimulation of mass consumption versus the self-reliant, centrally planned economy of shortage. These sharp contrasts reflected deeper changes in people's ideologies and values in China.

In a special issue on China, *Time* magazine titled one of its articles 'Time for the "Me Generation"'.[65] The article vividly described how one thousand young people, mostly under the age of thirty, spent a night at JJ's (a popular disco in Shanghai). They paid about US$4.5 for a ticket (a lot of money in China for a ticket), wore smart, imported designer clothes and, accompanied by fashionably dressed young women, sipped foreign drinks while making calls on cellular phones. Some of the bar tenders had actually dropped out of universities to earn four times as much money as a university graduate would normally earn in a state owned organization. The values and ideologies of these young people are in sharp contrast to Mao Zedong's Red Guards during the cultural revolution.

A friend of ours recently went back to his home village in China after spending ten years in the USA and Europe. His home village was in a very remote mountainous area, which was extremely isolated from the rest of the world before the reform. He expected his home village to be different, but to his great surprise, what he saw were not only new houses and new village factories (some of them foreign owned), and tractors, motor cycles, telephones and cars, but also young people in fashionable clothes, listening to Michael Jackson and Madonna whilst playing snooker in the village club. The smoke over small houses in his village and the faint music from shepherds' flutes had all disappeared. He was happy that people in his home village could now enjoy some products of modernization, but he was also sad that the traditional rural culture and related values he cherished so much had simply vanished – especially with the younger generation. Through modern communications, international trade and most directly, FDI, western influences have penetrated into even some of the most remote and isolated places in China.

Such new phenomena represent radical changes in people's ideologies and values. The slogan of 'politics in command' was replaced by 'economy in command' a long time ago,[66] and the famous slogan of 'hard work and plain living' (*Jian Ku Pu Su*) was replaced by a more popular but fundamentally different one – 'to get rich is glorious'. Such ideological and value changes would have been unimaginable only two decades ago in China.

Clearly, FDI is only one of many factors which have contributed to the ideological and value changes in China, and the clash between Chinese and foreign ideologies, values and culture has happened through many different means, such as the mass media, cultural exchanges and international trade, but perhaps none of these channels are as direct and profound as FDI. The rapid growth of FDI in China provided new opportunities for Chinese people to develop a deeper understanding of foreign values, ideologies and culture through direct and frequent contacts with foreign expatriates and their families.

In the contemporary world, the ideologies and values, and indeed, the culture of the advanced capitalist world are more influential (but not necessarily better or morally more correct) than that of the centrally planned societies, in the sense that elements of the former are increasingly penetrating into, and accepted by, the latter. The collapse of the Eastern bloc and the disintegration of the Soviet Union further enhanced this pattern. To speed up its economic development, China has decided to transform its centrally planned economic regime to a market system. Accompanying this transition, certain established values and ideologies in Chinese society need to be abandoned and new ones accepted. The development process of the western capitalist world has been regulated by a series of basic rules based on certain values and ideologies developed since the Industrial Revolution, many of which are in contradiction to the mainstream values and ideologies in China. If China intends to be part of this development process, it has to understand, and learn to play by, some of these rules. Strong external influences – sometimes uncomfortable influences – in Chinese society are, therefore, inevitable. This is not to say China should not protect its culture and values, but to participate in the world market China has to observe certain basic rules by accepting certain new values and compromising in other aspects. Only through participation can China develop its economy rapidly, thereby increasing its influence in this new world.

China needs FDI for its economic development, but to attract foreign investment it has to satisfy some basic requirements of foreign investors. Although the precise influences are difficult to evaluate, FDI has certainly contributed to the ideological and value changes in Chinese society by bringing new ideas and new concepts into

China – such as western style democracy, freedom, human rights, rule by law rather than by man, materialism and consumerism. Other key areas include private property rights, employment policies, mobility between jobs and places, the provision of social welfare, attitudes towards work and a whole series of other changes. Some of these ideas and associated values are increasingly accepted by Chinese people whilst others clashed with those in Chinese society. It is also interesting to notice that some traditional Chinese values and western values co-exist side-by-side in contemporary Chinese society.

Within the centrally planned regime in China, the purpose of production was political (ideologically determined) rather than economic (efficiency and profit) in nature. The main incentives for people to work hard were ideological rather than financial. Many people were not motivated to work hard, because the salary for everyone was fixed (often depending on how long one had worked in a state-owned organization and his/her rank). Promotion was strictly related to one's age, political background, working experience and, most importantly, *guanxi* (relations with key figures of the Communist Party at the relevant level). In addition, almost all jobs in state-owned organizations were permanent before the reform, and the mobility between jobs was extremely low. All permanent employees and some of their immediate families (for example, children and parents) were automatically entitled to a wide range of welfare such as free medical care, housing and education – mostly provided by the employer rather than by the government. The transfer of someone from a senior position to a lower position seldom occurred unless one made mistakes or committed crimes.

In sharp contrast, foreign investors came to China to make profits and to take advantage of the vast (potential) market. The salary in foreign invested enterprises is related directly to an employee's talent and performance, therefore people are motivated to work hard and to be responsible. Not all employees in foreign invested enterprises are permanent, and the rules of promotion and removal have also changed. Some of the social welfare benefits are simply unavailable and employees have to purchase them from the market if they need them (although this is changing in recent years). The attitudes towards work also need to change to meet the demands of foreign invested enterprises. In addition, FDI also helps to create a new, relatively rich, social group. The new social and economic status of this group not only affects their ideologies and values, but also their ways of life and behaviours. They have to work hard, but the economic rewards allow them to enjoy the happiness of wealth associated with middle-class western lifestyles. This group is also economically independent from the state provision, so their freedom in many other aspects is also increased.

More recently, the Chinese government decided to phase out a wide range of welfare benefits traditionally provided by employers at the organizational level, and in the future such benefits will be provided at the society level.[67] Private sector employers, including foreign investors, are required to pay into five different government funds: pension, medical care, maternity, unemployment and disability. Many foreign investors also offered housing to their employees as a lure for the workers they wanted.[68] In other aspects, the political control over ideologies and the mass media remains tight, as it is regarded as essential to the social and political stability in China. The Chinese authority has also made a number of attempts to protect Chinese culture and 'stop the invasion of foreign culture'. Apart from insisting on using Chinese *Pin Yin* to spell all names of people and places in English publications in China (for example, Peking should be spelt as Beijing), China also started to give official government press releases in Chinese (rather than in English). A number of other measures have been adopted to protect the purity of the Chinese language.

These contrasting phenomena reflect the strong clashes between Chinese and foreign values, ideologies, and culture in contemporary Chinese society. FDI is an important factor that has contributed to this profound social transformation although its precise role is difficult to specify. Some of the ideologies associated with the centrally planned economy are increasingly being replaced by that of a market system; many traditional values are increasingly abandoned while elements of western values are increasingly being accepted. These changes have profound implications for the reform and further opening up, and for the quality of the soft environment for FDI, in China.

FDI and the re-fabrication of Chinese society in the context of reform and opening up

Closely related to the ideological and value changes, the rapid growth of FDI in China has also facilitated significant structural changes in Chinese society. In particular, FDI is playing an important role in the formation of a new social group who no longer rely directly on the state for the provision of basic necessities and services, which serves to increase the social, and to a less extent, political, autonomy of this group in China.

After 1949, the collectivization of agriculture and the nationalization of industry left Chinese citizens fully dependent on the political authority and the work units (*Dan Wei*) for the provision of basic necessities and welfare. However, the reform and opening up paved the way for the emergence of new, more diverse social groups in Chinese society. Peasants once engaged in subsistence farming under the authority of the commune became independent farmers producing cash crops on their own fifteen- to thirty-year leaseholds. Rural entrepreneurs began to run their own small factories; and in urban areas, a small army of private shopkeepers and peddlers emerged to compete with state run stores. Many employees of state owned organizations gave up their permanent jobs to set up their own businesses. The private sector has been growing much faster than the state owned sector. As a result, many people are now freed, or partially freed, from direct dependence on party state, thereby having a degree of social and economic autonomy. In fact, it has even been argued that the growing autonomy of society and its progressive alienation from official norms and structures point the way towards a civil society in China.[69]

The role of FDI in the process is very profound. During the early days of reform, Chinese entrepreneurs operated in an insecure environment, and even the most successful companies needed government connections because they lacked formal legitimacy. For example, much of an urban merchant's property and resources were technically state property, for which the state held a lease. In fact, the social autonomy of the new social groups in China depends on the tolerance of the authorities or the government's indifference.[70] The legal framework in China was not complete enough to protect them effectively (though this situation has changed considerably in recent years).

However, foreign invested enterprises are very different. They not only allow many Chinese employees to be freed from dependence on the state, they are also part of multinational operations originating from other parts of the world, and therefore these enterprises are under the protection of international laws and their own countries of origin. In this sense, the control by the Chinese government over such enterprises is much looser than other private or quasi-private enterprises. The strong desire of the Chinese central and local governments to attract more FDI has also urged them to restrict interference in the affairs of foreign invested enterprises and their employees. FDI also directly enhances the private sector in the Chinese economy and hence changes the ownership structure in China, although the predominance of state ownership in China is not fundamentally affected. As FDI continues to grow rapidly, the influences of FDI on the social structures of Chinese society will continue to increase.

The rapid completion of FDI-related legal systems and the improvement in relevant government services

The influences of FDI on Chinese society are clearly reflected in a wide range of phenomena. For most foreign investors, their investments in China are only part of their international operations. To be successful, these ventures in China need to adapt to the specific local conditions, but some of their essential demands also need to be met by China – otherwise they will go somewhere else. One of these demands is the protection of an adequate legal framework – which was very inadequate during the early days of the opening up, but has been improving very rapidly since the mid-1980s. As has been discussed in Chapter 3, the development of FDI related laws, regulations and policies in China was characterized by a reactive process until the early 1990s, and since then a more proactive and more selective approach has been adopted. Today, a large body of laws and a coherent legal framework have been developed in the area of foreign economic relations (including FDI). Relevant issues have been discussed in detail in Chapter 6.

   A second demand by foreign investors is in the area of FDI-related government services at various levels. The Chinese government has traditionally been characterized by bureaucraticism and low efficiency, but in order to attract more FDI, both the local and central governments have simplified procedures and improved the efficiency of their services for foreign investors. The power of local governments in approving FDI projects has increased significantly since the mid-1980s, and specialized departments have been set up in most provinces and cities to deal with FDI-related issues, such as the approval of projects, arranging regular supply of materials, and many other legal, insurance, skilled labour supply, foreign currency and consultancy services – increasingly in accordance with international practice.[71] The rapid completion of FDI-related legal systems and the rapid improvements in FDI-related government services may facilitate the improvements of the legal environment and government services in China in general.

SUMMARY OF THE CHAPTER

This chapter has examined the economic and social influences of FDI in China. FDI has clearly contributed to the rapid development of the Chinese economy by relieving capital supply bottlenecks and by bringing new technologies and management techniques to China, but it also contributed to problems such as growing regional disparities and uneven distribution of personal incomes both within and between regions. The enormous difficulties faced by state owned enterprises are at least to some extent the result of growing competition from foreign invested enterprises in China.

The rapid growth of FDI has also contributed to the profound social transformations in Chinese society, which are reflected in a wide range of new phenomena in China. Although its precise role is difficult to specify, FDI has clearly contributed to changes in the mainstream values and ideologies of Chinese people, in the social structures of China, and in many other aspects – such as the rapid completion of FDI-related legal systems and the rapid improvements in FDI-related government services. Such changes are also having wider implications in Chinese society. However, since China only opened its door to foreign investors in the late 1970s, and only since the early 1990s that FDI began to grow rapidly, many social and economic consequences of FDI in China may have not fully emerged. More time, and more systematic studies, are needed to develop a comprehensive understanding of FDI's full impacts on Chinese society and economy. The economic and social changes facilitated by FDI, and people's perception and reactions towards such changes, will be reflected in the soft environment for FDI in China.

Notes

1. Li, Peng (1991) 'Report of the outline of the ten year national economic and social development plan and the eighth five year plan' (*Guan Yu Guo Min Jing Ji He She Hui Fa Zhan De Shi Nian Yuan Jing Gui*

Hua He Ba Wu Ji Hua De Bao Gao), *The People's Daily* (Overseas edition), 11 April 1991, p. 1. See Chapter 1 for a more detailed discussion.

2. For example, Shen, Xiaofang (1990) 'A decade of direct foreign investment in China', *Problems of Communism*, March–April, 1990; Lu, Luping (1992), 'Promoting China's opening up to the outside world to a higher level' (*Nu Li Ba Dui Wai Kai Fang Ti Gao Dao Xin De Shui Ping*), *Qiushi*, 1992 (8), pp. 19–24; Kamath, Shyam J. (1990) 'Foreign direct investment in centrally planned developing economy: The Chinese case', *Economic Development and Culture Change*, Vol. 39, No. 1, October, 1990; *Beijing Review*, 30 December 1991–5 January 1992, 'Open policy brings achievements'.

3. *The People's Daily* (Overseas edition), 9 June 1997, 'The total number of foreign invested enterprises exceeded 280 000, by the end of last year total utilized FDI exceeded US$176.5 billion' (*Wo Guo Wai Qi Yi Da 28 Wan Duo Jian, Jie Zhi Qu Nian Di Shi Ji Li Yong Wai Zi Yu 1765 Yi Mei Yuan*), p. 1. Figures were released by a senior official from the Ministry of Foreign Trade and Economic Co-operation (MOFTEC).

4. *The People's Daily* (Overseas edition), 3 April 1997, 'Attracting foreign investment – A rapidly booming area' (*Xi Yin Wai Zi – Yi Ge Fang Xing Wei Ai De Ling Yu*), p. 2; *The Economist*, 8–14 March 1997, 'The importance of foreign-devil money', *China Survey*, p. 9.

5. *The Economist*, 8–14 March 1997, *op. cit.*

6. *The Economist*, 21–27 June 1997, 'The China syndrome', pp. 79–80.

7. *The Economist*, 17–23 August 1996, 'China – A funny looking tiger', pp. 17–19.

8. Shen (1990) *op. cit.*; Kueh, Y.Y. (1992) 'Foreign investment and economic change in China', *China Quarterly*, September 1992, No. 131.

9. Williams, Ann (1992), 'China's booming "special economic zones"', *Geographical*, March 1992; *Fortune*, 5 October 1992, 'A new China without borders', pp. 40–44.

10. *The Financial Times*, 20 May 1994, information obtained from Ministry of Foreign Trade and Economic Co-operation (MOFTEC).

11. *Beijing Review*, 30 December 1991–5 January 1992, *op. cit.*

12. *The People's Daily* (Overseas edition), 25 September 1996. 'China is the second largest destination for foreign capital (*Zhong Guo Xi Yin Wai Zi Liang Ju Shi Jie Di Er*)', p. 6. It was reported in the United National World Investment Report published on 24 September 1996 that China attracted a total of US$37.5 billion foreign capital in 1995 (increased from US$33.8 in 1994), three years in a row to be the second largest destination for foreign capital after the USA.

13. Shen (1990) *op. cit.*

14. *The People's Daily* (Overseas edition), 6 May 1997, 'Last year Beijing newly approved over 800 foreign invested enterprises, with a total FDI exceeding of US$2.2 billion' (*Beijing Qu Nian Xin Pi San Zi Qi Yie Ba Bai Duo Jia, Wai Shang Zhi Jie Tou Zi Yu 22 Yi Mei Yuan*), p. 1.

15. *The People's Daily* (Overseas edition), 6 May 1997, 'Tianjin: Income by foreign invested enterprises increasing rapidly' (*Tianjin: Wai Qi Shou Ru Kuai Su Zeng Zhang*), p. 2.

16. Figures from Australian Ministry of Foreign Affairs and Trade, *The Economist*, 3–9 May 1997, 'Shanghai takes shape', pp. 67–68.
17. *The People's Daily* (Overseas edition), 12 August 1997, 'On the course opened up by the great man – Deng Xiaoping's theory on developing socialism with Chinese characteristics and Shanghai's reform and opening up' (*Zai Wei Ren Kai Pi De Hang Dao Shang – Deng Xiao Ping Jian She You Zhong Guo Te Ce De She Hui Zhu Yi Li Lun He Shang Hai De Gai Ge Kai Fang*), p. 1.
18. *Beijing Review*, 20–26 January 1992, 'Third foreign investment high tide', p. 29.
19. *The Financial Times*, 14 June 1993.
20. Wu Yi (who is the Minister for Foreign Trade and Economic Co-operation) announced these figures at the State Council news conference, *The People's Daily* (Overseas edition), 29 January 1994. The Working Conference for Registration Management of Foreign Invested Enterprises also released some of the figures in *The People's Daily*, 26 April 1994. *The Financial Times*, 14 June 1993, 'Lure of the billion-buyer market'.
21. Figures released in 'The People's Republic of China National Statistical Bureau Report on China's Economic and Social Development' for 1993, 1994, 1995, 1996 *[Zhong Hua Ren Min Gong He Guo Guo Jia Tong Ji Ju Guan Yu 1993 (1994, 1995, 1996) Nian Guo Min Jing Ji He She Hui Fa Zhan De Tong Ji Gong Bao]*, in *The People's Daily* (Overseas edition), 4 March 1994; March 2 1995; March 5 1996; 7 April 1997, p. 2.
22. *The Economist*, 1–7 March 1997 'Foreign investment: Not quite so sparkling China', p. 72.
23. *The People's Daily* (Overseas edition), 22 May 1997 'New characteristics in China's utilisation of foreign investment' (*Zhong Guo Li Yong Wai Zi Cheng Xian Xin Te Zheng*), p. 2.
24. Figures from *China Statistical Yearbook*, 1983–1996; *The Economist*, 8–14 March 1997, *op. cit. The People's Daily* (Overseas edition), 4 March 1994; March 2 1995; March 5 1996; 7 April 1997, *op. cit.*
25. *The People's Daily* (Overseas edition), 1 July 1995, 'Regulation on Guiding the Direction of Foreign Investment' (*Zhi Dao Wai Shang Tou Zi Fang Xiang Zan Xing Gui Ding*) and 'Index of Foreign Investment Industrial Guide' (*Wai Shang Tou Zi Chan Ye Zhi Dao Mu Lu*), p. 2.
26. *The People's Daily* (Overseas edition), 27 January 1997, 'The main focuses for attracting FDI in China this year' (*Zhong Guo Que Ding Jin Nian Xi Yin Wei Zi Gong Zuo Zhong Dian*), p. 2.
27. *The People's Daily* (Overseas edition), 3 May 1997, 'China adopts a series of new preferential policies and measures to encourage foreign businessmen to invest in the middle and western regions' (*Zhong Guo Cai Qu Xi Lie You Hui Zheng Ce Cuo Shi Gu Li Wai Shang Dao Zhong Xi Bu Di Qu Tou Zi*), p. 2.
28. *The People's Daily* (Overseas edition), 3 April 1997, *op. cit.*
29. Guo, Aimin and Robert Akroyd (1996) 'Overcoming barriers to technological transfers into China', in Child, John and Yuan Lu (eds) *Management Issues in China: Volume II, International Enterprises*, Routledge, London, pp. 30–51.

30. Pomfret, Richard (1991) *Investing in China*, Harvester Wheatsheaf, New York; Shen (1990) *op. cit.*; The Economist Intelligence Unit and Andersen Consulting (1995) *Moving China Ventures out of the Red into the Black: Insights from best and worst performers*, The Economist Intelligence Unit, London.
31. Euromonitor (1994) *China: A Directory and Source Book 1994*, Euromonitor Plc, London; Brahm, Lawrence and Li Daoran (1996) *The Business Guide to China*, Butterworth-Heinemann Asia, Singapore.
32. *The People's Daily* (Overseas edition), 13 August 1992.
33. *The People's Daily* (Overseas edition), 29 March 1994.
34. *The People's Daily* (Overseas edition), 20 August 1997 'Early movers versus new comers: A brief report of the competition between multinational car manufacturers in the Chinese market' (*Zhang Wo Xian Ji Yu Hou Lai Ju Shang – Qi Che Kua Guo Gong Si Jing Zheng Zhong Guo Shi Chang Ce Ji*), p. 2; also see *The People's Daily* (Overseas edition), 22 January 1992; *Financial Times*, 28 May 1993.
35. *The People's Daily* (Overseas edition), 19 February 1992.
36. *The People's Daily* (Overseas edition), 11 August 1997, 'The five major car groups set targets for the "ninth five year plan"' (*Wu Da Jiao Che Ji Tuan Que Ding "Jiu Wu" Mu Biao*), p. 2; *The People's Daily* (Overseas edition), 20 August 1997, 'The First Automobile Corporation Volkswagen new car production line checked and accepted' (*Yi Qi Da Zhong Jiao Che Xiang Mu Tong Guo Yan Shou*), p. 1.
37. Shen (1990) *op. cit.*
38. The Economist Intelligence Unit and Andersen Consulting (1995) *op. cit.*; *The People's Daily* (Overseas edition), 20 August 1997, p. 2, *op. cit.*
39. *The People's Daily* (Overseas edition), 22 January 1992.
40. *The People's Daily* (Overseas edition), 18 August 1997, 'China launches major plan to transfer and absorb new technologies' (*Guo Jia Zhong Da Yin Jin Ji Shu Xi Shou Ji Hua Que Ding*), p. 2.
41. The Economist Intelligence Unit and Andersen Consulting (1995) *op. cit.*; *The Economist* 3–9 December 1994, 'How not to sell 1.2 billion tubes of toothpaste', pp. 95–96.
42. *The People's Daily* (Overseas edition), 22 January 1992; *Gallup Survey* (1995), the first foreign sponsored national study of consumer attitudes and lifestyle trends of the People's Republic of China, conducted during May–September 1994 and results released by Gallup Organization on 15 February 1995 in New York.
43. *The People's Daily* (Overseas edition), 18 August 1997, *op. cit.*
44. Child, J. (1994) *op. cit.*; Child, John and Yuan Lu (1996) 'Introduction: China and international enterprise', Child, John and Yuan Lu (eds) *op. cit.*
45. Child, John and Yuan Lu (1996), *op. cit.*, p. 3.
46. The Economist Intelligence Unit and Andersen Consulting (1995), *op. cit.*; *The People's Daily* (Overseas edition), 18 August 1997, 'Creating high quality managerial staff – The views of enterprises in the east coastal region on human resources' (*Zao Jiu Gao Su Zhi Jing Ying Zhe Dui Wu – Dong Bu Yan Hai De Qi Ye Ren Cai Guan*), p. 1.
47. Tsang, Eric (1994) 'Human resource management problems in Sino–foreign joint ventures', *International Journal of Manpower* 15 (9/10):

4–21; Warner, Malcolm (1996) 'Managing China's enterprise reforms: A new agenda for the 1990s', *Journal of General Management* 21(3): 1–18, Spring 1996.

48. The Economist Intelligence Unit and Andersen Consulting (1995), *op. cit.*
49. *The People's Daily* (Overseas edition), 25 December 1991; Shen (1990) *op. cit.*
50. *Beijing Review*, 6 March 1989; page 25.
51. *The People's Daily* (Overseas edition), 18 January 1992.
52. *The People's Daily* (Overseas edition), 18 May 1994 'The future is bright, the potential is enormous', (*Qian Jing Guang Kuo, Da You Ke Wei*)' p. 1 and 3.
53. *The Economist*, 17–23 August 1996, *op. cit.*
54. *The People's Daily* (Overseas edition), 18 January 1992.
55. *The Economist* 16–22 September 1995, 'The private life of a Chinese', pp. 87–88.
56. *The People's Daily* (Overseas edition), 7 August 1992.
57. Aiello, Paul (1991) 'Building a joint venture in China: The case of Chrysler and the Beijing Jeep Corporation', *Journal of General Management*, Vol. 17(2) Winter 1991.
58. Li, Ling (1996) 'The main causes for the widening gap between the east and the west and some possible solutions', *China Opening Herald*, August 1996, Vol. 26 No. 8: 5–11; The Development Institute (1996) 'Regional economic disparities in China: Current situation, main causes and policy responses', *China Opening Herald*, September 1996, Vol. 27 No. 9: 5–15.
59. *The People's Daily* (Overseas edition), 19 September 1992.
60. *The People's Daily* (Overseas edition), 26 April, 1994.
61. *The People's Daily* (Overseas edition), 5 June 1992.
62. *The Economist*, 6–13 June 1992, 'Soaking the rich'; *The People's Daily* (Overseas edition), 22 January 1992.
63. A paper by David S.G. Goodman (1992), 'Reforming China: Foreign contacts, foreign values?' published in *The Pacific Review*, Vol. 5 No. 1, 1992, pp. 25–38, touched upon some issues related to the penetration of foreign values in China, but it is not exclusively about FDI and value changes. Child (1994) *op. cit.* also discussed some relevant issues.
64. Euromonitor (1994) *op. cit.*; Brahm and Li (1996) *op. cit.*
65. *Time*, China Special Report, 10 May 1993.
66. Schram, S.R. (1984) *Ideology and Policy in China since the Third Plenum, 1978–84*, Contemporary China Institute, London.
67. Sun, Jiupeng (1996) 'Reforms in China's social security system', *China Opening Herald*, July 1996, Vol. 25 No 7: 18–21.
68. *The Economist*, 16–22 September 1995, *op. cit.*
69. Rosenbaum, Arthur Lewis (ed.) (1992) *State and Society in China: The consequence of reform*, Westview Press, Boulder, Colorado, USA.
70. Shen (1990) *op. cit.*
71. *The People's Daily* (Overseas edition), 29 July 1992.

9 Conclusions: Foreign Investment Environment in China Under the Open Door Policy

For many foreign investors, developing a comprehensive understanding of China poses a major challenge. China is a complex society, by virtue of its deeply embedded and multi-layered cultural heritage, its long history, its diverse social and political development, and its vast geographical scale which encompasses both national common characteristics and strong local identities, traditions and distinctive dialects. This complexity, combined with the rapid changes in the country at present, makes it extremely difficult to reach an adequate understanding of contemporary developments. As Child pointed out,[2] foreigners often find it difficult enough simply to secure valid descriptions about China, let alone comprehensive understanding. This book is our attempt to help (potential) foreign investors to understand contemporary developments in China in the broad area of foreign investment environment.

For almost two decades, China has had the fastest growing economy in the world, providing some of the most attractive commercial opportunities for foreign investors. Although the Chinese government has faced extremely difficult challenges (such as controlling high inflation, reforming the loss-making state owned enterprises and the banking system, reducing the rapidly growing unemployment and regional disparities), the social and political stability in China has so far been effectively maintained. Many experts, commentators and international organizations (such as the World Bank and the IMF) have predicted that China will continue to grow rapidly for the next twenty years.

The perceived risks of investing in China have plummeted and, since the mid-1980s, China's legal framework, regulatory system and its business and physical infrastructure have been strengthened. Bureaucrats, business people, workers and consumers in China have

231

all become more comfortable with the ethics and values of a market economy. Foreign and Chinese firms in legal practice, accounting and advertising have been established. A pool of competent local managers, technical staff and workers has emerged. Combined with its enormous market potential and unlimited supply of cheap labour, China will continue to attract top companies from all over the world. However, foreign investors need to be fully prepared to face the enormous difficulties in doing business in China.

The future growth of China will depend critically on stability in its domestic and international affairs. Failure in either area will significantly undermine international business confidence in China and the quality of China's foreign investment environment. This chapter summarizes the main findings of the book, and speculates on the future prospects of the Chinese economy and the foreign investment environment in China.

THE FOREIGN INVESTMENT ENVIRONMENT IN CHINA

In Chapter 2 we identified the main attractions of China for different types of foreign investors, and analysed the key motivations of foreign investors for investing in China under the contemporary world economic climate. The main attractions of China, among many other factors, include its enormous market size and the even greater future potential, its abundant supply of cheap (but reasonably educated and well-disciplined) labour and the preferential taxation and other policies adopted by the central and local governments to attract foreign investors.

The motivations of foreign investors in China vary significantly, but a number of common features have been identified, including entering a new market, exploiting locational advantages (such as, cheap labour), and securing the supply of raw materials (including coal and oil). In some cases, FDI in China has been the result of industrial restructuring in developed economies. For most large investors (such as some world-leading multinational companies), FDI has often been intended to help them to set a foot in China in order to secure a slice of this rapidly growing market.[3] A number of differences were identified between investors from developed economies (the USA, Japan and Europe) and those from newly industrializing economies (such as Hong Kong, Taiwan and Singapore). The motivations of foreign investors to some extent determine what constitute the key elements of the foreign investment environment in China.

In Chapter 3 we examined the evolution of China's open door policy in respect of FDI. Major FDI-related laws and regulations were highlighted and their implications for foreign investors in China were discussed. The terms made explicit by these laws and regulations lay down the basic legislative and institutional framework for FDI in China. By examining the key factors that facilitated or led to the major changes in FDI-related laws and regulations, the book concluded that the key dynamics of China's evolving open door policy have been the strong desire of the Chinese leadership (and Chinese people) to achieve rapid and steady economic development, and the interactions between various internal and external forces. Such processes have resulted in what was known as 'reactive policy making' in much of the 1980s. The general tendency was that an increasingly relaxed foreign investment environment was created both for the starting up and the operation of foreign invested enterprises. Improvements in the legal environment and government services for FDI have been particularly significant. In the 1990s, the focus of China's opening up is shifting from quantity to quality, and an increasingly selective and proactive approach has been adopted to attract specific types of FDI into selected sectors and locations. Such a policy shift has profound implications for future opportunities in China for foreign investors.

The foreign investment environment in China is divided into the hard environment and the soft environment. Chapter 4 assessed the characteristics and conditions of China's hard environment for FDI. Major problems restricting the operation and development of foreign invested enterprises, including energy shortage, the insecure supply of raw materials, and the inadequate transportation and telecommunications infrastructure were identified, and their current situation and future prospects were discussed. Although the Chinese government has been working hard to tackle these problems, and some serious problems of the 1980s have been greatly relieved today (such as telecommunications), many problems will continue to affect foreign invested enterprises. The rapidly growing Chinese economy means improvements in certain infrastructures have often lagged behind the even faster growth in demand, so some existing problems may even deteriorate in certain areas in the near future.

China is a poor, large, developing country. Despite nearly twenty years of rapid growth, the general condition of China's hard environment cannot be improved to a level comparable with the developed economies in the short term. Nevertheless, improvements in certain sectors (such as telecommunications) and locations (for example, the special economic zones and some open cities along the coast) have been very impressive. Since the early 1990s, new sources of finance have been sought and foreign investors are increasingly encouraged to participate directly in the development of China's infrastructure (which has in fact provided some very lucrative investment opportunities). Continuous improvements in the hard environment are therefore inevitable, but many problems will remain for some time to come.

From the historical, political and social perspectives, Chapter 5 assessed the general context of China's soft investment environment. The historical perspective demonstrated the close relationship between China's opening up and economic prosperity, and its inward-looking, overly self-reliant mentality and national economic decline. The lessons from China's own history strongly support an opening-up scenario if China intends to achieve economic prosperity and continuous growth. From a political perspective, the book concluded that despite reoccurring fluctuations and short-term stagnation or set-backs, the reform and the opening up is going to continue – indeed, China has perhaps reached a stage of 'no turning back'. The question is how the reform and opening up will proceed, and at what speed. From a social perspective, the book argued that even under a stable political environment, the success of a foreign invested enterprise in China is still not straightforward. The unique culture and social structures in China will exert considerable influences on the operation and management of foreign invested enterprises. Many time-proven management techniques elsewhere may simply not work in China. We have particularly highlighted the critical importance of *guanxi*, examined the institutional and cultural roots of this phenomenon, and discussed the relevance of *guanxi* to foreign investors in China.

Chapter 6 continued to examine China's soft environment by analysing some operational problems encountered by foreign investors in areas ranging from insufficient foreign exchange facilities to incomplete legal systems. Many such problems are closely related to China's transition from a centrally planned economy to a market system. Today, most tactical problems in relation to the incompatibility between central planning and a market economy have been (even if only temporarily) resolved or greatly relieved, but many politically-sensitive issues have been deliberately put aside and their resolution depends on the success of the next round of reforms – some of which have begun in the mid-1990s (for example, reforming the loss-making state owned enterprises and the banking system). A comprehensive understanding of these factors is essential for foreign investors to make valid judgements about the quality of China's investment environment and the potential risks involved.

Although China is a large and rapidly growing market, getting products to consumers is a daunting task. Distribution and marketing, therefore, have posed serious challenges to foreign invested enterprises, and the unique, geographically varied, and rapidly changing consumer behaviours that characterize a market in transition makes the challenges even greater. Chapter 7 of the book thus examined a wide range of issues in this broad area, discussed their implications for foreign invested enterprises, and concluded that distribution and sales will continue to pose serious challenges to foreign invested enterprises. Because China is still in transition, administrative and market forces will continue to affect the operation of both Chinese and foreign companies in China. At the current stage, the state distribution system of the centrally planned economy has crumbled, but the new distribution system of the market economy has not been fully established. The poor transportation infrastructure and various government regulations and restrictions will continue to affect the development of a fast, reliable, and efficient distribution system. Although improvements since the early 1990s have been significant, and foreign invested enterprises now have a wide variety of options available to them in formulating a distribution and sales strategy, the challenge remains.

The Chinese market is huge and rapidly growing, but the exact size of the market is difficult to estimate. On purchasing power parity (PPP) basis, the World Bank put China's GDP per capita at US$2500 in 1994,[4] but in a following report, the figure was revised to US$1800, reducing the size of the Chinese economy by over one quarter.[5] Even so, the Chinese economy remains huge. The ownership of consumables in Chinese households is considerably higher than it was in most other countries when they were at China's current level of economic development. The Chinese consumer behaviours are in many ways very different from people in the West, and such characteristics should be taken into account when formulating a marketing strategy. Many well-tested techniques elsewhere simply do not work (indeed, may even be damaging) in China. To win a slice of the Chinese market, foreign investors not only have to find ways to distribute products efficiently and quickly to different parts of China, but also to market their products in ways which appeal to the Chinese consumers.

Chapter 8 examined the economic and social influences of FDI in China, which can significantly affect people's perception of and attitude towards FDI. Since 1978, FDI has been playing an increasingly important role in the development of the Chinese economy, but recently some negative economic influences of FDI have also been recognized. Moreover, FDI is facilitating radical changes in Chinese society. Changes in the social structures and in people's ideologies and values have been particularly dramatic. These changes will inevitably be reflected in China's future policies and regulations for FDI, and in China's open door policy in general.

Many findings of the book are tentative. China is still in the process of rapid change, and the full effects of many reforms which have been implemented since the early 1990s are not yet fully developed. More systematic studies, and more time, are required to understand the profound transformation. The challenges facing Chinese reformers are extremely difficult. The international environment is becoming more complex and uncertain; and in transforming China's planned economy into a market system, a wide range of political, social, ideological and economic barriers have to be overcome. The removal of old control mechanisms and the creation of new ones will not happen smoothly, especially when China is 'crossing the river by feeling the stones on the river bed'. The temporary 'vacuum' in political and economic control during the transition may lead to major economic and political fluctuations, thereby affecting China's foreign investment environment.

Recently, the attitude of the Chinese authority towards FDI has gone through a major change. Only a few years ago, all foreign investors that entered China were greeted with open arms, partly because China wanted some showpieces, but mainly because China needed the capital, technology and management techniques to develop its national and regional economies. Today, China has become much more sophisticated and selective about foreign investment. It is still prepared to offer incentives to attract FDI into specific industries (for example, high-tech) in selected locations (the middle and west of China), but it also has implemented restrictions to protect certain Chinese industries.[6]

Moreover, China is increasingly prepared to punish those foreign investors who violate Chinese regulations and those who make profits through cheating – which in the past China was reluctant to do because of the potential negative publicity. It has been reported that some foreign investors used loopholes in China's legal and taxation systems to make huge profits (a wide range of tricks has been identified); and some profit-making companies simply claimed to be making big losses in order to avoid taxes.[7] In some joint ventures, the profits made by foreign partners were achieved at the expense of the Chinese partners. To tackle such problems, the Chinese government developed new methods of gathering relevant business information, and those found guilty were punished. These are indications that policy making in the area of FDI is changing, and is now focusing on actively identifying problems and Chinese requirements and emphasizing mutual benefits and long-term commitments by foreign investors to the Chinese market.

FDI AND THE CHINESE ECONOMY: PROBLEMS AND FUTURE PROSPECTS

China's extraordinary economic boom has attracted major attention from the international business community. Since 1992, China has been on the cover of several influential magazines, including *Time, Business Week* and *The Economist*. Phrases such as 'the next superpower', 'the emerging economic powerhouse' and 'the greatest economic miracle ever' have been used to describe the future prospects for this rapidly growing economy. In spite of problems such as the economic over-heating and the reoccurring cycles of boom and bust, the general feeling about China's future has been optimistic.[8]

FDI in China: emerging problems and new trends

The Chinese government has increasingly recognized the enormous contributions made by FDI to the Chinese economy, and since the early 1990s renewed efforts from both the central and local governments have been initiated to attract more high quality FDI. So far, the result has been impressive. By the end of 1996, China had attracted over 280 000 foreign invested enterprise, with a total utilized FDI of US$176.59 billion (US$469.39 billion contracted), making

China, for four years in a row, the second largest destination for FDI in the entire world.[10] A growing amount of FDI, particular that from large, well-known multinational corporations, has been committed to China.[11] Many foreign invested enterprises have begun to achieve good financial results, providing employment opportunities and contributing to China's export and government revenue.[13]

Some problems also began to emerge, however. For example, over 80 per cent of all foreign investment has concentrated in the coastal regions.[14] By the end of 1994, the eighteen provinces and autonomous regions in the middle and west of China had only attracted 39 363 foreign investment projects (17 per cent of national total), with a total investment of US$10.42 billion (10 per cent of the national total).[15] Given the extraordinary growth rate by such enterprises and their enormous contribution to government revenue and exports, this pattern of FDI distribution has certainly contributed to the growing disparities between the east coast and the rest of China. Although after the mid-1990s, western provinces began to make breakthroughs in attracting foreign investors, using their natural resource advantages and government preferential policies,[16] the overall pattern in the geographical distribution of FDI in China will not change in significant ways in the near future. The Chinese government's concern about this issue has been increasingly reflected in China's policies and regulations for FDI.

China is a huge country with over 1.2 billion people. Although it has attracted a huge amount of FDI, the per capita FDI in China is still very low compared with many other countries (such as Singapore).[17] Between 1978 and 1993, total utilized FDI in China was US$56.48 billion, which translating into per capita FDI was less than US$50 per person. Even by the end of 1996, the figure was still less than US$150 per person. As such, continuous efforts are needed to attract more FDI in China, and the potential for further growth is enormous. In order to do so, however, the Chinese government will have to undertake some extremely difficult reforms, in both its economic regime and political system, and significantly improve the quality of its hard and soft investment environment.

In terms of the origin of FDI in China, more than half of the 'foreign' investment in China has come from Hong Kong and Macao. Between 1978 and 1993, US$38.51 billion, out of a total of US$56.48 billion FDI (utilized) attracted to China (or 68.18 per cent), originated from Hong Kong and Macao.[18] By the end of 1994, investors from this area established over 129 900 projects in China, with a total investment of over US$60.05 billion, representing 62.83 per cent of all utilized FDI in China (US$95.57 billion), which further increased to US$78.32 billion in 1995, although its share in China's utilized FDI decreased to 58.8 per cent.[19] Since early 1992, Taiwan has surpassed the USA and Japan and became the number two investor in mainland China (8.7 per cent of China's total utilized FDI between 1979 and 1995), and Singapore has moved to number five in the league table (ahead of both the UK and Germany, the largest European investors in China).[20] Collectively, overseas Chinese from Hong Kong, Macao, Taiwan and Singapore have been by far the largest 'foreign' investors in China. However, unlike investment from the developed economies such as the USA, Japan or Western Europe, the investment from Hong Kong, Macao and Taiwan tends to be in small scale (usually under US$1 million), low tech, labour-intensive operations.[21] Larger projects from these areas tend to be in non-productive sectors (such as real estate). The dominance of overseas Chinese in China's FDI is unlikely to change in the near future.

Investment from developed economies has also been increasing steadily in recent years.[22] Many world-leading companies from the developed countries which were reluctant to become involved in China during the 1980s have begun to make more substantial investment since the early 1990s.[23] Such investment tends to be large scale and long term and often involves transferring new technologies to China. The proportion of capital and/or technology intensive projects and investment from large multinational corporations has also been increasing rapidly.[24] By the end of 1994, over 200 of the top 500 world-leading multinational corporations from developed countries had invested in China.[25] By mid-1995, nine out of the top ten largest German companies, and seventeen out of the top twenty largest Japanese companies had invested in China.[26]

Investment from multinational corporations has gone through a number of major changes since the early 1990s. It was found that, before 1994, multinational corporations tended to invest in single, stand-alone projects.[27] However, after nearly two decades of observation and experiment, China has increasingly been regarded as an attractive place for investment, and many multinational corporations are systematically implementing their China business strategy. In many cases, holding companies and company groups are being established by such corporations to co-ordinate their operations and development in different parts of China and in different industries.

Holding companies and company groups in China tend to perform a wide range of functions including investment and re-investment, marketing and sales, personnel training, information provision and capital support. By doing so, different ventures in the group are increasingly integrated and systematically co-ordinated, which increases the strength and competitiveness of the group as a whole. Such groups tend to expand rapidly along value chains (from different stages of production to sales, marketing, after-sale services and training) and diversify into a wide range of industries (from manufacturing to banking, insurance, consultancy, retailing and transportation). More importantly, some multinational corporations have now completed their strategic re-orientation in the Chinese market, and are systematically expanding operations from the east to the west. Production, new product development, and components supply are increasingly localized, and technical and management personnel are increasingly recruited locally. Such new development will have major impacts on the Chinese economy, particularly in respect of capital investment, employment, market competition, government revenue, export, and technology transfer. The number of new ventures involving only foreign capital (that is, wholly foreign owned ventures) has also been increasing rapidly.

The Chinese economy and society: problems and future prospects

The Chinese economy has been growing very rapidly for nearly two decades, and the national GDP in 1995 quadrupled that in 1980, five years ahead of plan, to meet the national economic target set for the year 2000 (some provinces, such as Guangdong, achieved the target in 1992, eight years ahead of plan).[28] The Chinese model of reform is one of incremental and experimental innovation, with the state retaining a major role in the overall regulation of the economy and a significant stake in the ownership of industrial property (in fact, state monopoly continues in many strategic industries). Economic reform has been accompanied by gradual political liberalization, and a more pluralistic society has slowly been created by the market system.

The Chinese government is undertaking an ambitious and complex social and economic transformation in China. Its success will offer valuable experience to other developing countries and to nations of the former Eastern block. Since 1978, changes in China's economic system, social structure and culture, political regime and many other aspects have been very radical, but there is little domestic and international experience that China can draw upon. In spite of the enormous achievement and the general optimism about China's future prospects, short-term fluctuations and set-backs, cycles of boom and bust, re-orientation of certain policies and regulations, are unavoidable.

China still has not overcome the legacy of central planning. The international uncertainty, the political uncertainty within China (particularly in terms of political liberalization), the growing polarization associated with China's enormous size (both in area and in the number of people), combined with the rapid pace of change, continue to threaten the country's social, political and economic stability.

So far, the reform in general has been highly successful in bringing about a rapidly growing economy. To continue the rapid growth of the last two decades, China will have to face up to a wide range of extremely difficult challenges in the next round of reform. During the 1980s and early 1990s, many sensitive issues have been deliberately put aside. Some of them have now become major obstacles to China's further economic development, and they can no longer be withheld. The accumulating effect of these problems means that very harsh and unpopular measures have to be implemented. Some of the dilemmas facing the Chinese central government (such as reforming the state owned enterprises while maintaining social stability, decentralizing economic autonomy while maintaining central control) are extremely difficult to resolve.

Since the mid-1990s, the Chinese central government implemented an extensive range of reforms in accordance with market economic principles in the macro-economic area, including reforming the fiscal, banking, taxation, foreign exchange and investment sectors. The focus has now shifted to micro-level issues, which are much more sensitive as many individuals will be directly affected and there will be clear winners and losers. One of the most sensitive tasks is reforming the loss-making state owned enterprises, without which many other reforms cannot be carried out (such as the commercialization of banks). Apart from the enormous complexity involved in turning these bloated, loss-making state owned companies around, there are also some extremely difficult political, ideological and social hurdles involved. Some of these hurdles seem to have been over-come by President Jiang Zemin's reiteration at the fifteenth Communist Party Congress of the theory that China will remain at 'the primitive stage of socialism' for a long time.

China has more than 100 000 state owned companies, employing two-thirds of China's urban workforce (some 90–100 million people in the mid-1990s). It was believed that between one-third and one-half of these companies are losing money. To avoid mass un-employment, the Chinese government has committed itself to keeping these companies afloat, which has created a mass of unpaid debts and enormous inflationary pressure, thereby undermining China's financial system. About 70 per cent of China's bank loans to industry go to the state sector, which produces only 34 per cent of China's industrial output.

Between 1990 and 1995, the national industrial growth averaged 17.8 per cent per annum, but state owned enterprises only grew at 7 per cent per annum (some put the figure at only 3 per cent). In contrast, non-state industry grew at an extraordinary 38.5 per cent, with foreign invested enterprises at 95.6 per cent between 1991 and 1994 (although from a low statistical-base)![29] This pattern of growth means that the proportion of the state owned sector in the national economy is reducing (albeit slowly), and some experts have argued that the rapid growth of the non-state sector may signifi-cantly relieve the difficulties involved in reforming the loss-making state sector in terms of employment and government revenue.[30]

During the ninth five year plan (1996–2000), China is concen-trating on reforming the 1000 largest state owned enterprises and industrial groups, while others have to find ways to survive in their respective markets (including entering joint ventures with foreign investors) or face bankruptcy.[31] Three new policy banks have been set up to deal with loans to the state owned sector and bad debts, leaving commercial banks to concentrate on commercial deals.[32] These are all significant steps in converting the Chinese economy into a market system. The 'soft landing' of the Chinese economy, from the 1993 boom, in 1995/96 also suggested that the Chinese government has developed better tools than the familiar adminis-trative measures in managing the economy according to market rules.

Another difficult task facing the Chinese government is to balance economic and political reforms. Ever since the mid-1980s, it has been argued that the political reform was too slow to accommodate new demands derived from the economic reform. Even today, after nearly twenty years of economic liberalization, many politically sensitive issues remain unresolved, and these have become major obstacles to China's economic and social progress. Over the past two decades, a high level of social and political discipline in Chinese society has been maintained by a comprehensive system of state and Party leadership. The high degree of state control, combined with a huge and rapidly growing market, has enabled China to attract an increasing amount of FDI while pursuing a relatively independent road towards economic development.[33] However, as the economy continues to grow rapidly and regional economic disparity widens, it becomes increasingly necessary to delegate economic and political autonomy to local governments, which increases the difficulty of effective central control.

Maintaining the balance between centralization and decentralization has always been a dilemma facing the Chinese government. China is very large in area, and the local conditions vary significantly. It is often impossible to accommodate the enormous regional variations in a single national policy, therefore decentralization of economic control and increasing local autonomy is essential to inject new vitality into regional economies. Decentralization is also essential for maintaining law and order and collecting taxes. However, whilst decentralization reduces the central government's ability to control the macro-economy, rapid economic development creates greater disparity, which simultaneously increases the need (and difficulties) for the central government in maintaining effective central control. Failure to control the national economy often leads to economic over-heating and inflation, which not only causes dissatisfaction among Chinese people, but also damages business confidence in the Chinese market. Therefore, striking a proper balance between centralization and decentralization is essential to China's social and political stability and rapid economic development.

Adding to the difficulty is that, today, many old measures of economic control of the planning system have been abandoned in China, yet new measures of the market system are still not fully established. In times of difficlty, the easiest way for the Chinese central government to curb macro-economic imbalances is to use the familiar measures of the planned system through recentralization, which inevitably holds back the pace of China's political and economic reform and affects business confidence in China. However, the soft landing of the Chinese economy in 1995/96 was achieved primarily with non-administrative measures. This indicated that the Chinese central government had gained considerable experience in decentralizing economic control to the local governments while maintaining macro-economic balance via market rather than administrative measures.

Demand for political liberalization has also been growing. Since 1978, China has moved a long way towards political liberalization. Although the 1989 student movement seemed to freeze China's political reform, the advent of village democracy has been very impressive. There are around 900 000 villages in China, home for over three-quarters of the Chinese population. Since 1988, over 80 per cent of villages have elected their village chiefs and committees, and the figure is to increase to over 95 per cent by the late 1990s. *The Economist* magazine claimed this movement as the 'most sweeping abdication of power' since the People's Republic of China was founded in 1949.[34] The process was initiated through a new law passed in 1987 by the central government to allow villages to elect their own chiefs and committees, so as to make the village authorities more responsive to local economic need, and enable local talent to get the rural economy going. This process may gradually spread upwards to towns, counties, provinces and then the central government. However, the difficulties and potential destabilizing factors involved in the process are enormous.

There are many other difficult problems facing the Chinese government. Corruption in central and local government and state owned enterprises remains a major problem, despite the government's repeated efforts to control it. Decentralization and political liberalization may also unleash separatism in some parts of China. All such issues are powerful time-bombs laid in the already difficult path of China's economic and political reform and opening up to the outside world. Mishandling any of them can cause serious damage to China's long march to economic prosperity.

Nevertheless, all available evidence seems to suggest that China is rapidly becoming a market economy, and despite serious problems, the long-term prospect is optimistic. With its 1.2 billion people and a rapidly growing economy, the Chinese market has become increasingly attractive to foreign investors. However, investing in China requires particularly careful planning, and both short-term economic returns and long-term strategic development need to be taken into account. This book examined the main characteristics of China's investment environment, but China is very large in area, and is still undergoing rapid changes. The conditions of the investment environment in different localities tend to vary significantly and change rapidly over time. A proper focus in time and geography is therefore needed in evaluating the quality of China's foreign investment environment. Many attractive, lucrative opportunities are clearly there in China, but it takes vision, courage, knowledge and many other talents to grasp and exploit these opportunities.

Notes

1. Wall, David (1993) 'China's economic reform and opening up process: The role of the special economic zones', *Development Policy Review* Vol. 11: 243–260.
2. Child, J. (1994) *Management in China during the Age of Reform*, Cambridge University Press, Cambridge.
3. *The Financial Times*, 28 May 1993, 'China is new priority: The German approach', in 'Survey on UK Relocation'.
4. The World Bank (1996) *World Development Report*, The World Bank, Washington D.C.
5. *The Economist*, 12–18 October 1996, 'How poor is China?', pp. 79–85. The World Bank (1996) *Poverty in China: What Do the Numbers Say?* The World Bank, Washington D.C.
6. *The People's Daily* (Overseas edition), July 1 1995, 'Regulation on Guiding the Direction of Foreign Investment' (*Zhi Dao Wai Shang Tou Zi Fang Xiang Zan Xing Gui Ding*) and 'Index of Foreign Investment Industrial Guide' (*Wai Shang Tou Zi Chan Ye Zhi Dao Mu Lu*), p. 2.
7. *The People's Daily* (Overseas edition), 15 May 1994.
8. *The Economist*, 17–23 August 1996, 'China – A funny looking tiger', pp. 17–19.
9. *The Financial Times*, 14 June 1993.
10. *The People's Daily* (Overseas edition), 5 March 1996 and 7 April 1997, 'The People's Republic of China National Statistical Bureau Report on China's Economic and Social Development' for 1995 (1996). [*Zhong Hua Ren Min Gong He Guo Guo Jia Tong Ji Ju Guan Yu 1995 (1996) Nian Guo Min Jing Ji He She Hui Fa Zhan De Tong Ji Gong Bao*], p. 2.
11. *The People's Daily* (Overseas edition), 29 October 1996, 'The systemisation of investment by multinational corporations in China' (*Kua Guo Gong Si Zai Hua Tou Zi Xi Tong Hua*), p. 2.
12. *The People's Daily* (Overseas edition), 26 July 1995, 'New Characteristics of foreign investment in China' (*Zhong Guo Li Yong Wai Zi Cheng Xin Te Dian*), p. 1.
13. *Ibid*.
14. Lu, Luping (1992), 'Promoting opening up to the outside world to a

higher stage' (*Nu Li Ba Dui Wai Kai Fang Ti Gao Dao Xin De Shui Ping*), *Qiushi*, 1992 (8), pp. 19–24.

15. *The People's Daily* (Overseas edition), 22 June 1995, 'China's great achievement in attracting foreign investment: Investment from Hong Kong and Macao top the league table with a total utilised investment of over US$60 billion' (*Zhong Guo Xi Shou Wai Zi Cheng Jiu Xian Zhu: Gang Ao Tou Zi Shu Liang Zui Duo Yu Liu Bai Yi Mei Yuan*), p. 2.

16. *The People's Daily* (Overseas edition), 'New wave of opening up in western China' (*Wo Guo Xi Bu Yong Dong Kai Fang Chao*), p. 1.

17. Lu (1992) *op. cit.*

18. Ministry of Foreign Trade and Economic Co-operations (Moftec), quoted from *The Financial Times*, 29 May 1994.

19. *China Statistics Year Book*, 1996; *The Economist*, 8–14 March 1997, 'The importance of foreign devil's money', in *China Survey*, p. 9.

20. *The People's Daily* (Overseas edition), 22 June 1995, *op. cit.; Chinese Science Newspaper* (Overseas edition), 25 April 1995, 'The league table of foreign investors in China' (*Dui Da Lu Tou Zi Zhe Pai Chu Zuo Ci*). *The Financial Times*, 14 June 1993; 'Multinationals in China: Slow car to China', in *The Economist*, 15 April 1994.

21. Lu (1992) *op. cit.*

22. *The People's Daily* (Overseas edition), 22 June 1995, *op. cit.; Chinese Science Newspaper* (Overseas edition), 25 April 1995, *op. cit.*

23. *The Financial Times*, 14 June 1993.

24. *The People's Daily* (Overseas edition), 29 January 1994.

25. *The People's Daily* (Overseas edition), 18 October 1995, 'Multinational corporations rush to invest in China' (*Kua Guo Gong Si Yong Yue Tou Zi Zhong Guo*), p. 2.

26. *The People's Daily* (Overseas edition), 29 October 1996, *op. cit.*

27. Reported in *The People's Daily* (Overseas edition), 29 October 1996, *op. cit.*

28. Reported in *The People's Daily* (Overseas edition), 6 March 1996, 'China's main targets for the next fifteen years' (*Zhong Guo Jin Hou Shi Wu Nian Zhu Yao Fen Dou Mu Biao*), p. 1; *The People's Daily* (Overseas edition), 30 December 1992, 'Guangdong's GDP exceeds 200 billion yuan, eight years ahead of plan to achieve the second stage strategic target' (*Guang Dong Guo Nei Sheng Chan Zong Zhi Yu Liang Qian Yi, Ti Qian Ba Nian Shi Xian Di Er Bu Zhan Lue Mu Biao*), p. 3.

29. Warner, Malcolm (1996) 'Managing China's enterprise reforms: A new agenda for the 1990s', *Journal of General Management* 21(3): 1–18, Spring 1996.

30. *The Economist*, 17–23 August 1996, *op. cit.*

31. *The People's Daily* (Overseas edition), 'Looking at China's enterprise reform from the perspective of "focusing on the large and increasing the autonomy of the small"' (*Cong 'Zhua Da Fang Xiao' Kan Zhong Guo Qi Ye Gai Ge*), p. 2.

32. *The Bankers*, March 1995, 'Beijing sheds some weight', pp. 48–50.

33. Child (1994) *op. cit.*

34. *The Economist*, 2–8 November 1996, 'China's grassroots democracy', pp. 81–85.

Bibliography

Aiello, Paul (1991) 'Building a joint venture in China: The case of Chrysler and the Beijing Jeep Corporation', *Journal of General Management*, 17(2), Winter

Almanac of China's Foreign Economic Relations and Trade (1990) 'Regulation of the State Council of the P.R.C. for encouraging Taiwan compatriots to invest in the mainland', Ministry of Foreign Economic Relations and Trade, Beijing

Amin, A. and M. Dietrich (1991) 'From hierarchy to hierarchy: The dynamics of contemporary corporate restructuring in Europe', in Amin, A. and M. Dietrich (eds), *Towards a New Europe*, Elgar, London

Amin, A., D. Charles, T. Frazer, J. Goddard and J. Howells (1992) 'Large firms and regional cohesion in the European Community', paper presented to DGXVI, Commission of the European Community, Brussels. This paper is available from CURDS, University of Newcastle upon Tyne, Newcastle upon Tyne, NE1 7RU, England

Asian Wall Street Journal, 7 January 1985, 'Chinese hotels testing foreign investors'

Asian Wall Street Journal, 12 March 1985, 'Shanghai snags are worrying foreign firms'

Ash, Robert and Y. Kueh (1992) 'Introduction', *China Quarterly,* September 1992, No. 31, Special Issue: The Chinese Economy in the 1990s

Banker, 18 March 1993, 'Follow the leader', p. 18

The Bankers, March 1995, 'Beijing sheds some weight', pp. 48–50

Barclays Bank (1990–96) *Barclays Economic Review*, published quarterly by Barclays Bank, London

Beijing Review, 30 December 1991–5 January 1992, 'Open policy brings achievements'

Beijing Review, 20–26 January 1992, 'Third foreign investment high tide', p. 29

Boltho, Andrea (1994) *China's Emergence: Prospects, Opportunities and Challenges*, The World Bank, Washington D.C.

Brahm, Lawrence and Li Daoran (1996) *The Business Guide to China*, Butterworth-Heinemann Asia, Singapore

Britain, Samuel (1992) 'Tour of world economy after Berlin wall', *The Financial Times*, 19 November 1992

Brown, Ronald C. (1993) 'The role of the legal environment in doing business in the People's Republic of China', in Kelley, Lane and Oded Shenkar (eds), *International Business in China*, Routledge, London, pp. 63–87

De Bruijn, J.D. and Jia Xianfeng (1992) 'Transferring technology to China via joint ventures: Product selection perspective', paper presented at the conference on *Current Development of Joint Ventures in PRC*, Hong Kong, June 1992

Bucknall, Kevin (1989) *China and the Open Door Policy*, Allen and Unwin, North Sydney

Bucknall, Kevin (1994) *Kevin B. Bucknall's Cultural Guide to Doing Business in China*, Butterworth Heinmann, Oxford

Cai Hangan (1991) 'On the financial position and function of the transnational management of enterprises groups', *Economic Research* (*Jing Ji Yan Jiu*), May 1991

Cannon, Terry and Alan Jenkins (1990) (eds) *The Geography of Contemporary China*, Routledge, London

Chai, Joseph (1983) 'Industrial co-operation between China and Hong Kong' in Youngson, A.J. (ed.), *China and Hong Kong: The Economic Nexus*, Oxford University Press, Oxford, pp. 104–55

Chan, J.C.M., N.Y. Li and D. Sculli (1989) 'Labour relations and foreign investors in the Shenzhen special economic zone of China', *Journal of General Management*, 14(4), Summer

Che, B., J. Ki, Y.K. Mok and S. Stewart (1985) 'Investors' perception of the advantages and disadvantages of investing in an SEZ: Shenzhen', Department of Management Studies, University of Hong Kong

Cheng, Elizabeth and Stracy Mosher (1992) 'Deng's distant vision', in *Far Eastern Economic Review*, 14 May 1992, pp. 23–24

Cheng, Jing (1992) 'A summary of the development of investment environment in the open region' (*Kai Fang Di Qu Tou Zi Huan Jing Gai Quang*). *The People's Daily* (Overseas edition), 24 January 1992

Child, John (1994) *Management in China During the Age of Reform*, Cambridge University Press, Cambridge

Child, John and Yuan Lu (1996) 'Introduction: China and international enterprise', in Child, John and Yuan Lu (eds), *Management Issues in China: Volume II, International Enterprises*, Routledge, London

China News Digest (CND, News Global), Monday, 18 September, 1995, 'CCP says "no admittance" to private business people'

China News Digest, 10 May 1996, 'State sector still strong in economy', p. 6

China Statistical Yearbook, 1983–96

Chinese Science Newspaper (Overseas edition), 25 April 1995, 'The league table of foreign investors in China' (*Dui Da Lu Tou Zi Zhe Pai Chu Zuo Ci*)

Chinese Science Newspaper (Overseas edition), 25 August 1995, 'China quickly marching towards modernisation: The national economic and social development in China underwent major changes during eighth five year plan' (*Zhong Guo Kuai Bu Zou Xiang Xian Dai Hua*), p. 3

Chinese Science Newspaper (Overseas edition), 25 August 1995, 'New characteristics in China's utilisation of foreign investment' (*Zhong Guo Li Yong Wai Zi Cheng Xin Te Dian*), p. 3

Chinese Science Newspaper (Overseas edition), 25 April 1997, 'The largest Sino-US joint venture will be set up in Pudong' (*Zhong Mei Zui Da He Zi Xiang Mu Jiang Luo Hu Pu Dong*), p. 3

Christofferson, Gaye (1991) 'Plan and market in Shanxi province: The long 'energy crisis' of the economic reforms', *China Information*, Documentation and Research Centre for Contemporary China, Arsenaalstraat 1, P.O. Box 9515, 2300 RA Leiden, Holland

Cline, William (1995) 'Evaluating the Uruguay Round', *The World Economy*, 18 (1), January 1995, pp. 1–24

Cohen, J. (1988) 'Legal framework for investment', in Lawson, E. (ed.) *US-China Trade: Problems and Prospects*, Praeger, New York

Dernberger, Robert F. (1988) 'Economic cooperation in the Asia-Pacific Region and the role of the P.R.C.', *Journal of Northeast Asian Studies*, Spring 1988, Vol. VII, No. 1

The Development Institute (1996) 'Regional economic disparities in China: Current situation, main causes and policy responses', *China Opening Herald*, September 1996, Vol. 27, No. 9: 5–15

Dittmer, Lowell (1989) 'The Tiananmen massacre', *Problems of Communism*, September–October 1989

Dittmer, Lowell (1990) 'China in 1989: The crisis of incomplete reform', *Asian Survey*, Vol. XXXI, No. 1, January 1990

Dong, Jie Li (1994) 'In China, an understanding of *guanxi* can help open doors', *The Asian Wall Street Journal Weekly*, 16 May 1994, 7A–B

Easterby-Smith, Mark, Danusia Malina and Lu Yuan (1995) 'How culture-sensitive is HRM? A comparative analysis of practices in Chinese and UK companies', *International Journal of Human Resource Management* 6(1): 31–59, February 1995

The Economist, 21–28 March 1992, 'Running to keep up with Deng', p. 71

The Economist, 6–13 June 1992, 'Soaking the rich'

The Economist, 28 November–5 December 1992, 'China: The titan stirs'

The Economist, 15–22 May 1993, 'Chinese puzzles', p. 95

The Economist, 15–22 April 1994, 'Multinationals in China: Slow car to China'

The Economist, 1–7 October 1994, 'Survey of the global economy'

The Economist, 3–9 December 1994, 'How not to sell 1.2 billion tubes of toothpaste', pp. 95–96

The Economist, 16–22 September 1995, 'The private life of a Chinese', pp. 87–88

The Economist, 2–8 December 1995, 'How and why to survive Chinese tax torture', pp. 89–90

The Economist, 2–8 March 1996, 'Has Europe failed Asia?', pp. 63–65

The Economist, 17–23 August 1996, 'China: A funny-looking tiger' pp. 17–19

The Economist, 12–18 October 1996, 'How poor is China?', pp. 79–85

The Economist, 2–8 November 1996, 'China's grassroots democracy', pp. 81–85

The Economist, 1–7 March 1997, 'Foreign investment: Not quite so sparkling China', p. 72

The Economist, 8–14 March 1997, 'The importance of foreign-devil money', *China Survey*, pp. 9–12

The Economist, 29 March–4 April 1997, 'Business: And never the twain shall meet . . . Building business relationships in Asia, and then keeping them, is proving far harder than foreign companies imagined', pp. 87–88

The Economist, 3–9 May 1997, 'Shanghai takes shape', pp. 67–68

The Economist, 21–27 June 1997, 'The China syndrome', pp. 79–80

The Economist, 19–25 July 1997, 'Reform in the air', pp. 59–60

The Economist Intelligence Unit (EIU) and Andersen Consulting (1995)

Moving China Ventures out of the Red into the Black: Insights from Best and Worst Performers, The Economist Intelligence Unit, London

Euromonitor (1994) *China: A Directory and Source Book 1994*, Euromonitor Plc, London

Fairband, J.K. (1992) *China: A New History*, The Belknap Press of Harvard University Press, London

Fairbank, John and Edwin Reischauer (1989) *China: Tradition and Transformation*, (Revised edition), Allen and Unwin, London

Fan, Weitang (1995) 'The development and future prospects of China's energy industries (*Zhong Guo Neng Yuan Gong Ye De Fa Zhan Yu Zhan Wang*)', in *Chinese Science Newspaper* (*Zhong Guo Ke Xue Bao*, Overseas edition), 25 August 1995, p. 5

Fang, Minsheng (1996) 'The prospect of China's consumer market at the turn of the century', *China Opening Herald*, Vol. 20, No. 2/3, pp. 31–33

The Financial Times, 24 September 1990, 'Financial Times Survey: The world economy'

The Financial Times, 31 March 1993, 'Everything to play for in China's Tarim basin'

The Financial Times, 14 May 1993, 'China puts the brake on rapid economic growth'

The Financial Times, 24 May 1993, 'China's unique path towards the free market'

The Financial Times, 28 May 1993, 'Christopher Parkes on the German approach: China is new priority', *Survey on UK Relocation*, p. 7

The Financial Times, 14 June 1993, 'Lure of the billion-buyer market'

The Financial Times, 2 June 1993, 'Investors move as Asia gets on phone'

The Financial Times, 28 June 1994, 'Ford plans $50m China investment'

The Financial Times, 22 September 1995, 'Myths of business in China debunked'

The Financial Times, 20 November 1995, 'China plans reforms to break trade stalemate: Beijing to cut tariffs and ease investment rules in attempt to join WTO'

The Financial Times, 21 June 1996, 'China advances plans for convertible Yuan', p. 4

The Financial Times, 31 July 1996, 'Consumerism's new citadel: Western companies are pouring into Russia to meet the rapidly increasing demand for consumer goods', reported by Roderick Oram, p. 19

The Financial Times, 29 November 1996, 'China moves to Yuan convertibility', p. 4

Fitzerald, C.P. (1961) *China: A Short Cultural History*, The Cressett Press, London

Frank, Andre Gunder (1980), *Crisis in the World Economy*, Heinemann Educational Books Ltd, London

Fortune, 5 October 1992, 'A new China without borders', pp. 40–44

Frankenstein, John (1995) 'The Beijing Rules: Contradictions, ambiguities and controls', *Long Range Planning* 28 (1): 70–80

Frisbie, John (1988) 'Balancing foreign exchange', *China Business Review*, March–April 1988, p. 25

Gao, Shangquan (1987) *Nine Years of Chinese Economic Reform (Jiu Nian*

Lai De Zhong Guo Jing Ji Ti Zhi Gai Ge), The People's Publishing Agency (*Ren Min Chu Ban She*), Beijing

Gallup Group (1995) *Gallup Survey of Consumer Attitudes and Lifestyle Trends in the People's Republic of China*, Gallup Group, New York

Geringer, J.M. (1991) 'Strategic determinants of partner selection criteria in international joint ventures', *Journal of International Business Studies* 20: 235–254

Goddard, J. (1992) 'New technology and the geography of the UK information economy', in Robins, K. (ed.) *Understanding Information: Business, Technology and Geography*, Belhaven, London

Goodman, David S.G. (1992), 'Reforming China: Foreign contacts, foreign values?', *The Pacific Review*, Vol. 5 No. 1, 1992, pp. 25–38

Grosser, Kate and Brian Bridge (1990) 'Economic interdependence in East Asia in the global context', *The Pacific Review*, Vol. 3 No. 1

Guo, Aimin & Robert Akroyd (1996) 'Overcoming barriers to technological transfers into China', in Child, John and Yuan Lu (eds) *Management Issues in China: Volume II, International Enterprises*, Routledge, London, pp. 30–51

Guo, J.H. and N. Macpherson (1996) 'Marketing practices in the People's Republic of China – the way ahead for the next millennium', *MEG '96 Conference*, Glasgow

Haggard, Stephan and Tunjen Cheng (1987) 'State and foreign capital in the East Asian economies' in Frederic C. Deyo (ed.) *The Political Economy of the New Asian Industrialism*, Cornell University Press, Ithaca, N.Y., pp. 84–135

Hall, Edward T. (1981) *Beyond Culture*, Doubleday, New York

Harwit, Eric (1992) 'Foreign passenger car ventures and Chinese decision-making', *Australian Journal of Chinese Affairs*, Issue 28, July 1992

The Henley Centre (1997) 'From Marxism to the market', *Global Futures*, Summer 1997: 12–16

Hepworth, M. (1989) *Geography of the Information Economy*, Belhaven Press, London

Ho, Samuel and Ralph Huenemann (1984), *China's Open-Door Policy: The Quest for Foreign Technology and Capital*, University of British Columbia Press, Vancouver

Howe, Christopher (1990) 'Asia and the Pacific: Recent trends', *The Far East and Australasia*, 1990, 2, Europa Publications Limited

Howells, J. and M. Wood (1991) *The Globalization of Production and Technology*, a report under the Programme of Forecasting and Assessment in the Field of Science and Technology (FAST), Directorate-General for Science, Research and Development, Commission of the European Communities. Available from CURDS, Newcastle University, Newcastle upon Tyne NE1 7RU, England

IMF (1980–96) *World Economic Outlook*, Published twice each year in May and October by the International Monetary Fund (IMF), Washington D.C.

Ishigami, Etsuro (1991), 'Japanese business in ASEAN countries: New industrialisation or Japanese?' *IDS Bulletin*, Vol. 22 No. 2

Ji, Chongwei (1987) 'The improvements in China's investment environment and its future prospects' (*Zhong Guo Tou Zi Huan Jing De Gai Shan Ji Qian Jing*), *Almanac of the Chinese Economy (Zhong Guo Jing Ji Nian Jian)*

Jiang, Mingqing (1992) 'The economic development of China's coastal region' (*Zhong Guo Yan Hai Di Qu de Jing Ji Fa Zhan*), *Liaowang*, 27 January 1992

Julius, DeAnne (1990) *Global Companies and Public Policy: The growing challenge of foreign direct investment*, Pinter Publishers Ltd, London

Julius, DeAnne (1991) 'Direct investment among developed countries: Lessons for developing world', *IDS Bulletin*, 1991, Vol. 22 No. 2

Kamath, Shyam J. (1990) 'Foreign direct investment in centrally planned developing economy: The Chinese case', in *Economic Development and Culture Change*, Vol. 39, No. 1, October 1990

Kenworthy, James L. (1989) *A Guide to the Laws, Regulations and Policies of the People's Republic of China on Foreign Trade and Investment*, William S. Hein and Co, Buffalo, New York

Kleinberg, Robert (1990) *China's Opening to the Outside World*, Westview Press, Boulder

Kueh, Y.Y. (1992) 'Foreign investment and economic change in China', *China Quarterly*, September 1992, No. 131

Lall, Sanjaya (1977), *Foreign Investment, Transnationals and Developing Countries*, Macmillan Press Ltd, London

Lardy, Nicholas R. (1995) 'The role of foreign trade and investment in China's economic transformation', *China Quarterly*, No. 144, pp. 1065–1082

Lee, Keun, Chung H. Lee, and Won Bae Kim (1990), 'Problems and profitability of direct foreign investment in China: An analysis of the survey data', *Journal of Northeast Asian Studies*, Vol. IX, No. 4, Winter 1990

Li, Feng (1995a) *The Geography of Business Information*, John Wiley and Son, Chichester

Li, Feng (1995b) 'Structural innovations through information systems: Some emerging tendencies in Europe' *Journal of Management Systems* 7(3): 53–65

Li, Feng and Chris Gentle (1995) *Corporate Location in the New Europe*, Henley Centre for Forecasting, London

Li, Ling (1996) 'The main causes for the widening gap between the east and the west and some possible solutions', *China Opening Herald*, August 1996, Vol. 26 No. 8: 5–11

Li, Peng (1991) 'Report of the outline of the ten year National Economic and Social Development Plan and the eighth five year plan' (*Guan Yu Guo Min Jing Ji He She Hui Fa Zhan De Shi Nian Yuan Jing Gui Hua He Ba Wu Ji Hua De Bao Gao*), *The People's Daily* (Overseas edition), 11 April 1991, pp. 1 and 4

Li, Peng (1992) 'China's economy in the 1990s'. Speech at the annual meeting of the World Economic Forum in Davos, Switzerland on 30 January 1992, in *Almanac of China's Foreign Economic Relations and Trade (1992/93)* pp. 9–12

Li, Peng (1997a) 'China's energy policy', *The People's Daily* (Overseas edition), 30 May 1997, p. 2. First published in *Qiushi* magazine No. 11, 1997

Li, Peng (1997b) 'Developing an integrated transportation system' (*Jian Li Tong Yi De Jiao Tong Yun Shu Ti Xi*), *Economic Daily* (*Jing Ji Ri Bao*), 5 August 1997

Li, Xiao Jun and E.J. Griffiths (1989), *The Long March to the Fourth of June*, London: Duckworth

Lin, Zhiling (1991) 'How China will modernise', in *American Enterprise*, July–August 1991

Liu, Zaixing *et al.* (1985) *The Theory of Allocation of Production* (*Sheng Chan Bu Ju Yuan Li*), The People's University of China Press (*Zhong Guo Ren Min Da Xue Chu Ban She*), Beijing

Lo, T.W.X. (1986) 'Foreign investment in the special economic zones: A management perspective', in Jao, Y.C. and C.K. Leung (Eds.) *China's Special Economic Zones: Policies, Problems and Prospect*, Oxford University Press, Hong Kong

Lockett, Martin (1987) 'China's special economic zones: The cultural and managerial challenges', *Journal of General Management*, Vol. 12 No. 3, Spring 1987

Lockett, Martin (1988) 'Culture and the problems of Chinese management', *Organisation Studies* 9 (4): 475–496

Lu, Luping (1992), 'Promoting China's opening up to the outside world to a higher level' (*Nu Li Ba Dui Wai Kai Fang Ti Gao Dao Xin De Shui Ping*), *Qiushi*, 1992 (8), pp. 19–24

Martinelli, F. and E. Schoenberger (1989) 'Oligopoly alive and well: Notes for a broader discussion on flexible accumulation'. Paper presented at the international conference on *Les nouveaux espaces industriels: un survol international*, Paris, 21–22 March, 1989

Martinsons, Maris and Paul Hempel (1995) 'Chinese management systems: Historical and cross-cultural perspectives', *Journal of Management Systems* 7(1): 1–11, special issue on *Management in Greater China*

McLaughlin, Bruce (1996) 'The way to market', *Chinese Business Impact* (*Ying Zhong Jing Ji Dong Xiang*), June 1996, Issue 19, p. 7 and p. 26, published by Si Yu Chinese Times Publication, Manchester

Moser, Michael J. (1984, ed.), *Foreign Trade, Investment and the Law in the People's Republic of China*, Oxford University Press, Hong Kong

National Council for US–China Trade (NCUSCT) (1987) *US Joint Ventures in China: A progress report*, Washington D.C.

Nguyen, Trien, Carlo Perroni and Rardall Wigle (1995) 'A Uruguay Round success?', *The World Economy*, 18 (1) January 1995, 25–30

Nyaw, Mee Kau (1993) 'Managing international joint ventures in China', in Kelley, Lane and Oded Shenkar (eds) *International Business in China*, Routledge, London

OECD (1990–96) *OECD Economic Outlook*, published twice each year in June and December by OECD, Paris

Pan, Xipan (1996) 'Will it cause great confusion if we abolish the household register system?' *China Opening Herald*, Vol. 30, No. 12: pp. 50–52

Pearson, Margaret M. (1991a) *Joint Ventures in the People's Republic of China: The control of foreign direct investment under Socialism*, Princeton University Press, Princeton

Pearson, Margaret M. (1991b) 'The erosion of controls over foreign capital in China 1979–1988', *Modern China*, Vol. 17, No 1, January 1991

The People's Daily (Overseas edition), 25 June 1992, 'Foreign capital extensively entering the tertiary sectors' (*Wai Zi Guang Fan Jin Ru Di San Chan Yie*), p. 1

The People's Daily (Overseas edition), 30 June 1992, 'The State Council of the central government decided to accelerate the development of the tertiary sectors' (*Zhong Gong Zhong Yang Guo Wu Yuan Zuo Chu Jue Ding, Jia Kuai Fa Zhan Di San Chan Yie*), p. 1

The People's Daily (Overseas edition), 12 August 1992, '220 foreign financial institutions set up offices in China' (*Wai Zi Jin Rong Ji Gou Zai Da Lu Yi She Dai Biao Chu 220 Jia*), p. 2

The People's Daily (Overseas edition), 13 August 1992, 'Real estate becomes a new hot spot for investment' (*Fang Di Chan Cheng Wei Tou Zi Xin Re Dian*), p. 1

The People's Daily (Overseas edition), 22 August 1992, 'Tertiary sector becomes a new area for foreign investment in the Changjiang Delta area' (*Di San Chan Yie Zai Chang Jiang San Jiao Zhou Cheng Wei Wai Shang Tou Zi De Xin Ling Yu*), p. 2

The People's Daily (Overseas edition), 30 December 1992 'Guangdong's GDP exceeds 200 billion Yuan, eight years ahead of schedule to achieve the second stage strategic target' (*Guangdong Guo Nei Sheng Chan Zong Zhi Yu Liang Qian Yi, Ti Qian Ba Nian Shi Xian Di Er Bu Zhan Lue Mu Biao*)

The People's Daily (Overseas edition), 4 March 1994; March 2 1995; March 5 1996; 7 April 1997 'The People's Republic of China National Statistical Bureau Report on China's economic and social development' for 1993, 1994, 1995 and 1996 [*Zhong Hua Ren Min Gong He Guo Guo Jia Tong Ji Ju Guan Yu 1993 (1994, 1995, 1996) Nian Guo Min Jing Ji He She Hui Fa Zhan De Tong Ji Gong Bao*], p. 2

The People's Daily (Overseas edition), 18 May 1994, 'The future is bright, the potential is enormous' (*Qian Jing Guang Kuo, Da You Ke Wei*)' pp. 1 and 3

The People's Daily (Overseas edition), 24 September 1994, 'Constructing the basic framework for the new building: Past experience and future prospect in reforming China's economic regime this year' (*Gou Zhu "Xin Da Sha" De Ji Ben Kuan Jia – Jin Nian Jing Ji Ti Zhi Gai Ge De Hui Gu Yu Zhan Wang*), p. 1

The People's Daily (Overseas edition), 7 February 1995, 'Modern times call for new trunk road' (*Shi Dai Hu Huan "Xin Gan Xian"*), p. 1

The People's Daily (Overseas edition), 20 April 1995 'How big is the scale of the "three gold" project?' (*"San Jin" Gong Cheng Gui Mo You Duo Da?*), p. 1

The People's Daily (Overseas edition), 15 April 1995, 'China speeds up national informatisation process' (*Wo Guo Jia Kuai Guo Jia Xin Xi Hua Bu Fa*), p. 2

The People's Daily (Overseas edition), 22 June 1995, 'China's great achievement in attracting foreign investment: Investment from Hong Kong and Macao top the league table with a total utilised investment of over

US\$ 60 billion' (*Zhong Guo Xi Shou Wai Zi Cheng Jiu Xian Zhu: Gang Ao Tou Zi Shu Liang Zui Duo Yu Liu Bai Yi Mei Yuan*)

The People's Daily (Overseas edition), 22 June 1995, 'Telecommunications services have been developing rapidly, consistently surpassed the speed of economic development in the past ten years' (*Wo You Dian Tong Xin Shi Ye Fa Zhang Xun Su, Lian Xu Shi Nian Chao Guo Guo Min Jing Ji Zeng Zhang Su Du*)', p. 1

The People's Daily (Overseas edition), 1 July 1995, 'Regulation on guiding the direction of foreign investment' (*Zhi Dao Wai Shang Tou Zi Fang Xiang Zan Xing Gui Ding*) and 'Index of foreign investment industrial guide' (*Wai Shang Tou Zi Chan Ye Zhi Dao Mu Lu*), p. 2

The People's Daily (Overseas edition), 22 July 1995, 'Who can occupy China's "sky"?' (*Shui Neng Qiang Zhan Zhong Guo "Tian Kong"?*), p. 2

The People's Daily (Overseas edition), 26 July 1995 'New characteristics of foreign investment in China' (*Zhong Guo Li Yong Wai Zi Cheng Xin Te Dian*), p. 1

The People's Daily (Overseas edition), 23 September 1995, 'Rapid railway construction in China, 5800km new lines in five years' (*Zhong Guo Tie Lu Jian She Tu Fei Meng Jin, Wu Nian Pu Jiu Tie Lu Xin Xian 5800 Gong Li*)', p. 1

The People's Daily (Overseas edition), 18 October 1995 'Multinational corporations rush to invest in China' (*Kua Guo Gong Si Yong Yue Tou Zi Zhong Guo*), p. 2

The People's Daily (Overseas edition), 20 October 1995, 'Great prospect for nuclear power development in China (*Zhong Guo He Dian Fa Zhan Qian Jing Kan Hao*)', p. 1

The People's Daily (Overseas edition), 10 November 1995, 'China will intensify the construction of legal systems in the area of foreign trade and investment, improve the transparency and impartiality of laws' (*Zhong Guo Jiang Qiang Hua Wai Mao Fa Zhi Jian She Ti Gao Fa Lu Tong Yi Xing He Tou Ming Du*), p. 1

The People's Daily (Overseas edition), 14 December 1995, 'The reform and development of China's social security system' (*Zhong Guo She Hui Bao Zhang Zhi Du De Gai Ge He Fa Zhan*), p. 1

The People's Daily (Overseas edition), 29 December 1995, 'China adjusts preferential tax policy for foreign invested enterprises: Creating better investment environment for foreign investors' (*Zhong Guo Tiao Zheng Wai Qi Shui Shou You Hui Zheng Ce Jiang Wei Wai Shang Chuang Zao Geng Hao Tou Zi Huan Jing*), p. 1

The People's Daily (Overseas edition), 30 December 1995, 'The rapid development of the electricity industry during the 'eighth five year plan' period' (*Dian Li Gong Ye "Ba Wu" Fa Zhan Xun Su*), p. 1

The People's Daily (Overseas edition), 20 January 1996, 'China's telecommunications achieved great leap forward (*Zhong Guo You Dian Shi Xian Da Kua Yue*)', p. 1

The People's Daily (Overseas edition), 23 January 1996, 'China's transportation infrastructure significantly improved during the eighth five year plan (*Ba Wu Hui Mou: Wo Jiao Tong She Shi Da Wei Gei Guan*)', p. 1

The People's Daily (Overseas edition), 24 January 1996, '"Ninth five year plan" sets target for telecommunications *(You Dian Tong Xin "Jiu Wu" Mu Biao Ni Ding)'*, p. 1

The People's Daily (Overseas edition), 6 March 1996, 'Our National GNP quadrupled five years ahead of plan' *(Wuo Guo Guo Min Sheng Chan Zong Zhi Ti Qian Wu Nian Fan Liang Fan)*, pp. 1 and 3

The People's Daily (Overseas edition), 6 March 1996, 'China's main targets for the next fifteen years' *(Zhong Guo Jin Huo Shi Wu Nian Zhu Yao Fen Dou Mu Biao)*, p. 1

The People's Daily (Overseas edition), 20 March 1996, 'The People's Republic of China National Economic and Social Development: Outline of the "ninth five year plan" and long term targets for the year 2010' *(Zhong Hua Ren Min Gong He Guo Guo Min Jing Ji He She Hui Fa Zhan 'Jiu Wu' Ji Hua He 2010 Nian Yuan Jing Mu Biao Gang Yao)*, p. 1

The People's Daily (Overseas edition), 23 March 1996, 'China adjusts preferential policies for special development zones and special economic zones, what could Pudong do?' *(Zhong Guo Tiao Zheng Kai Fa Qu He Te Qu Yiu Hui Zheng Ce, Pu Dong Ze Mo Ban?)*, p. 1

The People's Daily (Overseas edition), 26 March 1996, 'Shenzhen progresses towards functional special economic zone' *(Shen Zhen Kua Xiang Gong Neng Xing Te Qu)*, p. 1

The People's Daily (Overseas edition), 27 March 1996, 'Modern enterprise system experiment in Sichuan achieving positive results' *(Sichuan Xian Dai Qi Yie Zhi Du Shi Dian Gong Zuo Jian Xiao)*, p. 1

The People's Daily (Overseas edition), 30 March 1996. 'General Motors has come to China: An interview with General Motors' China Chief Executive' *("Tong Yong" Lia Dao Zhong Guo Lai)*, by Lin Gang (Journalist), p. 2

The People's Daily (Overseas edition), 1 April 1996, 'Over 100 foreign financial institutions set up in China's coastal region' *(Bai Jia Wai Zi Jing Rong Ji Gou Zai Wo Yan Hai Xing Cheng Qi Hou)*, p. 1

The People's Daily (Overseas edition), 2 April 1996, 'The first fast passenger train in operation, top speed 140km per hour' *(Wo Shou Lie Kuai Su Ke Che Ying Yun Zui Gao Shi Su Wei 140 Gong Li)*, p. 1

The People's Daily (Overseas edition), 2 April 1996, 'Jing-Jiu railway becomes fully operational for cargo' *(Jing Jiu Tie Lu Quan Xian Tou Ru Huo Yun)*, p. 1

The People's Daily (Overseas edition), 3 April 1996, 'China actively constructs new types of wage system, intensify macro control of wages' *(Zhong Guo Ji Ji Gou Jian Xin Xing Gong Zi Guan Xi, Jia Qiang Lao Dong Gong Zi Hong Guan Tiao Kong Li Du)*, p. 4

The People's Daily (Overseas edition), 4 April 1996: 'Li Peng speaks at State Council Special Economic Zone Working Conference: Special economic zones should re-invent themselves, create new advantages and achieve further progress' *(Te Qu Yao Yi Er Ci Chuang Yie Jing Shen Zeng Chuang Xin You Shi Geng Shang Yi Ceng Lou)*, p. 1

The People's Daily (Overseas edition), 19 April 1996. 'The labour contract employment system will be established throughout China before the end of the year' *(Wo Nian Nei Quan Mian Jian Li Lao Dong He Tong Zhi)*, p. 1

The People's Daily (Overseas edition), 15 May 1996, 'China intends to invest 90 billion yuan in telecommunications' (*Guo Jia Ni Tou Zi You Dian Tong Xin Jiu Bai Yi Yuan*)', p. 2

The People's Daily (Overseas edition), 20 May 1996, 'China demands foreign invested enterprises sign collective employment contract' (*Zhong Guo Yao Qiu Wai Qi Qian Ding Yong Gong Ji Ti He Tong*), p. 2

The People's Daily (Overseas edition), 8 June 1996, 'Civil airports developments entered the fast lane in China' (*Wo Guo Min Hang Ji Chang Jian She Jin Ru Kuai Che Dao*)', p. 8

The People's Daily (Overseas edition), 12 June 1996, 'Total assets owned by foreign banks in China exceed US$19.1 billion' (*Zai Hua Wai Zi Yin Hang Zong Zi Chan Da Yi Bai Jiu Shi Yi Yi Mei Yuan*), p. 1

The People's Daily (Overseas edition), 15 June 1996, 'A summary of Chinese laws in the areas of foreign relations' (*Zhong Guo She Wai Fa Lu Gai Kuang*), by Zhang Shijin, p. 4

The People's Daily (Overseas edition), 19 June 1996, 'China establishes new employment system' (*Zhong Guo Jian Li Xin Xing Lao Dong Yong Gong Zhi Du*), p. 4

The People's Daily (Overseas edition), 21 June 1996, 'Foreign invested enterprises will buy and sell foreign exchange through the banking system, making yuan fully convertible on the current account before the end of the year' (*Wai Zi Qi Yie Jiang Shi Xian Yin Hang Jie Shou Hui, Jin Nian Nian Di Qian Shi Xian Ren Min Bi Jing Chang Xiang Mu Ke Dui Huan*), p. 1

The People's Daily (Overseas edition), 10 August 1996, 'An important step in vitalising the state owned economy' (*Gao Huo Guo You Jing Ji De Zhong Yao Yi Bu*), p. 1

The People's Daily (Overseas edition), 13 August 1996, 'Commentary: We are determined to utilise foreign investment effectively' (*Jian Ding Bu Yi Yong Hao Wai Zi*), p. 1

The People's Daily (Overseas edition), 4 September 1996, 'What have multinational corporations brought to China?' (*Kua Guo Gong Si Gei Zhong Guo Dai Lai Le She Mo?*), p. 2

The People's Daily (Overseas edition), 25 September 1996, 'United Nations Trade and Development Report indicated China as No. 2 in attracting foreign investment' (*Lian He Guo Mao Fa Hui Bao Gao Xian Shi Zhong Guo Xi Yin Wai Zi Liang Ju Shi Jie Di Er*), p. 6

The People's Daily (Overseas edition), 29 October 1996, 'The systemisation of investment by multinational corporations in China' (*Kua Guo Gong Si Zai Hua Tou Zi Xi Tong Hua*), p. 2

The People's Daily (Overseas edition), 1 November 1996, 'Hebei deepens its pilot reform in modern enterprise system' (*He Bei Shen Hua Xian Dai Qi Ye Zhi Du Shi Dian Gai Ge*), p. 1

The People's Daily (Overseas edition), 4 November 1996, 'Savings by Chinese urban and rural citizens increasing steadily, total saving reached 3708.5 billion Yuan by the end of September 1996' (*Quan Guo Ge Di Cheng Xiang Ju Min Chu Xu Cun Kuan Zeng Zhang Wen Ding, Dao Jiu Yue Di Chu Xu Yu E Da 37085 Yi Yuan*), p. 1

The People's Daily (Overseas edition), 4 November 1996, 'Our national foreign exchange reserves exceed US$95 billion' (*Wo Guo Wai Hui Chu Bei Yu Jiu Bai Wu Shi Yi Mei Yuan*), p. 1

The People's Daily (Overseas edition), 6 November 1996, 'The enormous potential in China's aviation market' (*Zhong Guo Hang Kong Shi Chang Qian Li Ju Da*), p. 4

The People's Daily (Overseas edition), 6 November 1996, 'Airbus AE100 project, China, Singapore and Europe reached agreement on share ownership' (*Kong Zhong Kuai Che AE100 Xiang Mu Zhong Xin Ou San Fang Gu Fen Que Ding*), p. 4

The People's Daily (Overseas edition), 29 November 1996, 'Renminbi will become convertible on the current account from next month' (*Xia Yue Qi Shi Xian Ren Min Bi Jing Chang Xiang Mu Ke Dui Huan*), p. 1

The People's Daily (Overseas edition), 30 November 1996, 'China's foreign exchange reserve exceeded 100 billion US dollars' (*Zhong Guo Wai Hui Chu Bei Tu Puo Qiang Yi Mei Yuan*), p. 1

The People's Daily (Overseas edition), 18 December 1996, 'Good start for the "ninth five year plan"' ('*Jiu Wu' Kai Ju Hao*), p. 1

The People's Daily (Overseas edition), 20 January 1997, 'National Electricity Corporation is established' (*Guo Jia Dian Li Gong Si Cheng Li*), p. 1

The People's Daily (Overseas edition), 20 January 1997, 'China will increase its use of foreign investment in the electricity industry' (*Zhong Guo Jiang Kuo Da Li Yong Wai Zi Ban Dian*), p. 1

The People's Daily (Overseas edition), 20 January 1997, 'China's public mobile telephones leapfrog to the top ranks in the world' (*Zhong Guo Gong Yong Yi Dong Dian Hua Yue Ju Shi Jie Qian Lie*), p. 2

The People's Daily (Overseas edition), 27 January 1997, 'The main focuses for attracting FDI in China this year' (*Zhong Guo Que Ding Jin Nian Xi Yin Wai Zi Gong Zuo Zhong Dian*), p. 2

The People's Daily (Overseas edition), 27 March 1997, 'The largest Sino-US joint venture signed, two automobile companies established in Shanghai' (*Zhong Mei Zui Da He Zi Xiang Mu Qian Yue, Liang Jia Qi Che You Xian Gong Si Zai Hu Cheng Li*), p. 1

The People's Daily (Overseas edition), 2 April 1997, 'China's trains systematically increased speed' (*Zhong Guo Lie Che Quan Mian Shun Li Ti Su*), p. 1

The People's Daily (Overseas edition), 3 April 1997, 'Attracting foreign investment – A rapidly booming area' (*Xi Yin Wai Zi – Yi Ge Fang Xing Wei Ai De Ling Yu*), p. 2

The People's Daily (Overseas edition), 3 May 1997, 'China adopts a series of new preferential policies and measures to encourage foreign businessmen to invest in the middle and western regions' (*Zhong Guo Cai Qu Xi Lie You Hui Zheng Ce Cuo Shi Gu Li Wai Shang Dao Zhong Xi Bu Di Qu Tou Zi*), p. 2

The People's Daily (Overseas edition), 6 May 1997, 'Last year Beijing newly approved over 800 foreign invested enterprises, with a total FDI exceeding US $2.2 billion' (*Beijing Qu Nian Xin Pi San Zi Qi Yie Ba Bai Duo Jia, Wai Shang Zhi Jie Tou Zi Yu 22 Yi Mei Yuan*), front page

The People's Daily (Overseas edition), 6 May 1997, 'Tianjin: Income by foreign invested enterprises increasing rapidly' (*Tianjin: Wai Qi Shou Ru Kuai Su Zeng Zhang*), p. 2

The People's Daily (Overseas edition), 9 May 1997, 'Chinese railways significantly increase speed' (*Zhong Guo Tie Lu Da Ti Su*), p. 2

The People's Daily (Overseas edition), 22 May 1997, 'New characteristics in China's utilisation of foreign investment' (*Zhong Guo Li Yong Wai Zi Cheng Xian Xin Te Zheng*), p. 2

The People's Daily (Overseas edition), 2 June 1997, 'The purchasing power per unit of money in eight cities in China' (*Zhong Guo Ba Cheng Shi Dan Wei Huo Bi Gou Mai Li Pai Xu*), p. 2

The People's Daily (Overseas edition), 5 June 1997, 'China and European Union sign joint statement on strengthening co-operation in the field of information and communications technologies' (*Zhong Guo Ou Meng Qian Shu Jia Qiang Xin Xi Yu Tong Xun Ling Yu He Zuo Lian He Sheng Min*), p. 4

The People's Daily (Overseas edition), 9 June 1997, 'The total number of foreign invested enterprises exceeded 280,000, by the end of last year total utilised FDI exceeded US$176.5 billion' (*Wo Guo Wai Qi Yi Da 28 Wan Duo Jian, Jie Zhi Qu Nian Di Shi Ji Li Yong Wai Zi Yu 1765 Yi Mei Yuan*), front page

The People's Daily (Overseas edition), 21 July 1997, 'China will become the world's largest investment market in infrastructure-related facilities' (*Zhong Guo Jiang Cheng Shi Jie Zui Da Ji Chu She Shi Tou Zi Shi Chang*), p. 2

The People's Daily (Overseas edition), 25 July 1997, 'Lian Tong's development enters new stage' (*Lian Tong Fa Zhan Bu Ru Xin Jie Duan*), p. 1

The People's Daily (Overseas edition), 26 July 1997, 'China's road network enters capital market' (*Zhong Guo Gong Lu Wang Zou Zin Rong Zi Shi Chang*), p. 2

The People's Daily (Overseas edition), 26 July 1997, 'Another very large scale hydro-electric project starting next year' (*Wo Guo You Yi Te Da Xing Shui Dian Gong Cheng Ming Nian Dong Gong*), p. 1

The People's Daily (Overseas edition), 28 July 1997, 'China has enormous potential in developing nuclear electric power' (*Zhong Guo Kai Fa He Dian Qian Li Ju Da*), p. 1

The People's Daily (Overseas edition), 6 August 1997, 'Establishing an integrated transportation system' (*Yao Jian Li Tong Yi De Jiao Tong Yun Shu Ti Xi),* p 1.

The People's Daily (Overseas edition), 11 August 1997, 'The five major car groups set targets for the "ninth five year plan"' (*Wu Da Jiao Che Ji Tuan Que Ding "Jiu Wu" Mu Biao*), p. 2

The People's Daily (Overseas edition), 12 August 1997 'On the course opened up by the great man – Deng Xiaoping's theory on developing socialism with Chinese characteristics and Shanghai's reform and opening up' (*Zai Wei Ren Kai Pi De Hang Dao Shang – Deng Xiao Ping Jian She You Zhong Guo Te Ce De She Hui Zhu Yi Li Lun He Shang Hai De Gai Ge Kai Fang*), p. 1

The People's Daily (Overseas edition), 18 August 1997, 'Creating high quality managerial staff – The views of enterprises in the east coastal region on human resources' (*Zao Jiu Gao Su Zhi Jing Ying Zhe Dui Wu – Dong Bu Yan Hai De Qi Ye Ren Cai Guan*), p. 1

The People's Daily (Overseas edition), 18 August 1997, 'China launches major plan to transfer and absorb new technologies' (*Guo Jia Zhong Da Yin Jin Ji Shu Xi Shou Ji Hua Que Ding*), p. 2

The People's Daily (Overseas edition), 20 August 1997, 'Early movers versus new comers: A brief report of the competition between multinational car manufacturers in the Chinese market' (*Zhang Wo Xian Ji Yu Hou Lai Ju Shang – Qi Che Kua Guo Gong Si Jing Zheng Zhong Guo Shi Chang Ce Ji*), p. 2

The People's Daily (Overseas edition), 20 August 1997, 'The First Automobile Corporation Volkswagen new car production line checked and accepted' (*Yi Qi Da Zhong Jiao Che Xiang Mu Tong Guo Yan Shou*), p. 1

Pomfret, Richard (1991) *Investing in China: Ten years of the open door policy*, Harvester Wheatsheaf, New York.

Qu, Guangmin (1997) 'China's oil and natural gas resources and their development strategy' (*Zhong Guo De You Qi Zi Yuan Ji Qi Kai Fa Zhan Lue*), in *Chinese Science Newspaper (Overseas edition)*, 25 May 1997, p. 5

Redding, Gordon (1995) 'Overseas Chinese networks: Understanding the enigma', *Long Range Planning* 28 (1): 61–69

Robins, K. and A. Gillespie (1992) 'Communications, organisation and territory', in K. Robins (ed.), *Understanding Information: Business, Technology and Geography*, Belhaven, London

Rong, Jingben, Qui Shufang and Liu Jirui (1987) *Shortage and Reform (Duan Que Yu Gai Ge)*, Hei Long Jiang People's Publishing House (*Hei Long Jiang Ren Min Chu Ban She*), Haerbin

Rosenbaum, Arthur Lewis (1992) (ed.) *State & Society in China: The consequence of reform*, Westview Press, Boulder, Colorado, USA

Schiffman, Leon and slie Kanuk (1994) *Consumer Behaviour* (fifth edition), Prentice Hall International, Englewood Cliffs, N.J.

Schram, S.R. (1984) *Ideology and Policy in China since the Third Plenum, 1978–84*, Contemporary China Institute, London

Schuster, Camille P. and Michael J. Copeland (1996) *Global Business: Planning for Sales and Negotiations*, The Dryden Press, Harcourt Brace College Publishers, Fort Worth, USA

Sekiguchi, Sueo (1991) 'Direct foreign investment and the Yellow Sea Rim', *Journal of Northeast Asian Studies*, Spring

Shambaugh, David (1991) 'China in 1990: The year of damage control', *Asian Survey*, Vol. XXXI No. 1, January 1990, pp. 36–49

Shao, A.T. and Paul Herbig (1994) 'Marketing inside the dragon, despite China's bureaucracy', *International Marketing Review* 12 (1): 65–76

Shen, Xiaofang (1990) 'A decade of direct foreign investment in China', *Problems of Communism*, March–April, 1990

Soete, L. (1991) *Technology in a Changing World*. A report of policy synthesis of the OECD Technology Economy Programme by MERIT, University of Limburg, Maastricht, Netherlands

Sun, Jiuping (1996) 'Reforming China's social security system', *China Opening Herald* 25 (7): 18–21

Sutter, Robert G. (1990) 'Changes in Eastern Europe and the Soviet Union: The effect on China', *Journal of Northeast Asian Studies*, Summer, 1990

Thoburn, John T., H.M. Leng, Esther Chau and S.H. Tang (1990), *Foreign Investment in China under the Open Policy: The Experience of Hong Kong Companies*, Avebury, Aldershot

Thoburn, John T. (1991), 'Investment in China by Hong Kong companies', *IDS Bulletin*, Vol. 22, No. 2

Tsang, Eric (1994) 'Human resource management problems in Sino-foreign joint ventures', *International Journal of Manpower* 15 (9/10): 4–21

Tseng, Choo-sin, Paula Kwan and Fanny Cheung (1995) 'Distribution in China: A guide through the maze', *Long Range Planning* 28 (1): 81–91

UBS (Union Bank of Switzerland) International Finance, Issue 15, Spring 1993, 'China's great leap forward', pp. 1–8

The United Nations (1983), *Economic Survey of Europe*, The United Nations (UN), New York

The United Nations (1992): *Foreign Investment, Trade and Economic Co-operation in the Asian and Pacific Region*, The Economic and Social Commission for Asia and the Pacific, The United Nations, New York

Wall, David (1993) 'China's economic reform and opening up process: The role of the special economic zones', *Development Policy Review* Vol. 11: 243–260

Wang, N.T. (1984), *China's Modernization and Transnational Cooperations*, Lexington Books, Lexington, Mass.

Wang, Qingxian and Rong Huang (1996) 'We start from here' (*Wo Men Cong Zhe Li Qi Bu*), *The People's Daily* (Overseas edition), 7 March 1996, pp. 1 and 3

Ward, Scott and Frederick E. Webster, Jr (1991) 'Organisational buying behaviour', in Robertson, Thomas S. & Harold H. Kassarjian (eds) *Handbook of Consumer Behaviour*, Prentice Hall International, Englewood Cliffs, N.J., 419–459

Warner, Malcolm (1996) 'Managing China's enterprise reforms: A new agenda for the 1990s', *Journal of General Management*, 21 (3) Spring 1996: 1–18

Wei Yuming (1983) 'Present situation in China's utilisation of foreign funds and suggestions concerning future work', *International Trade (Guo Ji Mao Yi)*, No. 19, July

Wiethoff, Bodo (1975) *Introduction to Chinese History: From Ancient Times to 1912*, Thames and Hudson, London

Williams, Ann (1992), 'China's booming "special economic zones"', *Geographical*, March 1992

Wong, Dorothy Suk Chee (1995) 'Understanding overseas Chinese businesses: Some barriers and traps'. Paper presented at the *Association of Management (AoM) 13th International Conference*, 2–5 August 1995, Vancouver, Canada

The World Bank (1990) *China: Between Planning and Market*, Country Study, The World Bank, Washington D.C.

The World Bank (1996) *World Development Reports*, The World Bank, Washington D.C.

The World Bank (1996) *Poverty in China: What do the numbers say?*, The World Bank, Washington D.C.

Wu, Yuguang *et al.* (1984), *The Economic Geography of China (Zhong Guo Jing Ji Di Li)*, Beijing Normal University Press (*Bei Jing Shi Fan Da Xue Chu Ban She*), Beijing

Yan, Rick (1994) 'To reach China's consumers, adapt to *Guo Qing*', *Harvard Business Review*, September–October 1994: 66–74

Yang, Qi (1997) 'China's coal resource' (*Zhong Guo De Mei Tan Zi Yuan*), *Chinese Science Newspaper (Overseas edition)* 25 May 1997, p. 5

Yue Gang (Guang Dong and Hong Kong) Information Times (Yue Gang Xin Xi Shi Bao), 1 March 1995 'An eye-catching research about China's investment environment' (*Yan Tao Zhong Guo Tou Zi Huan Jing, Yi Xiang Cheng Guo Bei Shou Zhu Mu*), p. 1

Zagoria, Donald S. (1991) 'The end of the cold war in Asia: Its impact on China', in *The Proceedings of the Academy of Political Science*, Vol. 38, No. 2

Zhang, Youwen, Duan Xiping, Jin Bu (1986), *The Opening Up of Our National Economy (Wuo Guo Jing Ji De Dui Wai Kai Fang)*, Shanghai Publishing House (*Shanghai Chu Ban She*), Shanghai

Zhang Wanqing, Yang Shuzhen, Gao Lianqing (1988), *Inter-Regional Co-operation and Economic Networks (Qu Yu He Zuo Yu Jing Ji Wang Luo)*, The Economic Science Press (*Jing Ji Ke Xue Chu Ban She*), Beijing

Zhao Ziyang (1984) 'The opening of China', in *Atlantic*, No. 6, December 1984, p. 24

Index

Alcatel 43, 107, 195, 210
Amoco 92
Arco 92
Avon 184
agricultural reform 4, 6
All China Federation of Trade
    Unions (ACFTU) 138, 145,
    168
Andersen Consulting 12, 139,
    161, 165, 187, 188
AT&T 43, 107, 195, 210
'Asian Dragons' 27, 30, 32, 44, 68
AT&T 43, 107, 195, 210

banking/financial sector
    reform 5, 7, 121, 129, 154,
    231, 241
British Petroleum (BP) 44, 92
British Telecom (BT) 106
Bucknall, Kevin 139, 146

centralization/decentralization/
    recentralization 5, 6, 11, 64,
    128, 241, 243
central planning 3, 4, 6, 57, 179,
    193, 211, 241, 243
Child, John 13, 15–16, 132,
    144–5, 181, 183, 212–213, 231
China Hotel (Guangzhou) 103
Chinese economy
    size 1, 28, 120, 121, 187–8
    growth rate 1, 30, 109, 120,
    121, 179, 242
    problems 237–40
    future prospect 240–5
Chinese Communist Party
    (CCP) 3, 56, 63, 76, 118,
    130, 132–6, 144–5, 157, 222
Chrysler-Beijing Jeep 17, 169,
    209–10
Confucius (Kongzi) 131, 155
consumer behaviour 3, 179,
    185–6, 188–90, 191–4, 197–8

corruption 4, 63–4, 151, 172, 244
'Cultural Revolution' 4, 126, 156,
    220
culture, Chinese 76, 130–9,
    140–3, 157, 159, 163, 170, 173,
    219–21, 223

Decentralization, see centralization
Deng Xiaoping 9, 10, 67, 73,
    121, 126, 144
distribution 180–4, 198

economic over-heating 1, 11,
    121, 243
economic reform 2, 4, 5, 6, 42,
    64, 71–3, 120–1, 162, 171,
    241–2
Economist Intelligence Unit 12,
    139, 161, 165, 187
enterprise reform 2, 4, 5, 69–70,
    137, 145, 171, 181, 215, 222,
    241–243, see also urban
    reform

'Face' 131, 136, 141, 170
financial sector reform, see
    banking reform
Five Year Plan 1, 120, 90–100
    Seventh (1985–1990) 89–90,
    100
    Eighth (1991–1995) 1, 30, 90,
    92, 97, 99, 100, 101, 106, 120
    Ninth (1996–2000) 70, 93, 97,
    98, 100, 137, 217, 242
Ford 104, 196, 210
foreign direct investment (FDI)
    amount 2, 10–11, 32–3, 61, 62,
    66, 91, 99, 101, 109–10, 123,
    124, 202, 205–7, 237–9
    forms 10, 51–2
    origin 31–2, 39–41, 44–5
    motivations 35–6, 38
    impact 33, 202–3, 204–18

foreign exchange   41, 61, 71, 75, 151–5, 207
foreign invested enterprises/ *Sanzi*   2, 10, 13, 51–3, 55, 60, 61, 62, 74, 75, 102, 117, 123, 124, 135, 138, 152, 157, 163, 165, 166, 168, 202, 208, 212, 214–15, 224, 237, 239
foreign investment environment definitions/concept   83–4, 116–17
   key elements/factors   82, 83, 84–5, 116–17
   condition   69–71, 83–4, 92, 108–9, 137, 163, 174–5, 207, 233
foreign trade (import/export)   10, 29, 31, 33, 72, 119, 121, 154, 164, 204, 214–15

Gallup Organization   187, 189, 194, 196, 197
General Motors   43, 104, 196, 210
Guandao, *see* corruption
Guanxi (connections/ networks)   12, 13, 117, 131, 136, 139–46, 159, 161, 166, 172, 174, 182, 222, 234

Han Fei   156
Honda   37
household registration system   135
Hu Yaobang   126
human rights   78, 222

Import/export, *see* foreign trade
intellectual property   78, 222
International Monetary Fund (IMF)   1, 42, 72, 231
'Iron Rice Bowl'   137, 169

Jian Zemin   73, 242
Joint ventures, *see* foreign invested enterprises
June 4th Tragedy in 1989, *see* Tiananmen Square tragedy

Klenberg, Robert   159–161
Kornai, Janos   105

Laozi   131, 155
legal framework for foreign investment   52, 54, 69, 77, 78, 116, 146, 151, 155–165, 225, 231, 233
Li Peng   93, 102
Li Xiannian   54
Lockett, Martin   13, 131, 136

Makro Stores   183
Mao Zedong   4, 126, 156, 220
management techniques   3, 74, 199, 211–214
McDonald   104
McKinsey   143, 188
NEC   107
Mencius (*Mengzi*)   131, 155
Mercedes Benz   210
MFN (most favoured nation trading status)   77
MOFTEC (Ministry of Foreign Trade and Economic Co-operation)   53, 160

National People's Congress   158
newly industrialising economies (NIEs)   38, 39, 44
Nissan   73, 104

open areas   8, 9, 70, 78, 163
open door policy
   key elements   5, 8, 120
   evolution   5, 8–9, 54, 73, 74, 78

Pearson, Margaret   14
Pomfret, Richard   14, 86
Procter and Gamble   196
Pudong Development Zone (Shanghai)   8, 9, 67–68, 173, *see also* special economic zone
purchasing power parity (PPP)   1, 187, *see also* Chinese economy, size

recentralization, *see* decentralization

Renault 104

Sanzi see foreign invested
    enterprises
Shanghai Pilkington Glass 103
Shell 44, 92
Siemens 107
social security and welfare 132,
    134–135, 138, 151, 167, 168,
    170–172, 138, 223
special economic zone (SEZ) 8,
    9, 67, 70, 71, 135, 136, 161,
    163, 233, *see also* Pudong
    development zone
stability, political, economic and
    social 6, 64, 69, 77, 123, 128,
    129, 175, 216–218, 232
State Council 4, 107, 144, 158,
    164
state owned enterprises/sector 2,
    5, 7, 64, 72, 121, 129, 132,
    135, 137, 167, 183, 203, 219,
    231, 241–242

Tarim Basin 68
technology transfer 7, 74, 127,
    129, 208–211, 240
Third Plenum (*San Zhong Quan
    Hui*) 4, 54, 63

Thoburn, John 13, 15
Three Gorges Dam (*San Xia*) 87,
    92
Tiananmen Square tragedy 10,
    14, 65–66, 121, 125, 126
Toyota 73, 104
town and village enterprises
    (*Xiang Zhen Qi Yie*) 4

Unico 92
Unilever 184
urban reform 5, 6, *see also*
    enterprise reform

Volkswagen (Shanghai) 17, 42,
    43, 103, 104, 187, 195, 209,
    210

Warner, Malcolm 13
wholly owned foreign
    ventures *see* foreign invested
    enterprises
World Bank 1, 28, 42, 208, 231
World Trade Organisation
    (WTO) 9, 31, 42, 71, 163
Wu Yi 164

Zhao Ziyang 122, 126
Zhou Enlai 4